ICONS OF THE LUSO-HISPANIC WORLD

2

MACHADO DE ASSIS

ICONS OF THE LUSO-HISPANIC WORLD

ISSN: 2633-7169 (print)
ISSN: 2633-7177 (online)

The Icons series includes books on a broad range of outstanding individuals – royalty, religious figures, explorers and leaders of indigenous resistance, inventors, scientists, politicians, revolutionaries, activists, authors, artists, musicians, philosophers, film directors, athletes – and occasionally groups of people, who have had a significant impact not only on Spanish- and Portuguese-speaking countries but on a broader, even global, scale. Books in the series offer an expertly researched overview of the impact these icons have made both within and beyond their native regions, considering their achievements, influence on contemporaries, and reception more widely. Focussing on key moments in an icon's life and work, these books trace the acquisition of iconic status. They explore an icon's legacy and image and afterlife(ves), showing how they have been interpreted, appropriated, and at times reimagined. Based on the most up-to-date scholarly research, books in the series explore how and why a Hispanic or Lusophone icon can also be considered an international icon.

Previously published in the series
1. *Federico García Lorca: The Poetry in All Things*, Federico Bonaddio (2022)
2. *Machado de Assis: The World Keeps Changing to Remain the Same*, Mario Higa (2022)
3. *María de Zayas and her Tales of Desire, Death and Disillusion*, Margaret R. Greer (2022)
4. *María Félix: A Mexican Film Star and her Legacy*, Niamh Thornton (2023)

MACHADO DE ASSIS

The World Keeps Changing to Remain the Same

Mario Higa

TAMESIS BOOKS

© Mario Higa 2022

All Rights Reserved. Except as permitted under current legislation
no part of this work may be photocopied, stored in a retrieval system,
published, performed in public, adapted, broadcast,
transmitted, recorded or reproduced in any form or by any means,
without the prior permission of the copyright owner

The right of Mario Higa to be identified as
the author of this work has been asserted in accordance with
sections 77 and 78 of the Copyright, Designs and Patents Act 1988

First published 2022
Tamesis Books, Woodbridge
Paperback edition 2025

ISBN 978 1 85566 362 6 (hardback)
ISBN 978 1 85566 421 0 (paperback)

Tamesis Books is an imprint of Boydell & Brewer Ltd
PO Box 9, Woodbridge, Suffolk IP12 3DF, UK
and of Boydell & Brewer Inc.
668 Mt. Hope Avenue, Rochester, NY 14620-2731, USA
website: www.boydellandbrewer.com

Our Authorised Representative for product safety in the EU is Easy Access
System Europe – Mustamäe tee 50, 10621 Tallinn, Estonia,
gpsr.requests@easproject.com

The publisher has no responsibility for the continued existence or accuracy
of URLs for external or third-party internet websites referred to in this book,
and does not guarantee that any content on such websites is, or will remain,
accurate or appropriate

A CIP record for this title is available
from the British Library

To
Paula, Julia, Sophia, and Olivia
(again and always)

To
Earl Fitz
(clever reader of Machado)

Contents

List of Illustrations		ix
A Note on Translations		xi
Acknowledgments		xiii
Chapter 1	"Better than Borges"	1
Chapter 2	Machado de Assis: Life and *Ethos*	37
Chapter 3	Translation, Poetry, and Drama: The Quest for Greatness	71
Chapter 4	Criticism and *Crônica*: The Quest for Greatness Continues	103
Chapter 5	Short Stories: The Dialectical Other	139
Chapter 6	Novels: Lights! Camera! Digression!	169
Chapter 7	The World Keeps Changing to Remain the Same	205
Chapter 8	The Machado Alphabet	221
Coda	Machado's Legacy	231
Appendix 1	Machado de Assis in English	235
Appendix 2	On Machado de Assis in English (Ten Books and a Bonus)	241
Bibliography		245
Index		249

Illustrations

1. Machado de Assis, c. 1864, by José Insley Pacheco, Academia Brasileira de Letras — 134
2. Machado de Assis, c. 1880, by Marc Ferrez — 135
3. Portrait of Machado de Assis, in O *Álbum*, Ano I, nº 2, January 1893 — 136
4. Carolina Augusta Xavier de Novais, when she was 44. Picture by Pacheco & Filho. Arquivo Nacional (Brasil), Fundo Correio da Manhã — 137
5. The house where Machado lived in the neighborhood of Cosme Velho — 137

The author and publisher are grateful to all the institutions and individuals listed for permission to reproduce the materials in which they hold copyright. Every effort has been made to trace the copyright holders; apologies are offered for any omission, and the publisher will be pleased to add any necessary acknowledgement in subsequent editions.

A Note on Translations

All translations are mine unless otherwise indicated.

Acknowledgments

Paula Higa
Margaret May
Megan Milan
Stephen M. Hart
Middlebury College

"Se vogliamo che tutto rimanga com'è, bisogna che tutto cambi."
(*If we want everything to remain the way it is, everything must change.*)
Giuseppe Tomasi di Lampedusa, *Il Gattopardo*

Chapter One

"Better than Borges"

An Opening Anecdote

It was the mid-1980s. I can't exactly recall the year. 1984, or maybe 1985. I had read in the newspaper that Décio Pignatari, one of the founders of the Concrete Poetry movement, was going to deliver a lecture in São Paulo. I was then a high-schooler crazy about soccer, music, and books, and living in my hometown of Santos. Despite the distance – Santos lies approximately 80 kilometers away from São Paulo – I decided to attend the talk. On the scheduled day, I took the bus, then the subway, rushed the streets a few blocks, and eventually arrived at the venue where Pignatari was about to speak. As I write these lines and walk down memory lane, I'm able to see a few pictures in my mind: the room with its huge windows, the high ceiling, lights, and chairs; the overwhelming number of people; the poet wearing his trademark Ben Hogan hat … But I can't remember the subject of the lecture. It was not about Machado de Assis, though. That's for sure.

It turns out that the most vivid memory I have of that night comes from the Q&A section when Pignatari, in answering a question from the audience, did approach the topic of Machado de Assis, and, while developing it, made a bold, provocative statement. Pignatari was known as a *provocateur*, so his statement should not have been taken *that* seriously. Yet, for some reason, I took it that way. That's why it stuck in my memory. Pignatari said – and I will try to replicate his words in translation as closely as possible – "Machado de Assis is not just Brazil's foremost author; he is unquestionably the greatest Latin American writer of all time … better than Borges."

As he spoke, Pignatari's disposition was brightly assertive, and his tone echoed this confidence. Nevertheless, Pignatari never documented what he said that night. Why not? Because he surely knew the consequences he would have faced had he *written* such a statement. Interestingly enough, during my college years in the late 1980s, I heard the same assertion – that Machado was better than Borges – a few more times. I heard it from my professors in hallway conversations or, informally, during a class. They usually approached the topic more like a rumor, or a secret wish, rather than a serious critical claim. No one really seemed to believe it, and, above all, no one was willing to stir up the hornet's nest by writing such an appraisal in an academic paper. The *rumor* only gained public ink in 1990 – and not in Brazil, nor by a Brazilian. It was Susan Sontag in an article for *The New Yorker*, who, while introducing Machado de Assis to an American audience, boldly called him "the greatest author ever produced in Latin America." As for Borges, Sontag, in the same article, referred to him as "the second-greatest writer produced on that continent."[1]

Let's Pause for a Second …

Let me clarify it straightaway: this book will not play the game of "who's better than who." Far from it! When Susan Sontag placed Machado over Borges in the Latin American canon, this, in fact, revealed more about Borges than Machado. In these pages, we'll focus on Machado, not on Borges. So, you may understandably ask: why did the author start off this introduction to Machado de Assis with an anecdote on Jorge Luis Borges? For two main reasons, I would say. First, for stylistic purposes. I wanted to make it clear from the outset that this book is not stylistically designed for "experts"; its target audience includes the general public, and the style, therefore, has been crafted and adjusted accordingly. Certainly, the topic of this book will lead us to venture into the academic terrain at times. However, these incursions into the *academic* will not prevent us, you and me, from having an informal, jargon-free conversation about literature, history, and criticism – or rather books, stories, and a nineteenth-century

---

[1] Susan Sontag, "Afterlives: The Case of Machado de Assis," *New Yorker*, May 7, 1990, 102. Curiously enough, when the article appears reissued in the volume *Where the Stress Falls* (New York: Farrar, Straus and Giroux, 2001), Sontag softens her language and calls Machado "the greatest *novelist* that Latin America has produced," and Borges, "the *other* supremely great writer produced on that continent." *Where the Stress Falls*, 39, emphasis added.

Brazilian writer named Machado de Assis. As I develop my arguments and thoughts, I'll write to answer unasked questions and to address your comments as I imagine them; I commit myself to exploring all possible avenues of this imagined dialogue between us. This book will be our *conversation*, as I best anticipate and conceive it. The opening section above, thus, tries to break the ice as we initiate our *chat*.

The second reason why I shared the story involving Machado and Borges has to do with the title of the series of which this volume is a part: *Icons of the Luso-Hispanic World*. While this book focuses on just one icon from the Lusophone world, I will try to make my case as broadly Luso-Hispanic as possible. In this respect, Borges and other Spanish-language writers (particularly Spanish Americans) will be called into our conversation whenever their presence casts light on the subject being discussed. Drawing parallels between Machado and other authors will help us understand certain aspects that would be harder to grasp if foregoing a comparative approach. In the specific case of Borges and Machado, the comparison is, in principle, justifiable for one simple reason: both occupy the top position in the Latin American and the Brazilian literary canon, respectively. A few critics, such as Sontag, place Machado over Borges. As I said, we won't take this approach. It can be revealing, though, to compare them both for what they have achieved and changed in literary history. Their achievements will provide us with a reliable, and somewhat objective, gauge to measure the greatness of their works. So, for the next few paragraphs, we'll be looking at Borges and Latin America, and then we'll gradually focus in on Machado and Brazil.

A Brief Note and a Trigger Warning

Given my mention of *literary canon* in the last paragraph, I would be remiss if I didn't address the criticism on this concept that's been unfolding over the last decades, particularly in the U.S. The concept of literary canon itself is a complex one, and the debate over it can be viewed as even more intricate.[2] We are not going to harp on these matters, as it would be tangential to our original plan. Suffice it to say, though, that the Western

---

[2] On the concept of literary canon, see John Guillory, "Canon," *Critical Terms for Literary Study*, ed. Frank Lentricchia and Thomas McLaughlin (Chicago: U of Chicago P, 1990), 233–49; and Wendell V. Harris, "Canonicity," *PMLA* (vol. 106, no. 1, Jan. 1991), 110–21. On the debate over canon, see Rachel Donadio, "Revisiting the Canon Wars," *The New York Times*, Sept. 16, 2007,

canon – from Homer to Joyce, from Socrates to Wittgenstein – which was once deemed to be "liberating," has been now regarded as "oppressive."[3] Why liberating? Why oppressive? In a few words, liberating because great texts are potentially capable of making their readers more intellectually autonomous, critical, and sensitive, more aware of themselves and the world in which they live. The charge of oppression, on the other hand, would stem from the issue of who decides which text is great and which is not. In this regard, the question that needs to be answered is, who controls the canon? The short answer is, people from the top of the social pyramid who, in theory, are blind, or tend to be blind, to the feelings of people at the bottom, whose voices have been muted. However, beyond this fierce dispute, there is one point that still remains unquestionable, that of the importance of having a literary canon as a reference available to the readers. Metaphorically speaking, canons function as compasses that guide travelers through the exploration of an unknown territory. The problem is that uncalibrated compasses can get us lost. Moreover, there is no such a thing as a *perfectly calibrated* canon. In the end, we can briefly conclude, without closing the discussion, that literary canons reveal the perspective of a certain group of readers whose values and worldview are conceived within the epistemological conditions of their social position and historical time.

Ultimately, I brought this topic into our conversation in order to clarify the way in which we are going to approach it; we are going to be using a *pragmatic* approach to literary canon. What does this mean? *Pragmatism*, in this context, corresponds to what a given literary work effectively *did* in history, and not simply to an *intrinsic* value that a community of readers, with an inherent dose of subjectivism, *ascribes* to it. Let me give you an example.

In pragmatism, the definition of a phenomenon, either natural or cultural, coincides with its properties and practical effects: how I perceive it with my senses; what it does.[4] For instance, if you asked a pragmatic the-

---

www.nytimes.com/2007/09/16/books/review/Donadio-t.html?searchResultPosition=1
3 John R. Searle, "The Storm Over the University," *The New York Review of Books*, December 6, 1990, www.nybooks.com/articles/1990/12/06/the-storm-over-the-university/
4 On the concept of pragmatism, see Catherine Legg and Christopher Hookway, "Pragmatism," *The Stanford Encyclopedia of Philosophy*, ed. Edward N. Zalta (Summer 2021 Edition), https://plato.stanford.edu/entries/pragmatism/#Bib

orist what gravity is, they would likely answer, "I don't know. But I know what gravity does, and, to me, what gravity *does* is ultimately what gravity *is*." The same logical reasoning could be applied to the definition of wine, politics, love, time, or art. Thus, when I say that Machado de Assis is regarded as the greatest Brazilian writer of all time, I'm referring not to an intrinsic value that his works may have, but rather to their *pragmatic* value, which is measurable through events in history. And here comes the big question (a drum-roll, please): what did Machado's literary works *do*, after all? To a large degree, this book was conceived and designed to answer this question. We need to know what Machado's works *pragmatically* did if we want to gauge their value. In this chapter, we'll start tackling this issue by comparing Borges and Machado in terms of the impacts their works had on literary culture. But before beginning our analysis, we have to draw a schema. And now, it's time for the trigger warning announced in the title of this section.

As the term indicates, a schema is an outline of a complex concept or idea. Schemata are not misconceptions, but they can lead to misconceptions. Notwithstanding, schematic ideas can be at times quite useful to provide a foundation on which we can develop more elaborate concepts. And that's exactly what we're going to do next: draw a schema about cultural geopolitics (i.e. center–periphery relationships) and rely on it in order to move forward into more complicated issues. I remind you, my dearest reader, that this book is not a treatise on, but instead an introduction to Machado de Assis. So here, I warn you: we have to rely at times on sketches, outlines, and generalizations. Nevertheless (and this is a huge *nevertheless*), whenever I feel that we are landing on helpful but too simplistic concepts, I will suggest additional reading in the footnotes – as I did a few lines above regarding literary canon and philosophical pragmatism (see footnotes 2 and 4). Deal?

Ethnocentrisms: Eurocentrism and U.S.-centrism

In general terms, Geopolitics Studies focus on the relationship between space and power. Think about this relationship as applied to three global regions: Latin America (mainly Portuguese and Spanish America, or Brazil and Hispanic America), North America (the U.S. and Canada), and Europe. Historically, what has been the power exchange among them? Overall, from an economic and cultural standpoint, Europe and North America have constituted central, dominant areas, whereas Latin America has played a secondary, peripheral role in this game. In other words, this means that Latin America has been greatly dependent on Europe and North America. What does this dependency say about the region in practical terms? It basically says that Latin America has been an importer more than an exporter of both commercial and cultural products. It also says that, as an importer, Latin America is constantly looking in three directions: towards North America, towards Europe, and towards itself. To put it differently, whenever Latin America creates a cultural product (like music, cinema, or literature), the creator has one eye upon North America, another upon Europe, and a third upon Latin America. This way of perceiving may be viewed, at first, as an advantage to Latin America. In São Paulo, for instance, people are aware of what is going on in New York, Berlin, and São Paulo. But, by and large, in New York or Berlin, people don't know what is happening in São Paulo. In Buenos Aires, people read and discuss the works of Margaret Atwood, Elena Ferrante, and Samanta Schweblin. But in Toronto or Milan, it is not that easy, I guess, to find readers interested in Samanta Schweblin. (By the way, have you read Samanta Schweblin yet? Believe me, you should!) From this standpoint, one could say, again, that Latin America has the advantage of surveying more options, or seeking out a wider field of vision, when compared to Europe and North America, whose eyes stare only at one another.

And yet, despite this "advantage," Latin America continues to be – over the years, decades, and centuries – culturally isolated and economically dependent upon the north-central areas. Why is this so? For several reasons, but I will briefly tackle one: colonialism, or rather, forms of colonialism. In principle, and also in practice, colonialism (has) favored Europe, the colonizer. By the same token, colonialism rendered the colonized (i.e. the Americas) widely vulnerable. However, history has shown that within the Americas, the North has been less vulnerable than the South; hence the wide economic gap that separates North and Latin America. Why this gap? How was it created? One possible answer is, again, colonialism. The way the English settled in and built up a new society (especially in New England) differs significantly from the same process as implemented by the Spanish and the Portuguese in the South.[5] Therefore, the economic discrepancy between North and Latin America has one of its roots in the colonial past. As for the specific factors that oppose these forms of colonialism, we will comment on a few of them later. It's important to put together general assumptions and specific, concrete examples, and I will. For now, however, it's worth noting that economics and culture go hand in hand.

---

5   I'm not including here the French or the Dutch, for this would fall out of our scope of analysis.

Up until the middle of the twentieth century, this means that, culturally speaking, Latin America was predominantly perceived as an exotic place through the eyes of Europe and North America. See, in this respect, how Disney Studios portrayed the region in the movies *Saludos Amigos* (1942) and *The Three Caballeros* (1944). Switching gears from cinema to sport, and backtracking to a few years earlier, the Brazilian national soccer team traveled to France in 1938 to participate in the third World Cup. When they arrived in Paris, the headline of the newspaper *Le Petit Parisien* read: "Voici les Brésiliens avec leur café et leur guitares" ("Here are the Brazilians with their coffee and their guitars").[6] Brazil was seen then as the land of coffee and popular music. Has this perception changed? Not much. For most Europeans and Americans, Brazil continues to be a place mainly associated with popular music (samba, Bossa Nova, Carnival), food (coffee, sugar, "caipirinha"), and soccer.[7] What about Latin America at large? Have the foreigners' perceptions changed? This is another different and more complex issue. In literary terms, the so-called Latin American Boom of the 1960s and 1970s definitely contributed to revamping the image of the region. However, it's worth observing that before the Boom phenomenon, there was Borges; and, before Borges, there was Machado de Assis. Or, as Salman Rushdie puts it, "If Borges is the writer who made García Márquez possible, then it is no exaggeration to say that Machado de Assis is the writer who made Borges possible."[8]

What About Africa in the Context of Nineteenth-Century Geopolitics?

Machado de Assis was of African descent from his father's side. Machado's paternal grandparents were born enslaved but were freed by their owners at some point in their lives – probably when they got married.[9] How Machado expressed his African roots in his personal life as well as in

---

6 *Le Petit Parisien*, May 17, 1938, 6. The picture that illustrates the news article indeed shows guitar cases among the luggage of the Brazilian delegation. No coffee is visible, though.
7 The dark side of the stereotype about Brazil also includes sexual tourism, unfortunately.
8 Apud Machado de Assis, *The Posthumous Memoirs of Brás Cubas*, trans. Flora Thomson-DeVeaux (New York: Penguin, 2020), iii.
9 Jean-Michel Massa, *A juventude de Machado de Assis*, trans. Marco Aurélio de Moura Matos (Rio de Janeiro: Civilização Brasileira, 1971), 32–33.

his literary works will be a matter of discussion in the next chapters. How Brazilians perceived Machado in terms of race will be also commented on later. Here, I want to briefly focus on Africa in the context of nineteenth-century geopolitics.

In Africa, the nineteenth century ends in the 1880s, when Europeans established the infamous *scramble* for the continent, the greatest land grab in history. Before the 1880s, Europeans and North and South Americans saw Africa, particularly West Africa, mostly as a supplier of slave labor. In 1807, "the British government prohibited the slave trade to British traders and converted the freed-slave settlement in Freetown into a Crown Colony and a base for a West Africa-wide naval campaign against the slave trade."[10] The British campaign and actions go along with the birth of abolitionist movements in Europe and the Americas. In Brazil, despite the arduous work of abolitionist groups, slavery remained legal until 1888.

Throughout the nineteenth century, but particularly during the second half, Brazil was the scene of a dispute between abolitionists and anti-abolitionists. Slavery, therefore, was a recurrent topic during Machado's lifetime. This does not mean, however, that overall interest in Africa from Brazilians, or Americans, or Europeans, went beyond economic issues, such as forced labor and colonialism. Beyond these points, Europeans and Americans (i.e. people from the Americas) were mostly, and blissfully, ignorant about Africa. This state of things, by the way, has not changed much, despite improvements in some areas. In Brazil, for instance, one relevant act in this regard was the signing of Law 10.639, which made it mandatory for private and public middle and high schools to include in their curriculums the History of Africa and Afro-Brazilian culture. This law was signed in ... 2003, that is to say, 115 years after the abolition of slavery in the country.[11]

As I write these lines, it wouldn't be inaccurate to say that Africa, its peoples and its cultures, still remains to be discovered by those who colonized the continent (Europeans) and those who used its workforce as slave labor (Europeans and Americans). It wouldn't be unfair as well to say that Brazil, the largest importer of African slave labor in history, has (or should have) more interest in *discovering* Africa than other countries.

---

10 J. F. A. Ajayi, "Africa at the Beginning of the Nineteenth Century: Issues and Prospects," *General History of Africa*, vol. VI, ed. J. F. A. Ajayi (Paris: UNESCO, 1989), 6.

11 Here are the terms of Law 10.639/2003 (in Portuguese): www.planalto.gov.br/ccivil_03/leis/2003/l10.639.htm

Why? Simply put, because the legacy of African culture for the formation of Brazil is enormous. Brazil as we know it is unthinkable without the contribution of Africa. However, Brazil *as we know it*, the country of samba, *capoeira*, and *feijoada*, the nation of the so-called "racial democracy," was largely invented in the 1930s during the administration of Getúlio Vargas.

The country in which Machado was born and grew up was a quite different one. Brazil during Machado's lifetime was a young nation in search of a mythology that could shape its national identity. In this regard, Romantic writers such as José de Alencar and Gonçalves Dias made efforts, respectively in the novel and in poetry, to create a foundational mythology for Brazil. In this mythology, both Alencar and Dias fictionally recreate the nation's past through the idealization of Native Indians. Romantic Indianism thus became the basis for Brazilian nationalism, the mirror into which the newly independent nation was supposed to look and feel proud of itself. As we shall see in Chapter Three, Machado himself embraced Indianism in *Americanas*, a poetry collection published in 1875.

Still in the context of Brazilian Romanticism, Castro Alves distinguished himself by writing abolitionist poetry. The abolitionist movement mobilized various types of discourse to achieve its political goals. In Brazil, poetry became one of the most notable in this regard. In the poetic discourse, black Africa and Africans were placed at the center of a humanitarian battle, a battle for freedom and justice. Africa and Africans, their culture and legacy, were then not seen as a component of Brazilian national identity. So, you may ask, when did African culture eventually begin to be acknowledged as a key part of Brazil's national identity? In order to address this topic, we need to approach it in two separate times: the 1840s and the 1930s.

In 1840, the then recently inaugurated Brazilian Historic and Geographic Institute offered a prize for the best essay that outlined a plan to write the history of Brazil. The winner was a German naturalist named Karl Friedrich Phillip von Martius. His essay, titled "How the History of Brazil Should Be Written," was published in 1844. In this work, von Martius proposed, for the first time, the idea of a racial history of Brazil. "Whoever takes on the task of writing the History of Brazil," von Martius states, "must never lose sight of those elements that converge there and that are part of the development of man." And he continues:

> These are, however, very diverse natural elements that have been brought together for man's formation of *three races*, namely, the copper-colored or American, the white Caucasian, and finally the black

or Ethiopian. Out of the encounter, the mixture, out of the mutual relations and the changes in these three races, today's population was formed, which is why its history has a very particular hallmark.[12]

Von Martius's statement was utterly visionary. His vision, however, foreshadowed interpretations that would gain historical and anthropological traction almost a century later. The central work in this respect is Gilberto Freyre's *Casa-Grande & Senzala* (translated as *The Masters and the Slaves*), published in 1933. To a great extent, Freyre's study provided a basis for Getúlio Vargas to establish a concept of national identity based on the re-evaluation (and appreciation) of the notion of "mestiçagem" (interracial unions).[13] To give just one example: in 1937, under Varga's regime, the practice of the Afro-Brazilian capoeira was decriminalized (capoeira had been a criminal act since 1890). This should not be seen as a chance happening. It was part of a whole project designed to popularize Afro-Brazilian culture and introduce a new set of national symbols. During the Vargas Era, Brazilians eventually embraced – or at least started the process of embracing – their African roots.

One additional note before going back to Machado. It is worth mentioning that prior to Gilberto Freyre and his *Casa-Grande & Senzala*, Mário de Andrade had already created a mythical hero who combines in himself the three races that historically formed Brazilian culture and identity: Macunaíma. Published in 1928, *Macunaíma* depicts a protagonist who is born Indian with black skin and who magically turns into a white man in the first half of the narrative. Mário de Andrade's Macunaíma synthesizes the virtues and vices – where vices can be virtues and virtues can be vices – of an Afro-Indian-European being who became a paradigmatic symbol of the multifaceted, multiracial, and carnivalesque concept of Brazilianess.

As we can see, there is a wide gap in the racial history of Brazil that goes from von Martius's 1844 essay up until Mário de Andrade's *Macunaíma*, in 1928. Or, as has already been said, von Martius's proposal of a history of Brazil that included the three races of its formation would end up drawing

---

[12] Carl Friedrich Phillip von Martius, "How to Write the History of Brazil," trans. Emma Wohl, *The Brazil Reader*, 2nd edn., eds. James N. Green, Victoria Langland, and Lilia Moritz Schwarcz (Durham, NC: Duke UP, 2019), 187–88. Emphasis added.

[13] I use the Portuguese word "mestiçagem" to avoid derogatory connotations associated with the English counterpart "miscegenation." In Portuguese, "mestiçagem" has no such connotations.

the attention of intellectuals almost a century later. Generally speaking, between von Martius and Mário de Andrade, Africa constituted a political topic related to European economic interests, and Africans were seen as a humanitarian cause to be supported. In the English language, we could think of two nineteenth-century fictional works that somehow sum up these two lines of thought: Harriet Beecher Stowe's *Uncle Tom's Cabin* (1852), which fueled the abolitionist movement in the Northern U.S., and Joseph Conrad's *Heart of Darkness* (1899), which denounced the horrifying methods and effects of colonialism in the region of Congo as a metonym for the African continent.

Machado de Assis wrote almost uninterruptedly from 1854 – ten years after von Martius's essay – up until his death in 1908 – twenty years before Mário de Andrade's *Macunaíma*. This places Machado's works, therefore, in the abovementioned gap where black Africa and enslaved Africans had no voice in the widespread game of power disputed by white Europeans and their American counterparts and descendants.

However, despite the gap that separates, in terms of racial perception, Machado from von Martius and Mário de Andrade, the three of them have at least one feature in common: von Martius was *the first* to put forward a project to write a history of Brazil based on the role played by the three races, or ethnic groups, that built the country: Native American, African, and European. Mário de Andrade was *the first* to bring this idea into the fictional realm before it became a general trend in sociological and anthropological studies. For his turn, Machado de Assis was *the first* ... Well, this issue will require a bit more space. Maybe another section ...

The First

Who was the first European navigator who travelled to the Americas? Using *the first* in this question introduces a historical category, and at times a slippery category as well. It was most likely not Christopher Columbus, the European who first encountered the native people of the Americas. Sometimes, though, this concept of *the first* is not as complicated. Who was the first man to step on the moon? Neil Armstrong, for sure. Let's unpack this category of *the first* a bit more.

Throughout the nineteenth century, European culture ruled sovereign and alone over the Western World. European culture and its products were confidently self-resourceful and, consequently, had no companion, or rather no need for a companion, from the New World. The first author from the Americas to break through the European blockade (a.k.a.

Eurocentrism) was Edgar Allan Poe. Charles Baudelaire's praise and translations into French of Poe's works are a historical landmark for the reception of American literature in Europe. This milestone opened the borders for other American writers – such as Emerson, Hawthorne, and Twain – to be appreciated, although timidly, on the Old Continent. Meanwhile, names such as Thoreau, Melville, and Dickinson – to mention just a few – were either ignored or underestimated by European readers. The history of the animosity towards American authors in Europe started gradually to change only after World War I.[14] In any case, this is the point I want to underline here: Poe was *the first* Western, non-European author whose work was recognized by a qualified European audience as having superior merit. Poe's achievement was of extraordinary historical significance, given the fact that Eurocentrism – or the European sense of cultural superiority – constitutes a solid barrier not easily transcended. Poe did it – and so did Borges, approximately one century later.

To be more specific, let me note two dates: 1848 and 1966. In 1848, Baudelaire published his first French translation of a Poe story, "Mesmeric Revelation." This event can be viewed as the starting point for the European "conquest" by the American writer Edgar Allan Poe, who, by the way, was still alive in 1848. Now, let's jump to 1966. During this year, Michel Foucault published his celebrated essay *Les Mots et les choses*, whose opening line reads: "This book first arose out of a passage in Borges."[15] What does this mean from a historical standpoint? This means that in 1966, Borges, who had already been translated into other languages, became the first Latin American author to be cited *as a source* by a world-class European thinker.

If you trace back in time, you'll see that Nietzsche admired Emerson; Freud read Shakespeare; Heidegger examined van Gogh; Adorno commented on Kafka; Gadamer quoted Rilke; and Lacan analyzed Poe. Foucault's tribute to Borges in *Les Mots et les choses* may be seen, therefore, as a symbol: a gesture that symbolically raised the status of (the Latin American) Borges up to the level of (the American) Poe, Emerson, (and the European) Shakespeare, van Gogh, Kafka, and Rilke. Foucault's gesture

---

14 See Joseph Remenyi, "American Writers in Europe," *The Georgia Review*, vol. 2, no. 4 (Winter 1948), 461–65.
15 Michel Foucault, *The Order of Things*, English edition by Tavistock Publications [1970] (London: Routledge, 2002), xvi.

also raised metonymically the status of Latin America in Europe.[16] When the so-called Latin American Boom began to export its authors in the late 1960s, the road had already been paved by Borges. The late 1960s was the time when European and American readers discovered and explored the works of Gabriel García Márquez, Julio Cortázar, Mario Vargas Llosa, Alejo Carpentier, and Carlos Fuentes, among others. From this point on, tourists' exotic image of Latin America would compete with another, more complex, modern, and sophisticated image. And what about Machado de Assis? That's a different story, full of ups and downs, which we will start examining now.

Machado was born in 1839 (ten years before Poe's death) and died in 1908 (nine years after the birth of Borges). Like both Poe and Borges, Machado shares the pioneering position of being the first to project a modern, non-exotic image of his country internationally through critically acclaimed literary works. He didn't do so as successfully as Poe and Borges, but this story is still unfolding, and new chapters are coming out (like the one you have in your hands, for instance). At this point, the question is: why has Machado not been as successful as Poe and Borges?

"I am astonished," Susan Sontag affirms about Machado, "that a writer of such greatness does not yet occupy the place he deserves."[17] The place to which Sontag refers is a seat at the table of world literature. This feeling of astonishment is shared by every scholar of Machado, inside and outside Brazil. "Arguably the major literary figure of all time in Latin American literature," David Jackson asks, "why should [Machado's] name remain a mystery to world literature and his works still be comparatively unknown?"[18] Does it have to do with the fact that Machado wrote in Por-

---

16 In this regard, Earl Fitz points out that the 1964 edition of *On Contemporary Literature*, edited by Richard Kostelanetz, contains studies on American, Canadian, French, German, Spanish (though not Portuguese), and British authors. In Kostelanetz's "widely disseminated book," Latin America has zero presence! The 1969 edition, though, relented "in its European reverie" and included one Latin American writer: Borges. And Fitz concludes: "Even by the late 1960s, it seems, not all American scholars and critics were concerned with Latin American literature or with granting it a seat at the world literary table." "The Reception of Machado de Assis in the United States during the 1950s and 1960s," *Luso-Brazilian Review*, vol. 46, no. 1 (2009), 22.
17 Susan Sontag, "Susan Sontag on Machado de Assis," *Mutual Impressions*, ed. Ilan Stavans (Durham, NC: Duke UP, 1999), 280.
18 David Jackson, *Machado de Assis: A Literary Life* (New Haven, CT: Yale UP, 2015), x.

tuguese, a marginalized language in the European context? Does it have to do with the translations of Machado's works into other languages? As you may imagine, there is no simple way to address these questions. But we can start with an overview of Machado's reception outside Brazil to help us better understand these issues. I'll be focusing on two main areas: France and the Anglo-American world. At the time of writing, Machado has already been translated into nineteen languages. By looking at his works translated into French and English, though, we can get a fair sense of how Machado has been treated by foreign readers.

Machado de Assis in Translation

The beginning of this story has three moments: 1882, 1888, and 1899. In 1882, Machado wrote a letter to his brother-in-law Miguel Novais, in which he stated that his novel *Memórias póstumas de Brás Cubas* (*Posthumous Memoirs of Brás Cubas*), published the previous year – and henceforth referred to as *Brás Cubas* – was being translated into German. This letter is unfortunately lost. It is possible, though, to infer what was in this letter from the response by Novais dated November 2, 1882.[19] For unknown reasons, the announced translation was not completed. Six years later, in 1888, Machado signed a document in which he granted permission for another German rendition of *Brás Cubas*. The translator was a certain Curt Busch von Besa, about whom modern scholars know nothing. This project somehow failed as well. Finally, in 1899, Machado received a letter in which a friend, Alfredo Ellis, informed him that Alexandrina Highland, a woman then living in São Paulo, had shown a willingness to translate Machado's works into German. We have no other information on who Alexandrina Highland was, nor which works she wanted to translate. We do know, however, that in January 1899, months before receiving the letter from Ellis, Machado had sold the copyright to all his titles but one – *Várias histórias* (*Assorted Stories*), published in 1896 by Casa Laemmert – to his publisher, Hippolyte Garnier. Therefore, Machado could not legally authorize the translation of his works – except for *Várias histórias*, which wasn't on the radar of any translator.

---

19 Along with others, Novais's letter was published in *O Estado de São Paulo*, June 20, 1964, 36. There, Novais says to Machado, in response to a previous letter: "I appreciated knowing that your *Brás Cubas* was being translated into German."

Machado then wrote to Garnier and urged the publisher to grant a copyright license to Ms. Highland. For his part, Machado affirmed that he would waive any pecuniary compensation from the agreement, "for I consider," he stated in French, "that it's an advantage per se to become known in a foreign language, whose market is so different and so far away from ours. I believe," he concludes, "this is an advantage for you as well."[20] In a letter from Paris a few weeks later, Hippolyte Garnier refused to comply with Machado's appeal. The reasons for Garnier's stance on such a decision are both clear and unclear. We won't go into this issue further for it would lead us down another road.[21] The point I want to highlight here is that, from 1882 to 1899, there were three frustrated attempts to translate Machado de Assis into German. At the time, Machado had already been widely acclaimed in Brazil, and his works, particularly *Brás Cubas*, had started to attract international attention. Despite Machado's efforts to make his books accessible to readers in other languages, the time for that to happen had yet to come.

The time eventually came in 1902, when a Spanish rendition of *Brás Cubas* by Julio Piquet appeared in *feuilleton* form on the pages of the Uruguayan newspaper *La Razón*. A few years after preventing the translation of Machado's works into German, Hippolyte Garnier decided to promote the author in Spanish and French. In 1905, in Buenos Aires, *Esaú e Jacó* (*Esau and Jacob*), originally published the year before, became the second of Machado's novels to appear in Spanish. The volume doesn't indicate the name of the translator. The Argentinian edition of *Esaú e Jacó* was the second and the last of Machado's works to be published in translation during his lifetime.

When Machado died in 1908, he was already widely celebrated as the national writer of Brazil, a position that he still holds in Brazilian culture. Given the greatness of his works, it was seen as a natural progression that he should become internationally known. At this time, at the beginning of the twentieth century, "internationally" meant primarily to France, or, better yet, to Paris, then the cultural center of the world. However, French hegemony in the field of arts and culture, albeit dominant,

---

20 Machado de Assis, *Correspondência de Machado de Assis*, vol. III, ed. Sérgio Paulo Rouanet (Rio de Janeiro: ABL, 2011), 378–79.
21 For those interested in this topic, see Lúcia Granja, "Três é demais! (Ou por que Garnier não traduziu Machado de Assis?)," *Machado de Assis em Linha*, no. 25 (2018), 18–32. Available at www.scielo.br/pdf/mael/v11n25/1983-6821-mael-11-25-0018.pdf

was being threatened by England, Germany, Italy, and the United States. For this reason, the French government had decided to launch a project called *latinité* (Latinness, Latinhood) at the end of the nineteenth century. Strategically designed and financially funded, *latinité* was planned to help France increase its influence around the world. The plan specified, among other goals, strengthening the bonds of France with its "sister republics" of Latin America.[22] It's in this context of political proximity and cultural exchange between France and Brazil that, in 1909, the diplomat and historian Oliveira Lima was invited to deliver a lecture at the Sorbonne entitled "Machado de Assis and His Literary Works." Taking advantage of this opportunity, Anatole France, while introducing Oliveira Lima, referred to Machado de Assis as an artist whose works genuinely represented the spirit of "le génie latin" ("the Latin genius").[23] It should be noted that, back then, the prestige held by Anatole France as a man of letters was enormous.

In 1909, Machado's works started to be translated into French. Poems and one story, "O enfermeiro" ("The Caregiver"), appeared in French journals. In 1910, Adrien Delpech translated *Várias histórias*. The next year, it was *Brás Cubas*'s turn, also translated by Delpech. Still in 1911, the Sorbonne offered a course on Brazilian studies for the first time. Everything in France seemed to conspire in favor of Brazil and Machado. What actually transpired, however, would belie all these good omens. Despite the actions to promote Machado, his works had little impact among French readers. Why? Well, let me focus on two possible reasons: translation and expectation.

Adrien Delpech's translation of *Brás Cubas* apparently failed to capture Machado's wry and ironic style. Moreover, Delpech awkwardly cuts off one chapter of the novel as well as the somber-sarcastic Brás Cubas's dedication: "To the worm that first gnawed at the cold flesh of my cadaver I dedicate as a fond remembrance these posthumous memoirs."[24] These opening words, vertically arranged on the page in a form that resembles an

22 See Jacqueline Penjon, "Machado de Assis: um século de traduções francesas," *E-letras com vida*, no. 2 (2019), 188–201.
23 See Oliveira Lima & Victor Orban, *Machado de Assis: son œuvre littéraire*, avec un préface de Anatole France. Available at www.gutenberg.org/files/57360/57360-h/57360-h.htm#LE_GENIE_LATIN
24 Machado de Assis, *Posthumous Memoirs of Brás Cubas*, trans. Flora Thomson-DeVeaux (New York: Penguin, 2020), xli. Both Thomson-DeVeaux's and Jull Costa & Robin Patterson's (New York: Liveright, 2020) recent translations of the novel are excellent to my taste. Whenever quoting *Brás Cubas* in

inscription on a tomb, sets the tone for the entire narrative. If readers don't step across this threshold to enter the book, they will likely get lost. For readers who do step across this threshold, the chances of getting lost are still high; but for those who don't, chances are – obviously! – even higher.

Expectation may be the second reason for Machado's unsuccessful reception in France. What did French readers, at the beginning of the twentieth century, expect to find in a Brazilian novel? Exoticism, or the wild appeal of the unfamiliar. French readers wished to see the picturesque, colorful landscape of the countryside, with its local and native characters, and their customs, attire, foods, beliefs, patterns of morality, and so on. They wished to read, let's say, an authentic, Latin American René de Chateaubriand, or, at the very least, some fictional, modern account in the lineage of Jean de Léry's *Histoire d'un voyage fait en la terre de Brésil* (*History of a Voyage to the Land of Brazil*). They wished, in sum, everything that Machado's fiction does not deliver, but the narratives of José de Alencar, Alfredo Taunay, and Coelho Neto would do instead. The result was that from 1896, as part of the *latinité* project, Alencar, Taunay, and Coelho Neto were being translated into French. *O Guarani* by Alencar, for example, was released in 1902, in a translation signed by Xavier de Ricard, with the suggestive title *Le fils du soleil* (*The Son of the Sun*). *Iracema*, another huge success by Alencar, was published serialized, in 1907, translated by Philéas Lebesgue. Furthermore, it's worth remembering that exoticism was a trend in France and, as a consequence, in Europe at that time. To give just two notable examples, think of the Orientalism in Debussy's music or the Africanism in Picasso's paintings.

Let's jump to the 1930s and focus on three events that occurred in 1934, 1936, and 1938. In 1934, the University of São Paulo was created. Scholars from all over the world were invited to teach there. Due to historical cooperation between France and Brazil – the *latinité* project was just one chapter of this cooperation – France was the country that sent the largest number of researchers. The French scholars played a pivotal role in bringing new methods of research and new critical theories to the newborn Brazilian academia. Names such as Claude Lévi-Strauss, Fernand Braudel, Pierre Monbeig, Paul Arbousse-Bastide, Martial Gueroult, and Roger Bastide helped shape and refine a brilliant generation of Brazilian intellectuals, such as Antonio Candido, Florestan Fernandes, and Fernando Henrique Cardoso, among others. To a certain degree, this second

---

this book, I'll be using Thomson-DeVeaux's version just as a matter of being consistent with one edition.

"French Mission" (the first was a group of French artists and architects who travelled to Brazil in 1816, under the patronage of the Portuguese royal family, who were living in Rio de Janeiro at the time) founded the University of São Paulo and re-founded Brazil. Lévi-Strauss, for instance, in exploring the backlands of Central Brazil, discovered an unknown country, which he reveals in *Tristes Tropiques* (1955). Roger Bastide, for his turn, working in the frontiers of sociology and literary criticism, discovered an unknown Machado de Assis, whom he revealed in a 1940 essay entitled "Machado de Assis, paisagista" ("Machado de Assis, the Landscape Painter" – See Chapter Eight, letter B).

In 1936, a French edition of Machado de Assis's *Dom Casmurro* came out, translated by Francis de Miomandre. When Roger Bastide read Machado for the first time, it was in Miomandre's translation, which he praised. Bastide also praised René Chadebec de Lavalade's new version of *Brás Cubas* released in 1944. Translation, thus, did not appear to be a setback for Machado's reception in France in the 1930s and 1940s. Moreover, Machado had a strong supporter in Bastide, who acted for years as a cultural mediator between Brazil and France, and, as such, advocated for Machado in his home country. Nevertheless, despite this conjunction of efficient translations with Bastide's continuing efforts, it was not the time for Machado to take off in French territory. This can be explained, albeit partially, by the fact that Machado had gained a weighty Brazilian rival there ...

In 1938, Éditions Gallimard released Jorge Amado's *Jubiabá*, translated by Michel Berveiller and Pierre Hourcade. The book became a tremendous success and awakened the interest of French readers in Brazil. Throughout the following years, particularly after World War II, names such as Euclides da Cunha, José Lins do Rego, Afrânio Peixoto, Graciliano Ramos, and Jorge Amado had some of their works published in France.[25] This selection of authors exhibited the continuing taste for exotic tropics (*exotic* and *sensual*, in the case of Amado) among French audiences. Machado, whom Bastide compares to Proust and Pirandello, was then viewed as too much of a "European."[26] Maybe *that* was the real obstacle preventing him from being widely accepted in Europe at that point. Europeans were eager, especially from the 1950s onward, to find the "Brazilianess" (whatever

---

25 For a complete list of Brazilian titles published in France from 1823 to 1993, see Teresa Dias da Cunha, "A literatura brasileira traduzida na França: o caso de *Macunaíma*," *Cadernos de Tradução*, vol. 1, no. 2 (1997), 309–26.
26 In 1939, Bastide refers to Machado as "l'original devancier d'un Proust ou d'un Pirandello" [*the original predecessor of a Proust or a Pirandello*]. Apud Jacqueline Penjon, "Machado de Assis: um século de traduções francesas," 196.

that might be) in the stories written by Brazilian authors. In this regard, Machado was not considered the best option.

Let's Pause for a Second ...

I bet you're thinking of ... Borges! Right? Like Machado, Borges, too, can be viewed as "European," or, on the scale of regionalism, as more "European" than "Latin American," or more "European" than "Argentinean." Well, Borges was indeed something of a European as he lived in Europe from 1914 to 1921, from the age of 15 to 22. The same cannot be said about Machado, who, during his lifetime, was barely able to stir from his hometown of Rio de Janeiro. The European experience for Machado came through his reading of European authors, his acquaintance with European people in Rio, and, above all, Carolina, his Portuguese wife. However, despite this difference in terms of experience, there is one point of intersection that creates a curious similarity between the two writers. Borges has been unanimously considered to be the national writer of Argentina. Nonetheless, there are other candidates for that position stronger than Borges: Domingo Faustino Sarmiento or José Hernández, for instance. (As a matter of fact, before Borges was placed at the top of the Argentinian canon, Hernández occupied it.) From a narrow perspective of nationalism, both Sarmiento and Hernández are more "Argentinian" than Borges. The same argument could be applied to Machado, the national writer of Brazil. José de Alencar or Mário de Andrade, for example, dug deep in search of the "authentic" Brazilian identity. From this angle, both Alencar and Andrade are more "Brazilian" than Machado.

Curiously enough, Borges and Machado tackled this issue in their critical writings. In a lecture delivered in 1979, at the University of Belgrano, Borges asserted that Dr. Johnson could have been chosen to represent England as its national writer. "But, no," argued Borges, "England has chosen Shakespeare, and Shakespeare is – let's say – the least English among the English writers." The case of Germany and Goethe followed a similar path as, in Borges' view, Goethe did not demonstrate much interest in "the concept of fatherland." As for Spain and Cervantes, Borges stated that the author of the *Quixote* – different from Lope de Vega, Calderón, or Quevedo – "is a man who has neither the Spanish virtues nor the Spanish vices."[27] For Borges, in sum, England, Germany, and Spain could have

---

27 Jorge Luis Borges, *Obras completas*, vol. IV (Buenos Aires: Emecé Editores, 2005), 181.

been better represented – again, from a strictly nationalist standpoint – by writers other than those that these countries had actually elected. Over a century before, in 1873, Machado de Assis developed analogous ideas in one of his central essays, "Instinto de nacionalidade" ("Instinct of Nationality"), which we will discuss in Chapter Four.

Back to Machado in France

Let's take a look at the results of a survey conducted in France between 1978 and 1980. In response to the question "Have you heard of these Brazilian authors?", only 1% of the general public replied "yes" for Machado de Assis, against 8% for Jorge Amado, and 3% for João Guimarães Rosa.[28] Thirsty for more statistics? In a thirty-year period, from 1969 to 1999, graduate students in French universities defended nine doctoral dissertations on Jorge Amado, five on Guimarães Rosa, and only three on Machado de Assis.[29] The first of these three was Jean-Michel Massa's *La jeunesse de Machado de Assis (1839–1870), essai de biographie intellectuelle* (*The Youth of Machado de Assis [1839–1870], Essay on Intellectual Biography*), defended in 1969 at the University of Poitiers. But although academic interest and numbers have been low for Machado in France, this does not reflect the quality of the works that were produced there. Since being published in Brazil in 1971, Massa's study has received continuous praise from critics for both the amount of research the author carried out and the robust results he achieved. Massa's *La jeunesse* indisputably occupies one of the top positions in the enormous bibliography on Machado de Assis. In addition to Roger Bastide, Massa is another name of utmost importance in regard to the history of Machado's reception in France.

Back to the Opening Anecdote

During Décio Pignatari's lecture, I remember that, while talking about Machado, he referred to Massa's work without mentioning his name. Pignatari said – and, again, I'll try to come as close to the original sentiment as possible:

---

28 See Jacqueline Penjon, "Machado de Assis: um século de traduções francesas," 198.
29 http://crbc.ehess.fr/docannexe/file/3193/litterature_1823_1999.pdf

Some enigmas involving Machado still remain, although some have already been unraveled. As for the latter, consider, for instance, the case of Carolina, who was 34 years old when she married Machado. The "official" history taught us that Carolina had come to Brazil from Portugal to take care of her sick brother, the Portuguese poet Faustino Xavier, who was then living in Rio. We naively bought this version. In part, because it was partially true. And, in part, because we didn't want to raise morally dangerous questions about Machado. Why was Carolina, as a 34-year-old woman in the mid-nineteenth century, still single? Did she have suitors in Portugal? She may have had one, or even more. Who was he, or who were they? Did some romantic imbroglio happen before she rushed to Brazil? Only recently, one century later, a French researcher came and solved the puzzle involving Machado's wife, Carolina.

I clearly recalled being shocked by Pignatari's words. Who was the "French researcher" who did the work that we, Brazilians, should have done? What did he find out about Carolina, to whom Machado was married for thirty-five years? I later discovered that the French researcher was Jean-Michel Massa. As for his findings on Carolina, those have to wait until the next chapter.

Final Note on Machado in France

Carolina played a crucial role in Machado's life, for a number of reasons that we'll also be examining in Chapter Two. After Machado's death, other women made invaluable contributions towards Machado's reception inside and outside of Brazil. Like Carolina, they are central figures in this story. The effectiveness and quality of their input into promoting Machado are beyond dispute. I'm specifically referring to three women: the Brazilian Lúcia Miguel-Pereira, whose critical works on Machado had immense impact in the 1930s and 1940s; the American Helen Caldwell, whose translations and critical studies projected Machado into the English-speaking world during the 1950s and 1960s; and the French Anne-Marie Métailié, whose publishing activities have circulated Machado's works in France through excellent editions from the 1980s to date.

In the 1960s, Anne-Marie Métailié studied Portuguese at the Sorbonne with the Brazilian literary critic Antonio Candido and Jorge Amado's French translator, Georges Boisvert. In these skilled hands, Anne-Marie, unsurprisingly, fell in love with Brazil and Brazilian literature, particularly that of Machado de Assis. In 1979, she founded the publishing house

Métailié, which specialized in authors from the Luso-Hispanic world. As part of a personal project, Anne-Marie commissioned a new translation of *Dom Casmurro* to be released in 1983. The novel received highly positive reviews. Following *Dom Casmurro*, Métailié published *L'aliéniste* (1984), *Esaü et Jacob* (1985), *La montre en or* [stories] (1987), *Mémoires posthumes de Brás Cubas* (1989), *Quincas Borba* (1990), *Ce que les hommes appellent amour* [Memorial de Aires] (1995), and *La théorie du médaillon et autres contes* (2002) [stories]. All these titles are new translations, except for *Brás Cubas*, which was a reprint of Chadebec de Lavalade's rendition. Anne-Marie selected a hand-picked team of translators. Each volume provides the reader with a fine introduction written by a notable critic. In sum, Anne-Marie's dedication to disseminating Machado's works in France eventually yielded results. Since the late 1980s, for instance, Machado has often been cited as a literary reference by renowned French theorists and scholars such as Gérard Genette (*Seuils*, 1987), Pascale Casanova (*La république mondiale des lettres*, 1999), and Tiphaine Samoyault (*La montre casée*, 2004). Due in large part to Anne-Marie Métailié, Machado de Assis has gained momentum in France.

Machado de Assis in the Anglo-American World

Machado de Assis found his way into the Anglo-American world as well. The English language, by the way, has done a lot for Machado. To justify this claim, let me begin, as did Brás Cubas in his memoirs, at the end. English is the only foreign language into which all nine of Machado's novels have been translated (in Spanish, only eight out of the nine have translations). *Brás Cubas*, for instance, has five renditions: William Grossman, 1951; E. Percy Ellis, 1955; Gregory Rabassa, 1997; Margaret Jull Costa & Robin Patterson, 2020; and Flora Thomson-DeVeaux, 2020. The latter, published in the prestigious Penguin Classics series, reached the #1 Amazon best-selling position in its category when released in June 2020. As I write these lines in September 2020, the Penguin edition of *Brás Cubas* occupies (I just checked) the #6 position ... with Borges as #7. The reviews of the two new *Brás Cubas*, Thomson-DeVeaux's and Jull Costa & Patterson's, both out in June 2020, were utterly positive.[30]

---

30 These are the links for the two reviews: www.nytimes.com/2020/06/16/books/review-posthumous-memoirs-bras-cubas-machado-de-assis.html?action=click&module=Well&pgtype=Homepage&section=Books;andwww.wordswith

The five translations of *Brás Cubas* make it the most translated Brazilian novel into English. In comparison, we count eleven in Spanish of *Brás Cubas* from 1902 to 2010. To the best of my knowledge, this makes *Brás Cubas* also the most translated Brazilian novel into Spanish.[31] That's definitely not irrelevant! Furthermore, out of the seventy-six stories (culled from over 200) that Machado selected to publish in book form, all of them have at least one English version. That's no small thing either! Anglo-American publishers, translators, scholars, and public intellectuals have definitely done their work. What Susan Sontag did in offering her words of unconditional praise to Machado, other heavyweight names such as Harold Bloom, Woody Allen, Philip Roth, Salman Rushdie, Elizabeth Hardwick, Allen Ginsberg, Jonathan Franzen, John Updike, John Barth, V. S. Pritchett, and Michael Wood, also did. The English-language club of Machado admirers is not half bad! The writers Machado is commonly paired with range from Sterne, Swift, Hardy, James, Melville, Beckett, Shakespeare, and Poe (from the Anglo-American world) to Flaubert, Dostoevsky, Kafka, Chekhov, Cervantes, Gogol, and Proust (from the non-English world).[32] That's not a lousy club either! Together, both clubs make Machado an unquestionable phenomenon of *succès d'estime*. His fine artistry has been enthusiastically applauded for decades by critical readers all over the world. Carlos Fuentes described him as a miracle; John Updike, a master; Harold Bloom, a genius.

Now, after the bright side, let's take a peek at the dark side of the moon. Here are some quotes from random reviewers from the Anglo-American press:

> The question that inevitably hovers over all the superlative references to Machado in English is how come so few English speakers in the 21st century have read him? (*Los Angeles Review of Books*, September 22, 2020)

> Though a literary titan in his native Brazil, he [Machado] is little read in English. (*Los Angeles Review of Books*, July 4, 2018)

---

outborders.org/book-review/machado-de-assis-gains-different-voices-in-new-translations-of-posthumous-m

31 See Pablo Cardellino Soto, "Traducciones de Machado de Assis al español," *Machado de Assis: tradutor e traduzido*, eds. Adréia Guerini, Luana de Freitas & Walter Costa (Florianópolis: PGET/UFSC, 2012), 129–59.
32 See Earl Fitz, *Machado de Assis* (Boston: Twayne, 1989), 10–22.

> He's one of Brazil's greatest writers. Why isn't Machado de Assis more widely read? (*The New Yorker*, July 9, 2018)
>
> It [*Brás Cubas*] is a glittering masterwork and an unmitigated joy to read, but, for no good reason at all, almost no English speakers in the twenty-first century have read it. (*The New Yorker*, June 2, 2020)
>
> Still neglected by English readers, the Brazilian writer [Machado] is one of the very greatest of the early modern era. (*The Guardian*, March 1, 2013)
>
> Elsewhere [outside of Brazil], he [Machado] remains little read. (*The Times Literary Supplement*, October 26, 2018)

The examples mentioned above are clear enough for us to identify an obvious contradiction that we have already touched on some lines ago: how can we reconcile the superb quality of Machado's novels and stories – as internationally acknowledged and praised by a number of renowned critics – with readers' overall reluctance or unwillingness to engage with these works? Or rather, how can we coherently conceive that excellence brings about obscurity? No easy answer ahead, of course. But we can approach this issue by briefly addressing two factors that interfere in this process: ethnocentrism, which we have already introduced, and engagement, which I will discuss in the context of my experience as a teacher.

History teaches us that ethnocentrism (Eurocentrism, U.S.-centrism) tends to lead to prejudice. We should not disregard this issue if we want to understand why the Brazilian Machado de Assis has been so invisible to American and European readers: "Had he [Machado] been French or English," asserts Roberto González Echevarría, "there is little doubt that his works would be prominently featured in the Western canon."[33] Earl Fitz, before González Echevarría, similarly said: "Had he written in French, German, or English, for example, Machado de Assis would be as well-known today as Flaubert, Goethe, and Shakespeare."[34] This has been a recurring claim in Brazil as well. The Brazilian writer Érico Verissimo, well before Fitz and González Echevarría, once stated: "Had he [Machado] written in French, English, German or Italian, he would have achieved universal fame and would be, as storyteller, in the company

---

33 Roberto González Echevarría, "Joaquim Maria Machado de Assis," *The Oxford Book of Latin American Short Stories*, ed. Roberto G. Echevarría (Oxford: Oxford UP, 1997), 95.
34 Earl Fitz, *Machado de Assis*, 11.

of such illustrious names as Balzac, Tolstoy, Dickens, and Dostoyevsky."[35] All these assertions ultimately point to the issue of ethnocentrism.

The oft-used rhetorical practice of what we could call the "colonizing shadow" is also ethnocentric. This practice occurs when one refers to, for instance, the composer Heitor Villa-Lobos as the "Brazilian Debussy." When one uses this framing device, they put the "colonized" (Villa-Lobos) in the shadow of the "colonizer" (Debussy). Moreover, this approach – aside from being inaccurate – says literally nothing about Villa-Lobos's marvelous music. To be accurate, Villa-Lobos is not the Brazilian Debussy; instead, Villa-Lobos is the Brazilian Villa-Lobos. By the same token, Horacio Quiroga is not the Uruguayan Edgar Allan Poe; Pablo Neruda is not the Chilean Walt Whitman; Borges is not the Argentinian Kafka; nor is Machado de Assis the Brazilian Sterne. If one views Machado – or Borges, Neruda, Quiroga, or Villa-Lobos – in that way, the sight will be distorted by a stereotyped image. After all, every tree in the forest is unique, and it should be appreciated for its uniqueness, even though the trees – obviously – share common features with the other trees. (Sorry for the cheap philosophy moment!)

Now, this does not mean that Machado didn't frolic in Sterne's spring. Machado did frolic in hundreds of Brazilian, American, and European springs, Sterne's being just one of them. The idea that Machado is a disciple of Sterne gained traction in the twentieth century. If we want to help Machado in the twenty-first century, let's get rid of this master–disciple approach. Machado is a master and a disciple of himself. The fact that he read and emulated European authors doesn't devalue his works *a priori*. We must move Machado out from other's shadows and allow him to bask in his own light.

Enough of ethnocentrism! If you want to learn more about it, especially in the context of the U.S., I highly recommend an article by Earl Fitz.[36] Now, let's move on to the argument of engagement.

Engagement

The reception of Machado's works in Europe and the U.S. could have been better, according to the arguments presented above. But what about Machado's reception in Spanish America? What about in Lusophone

---

35 Érico Veríssimo, *Machado of Brazil: The Life and Times of Machado de Assis*, José Bettencourt Machado (New York: Bramerica, 1953), v.
36 Earl Fitz, "The Reception of Machado de Assis in the United States during the 1950s and 1960s," 16–35.

Africa? What about in Portugal, a European country that has close historical ties with Brazil? Has the reception of Machado in these areas been different from Europe and the U.S.? It has, of course, but not by much. And, here, we cannot lay the blame on ethnocentrism. No; we must find another rationale through a comparative approach.

There are arguably three colossal novelists in the Portuguese language: the Brazilian Machado de Assis, and the Portuguese Eça de Queirós and José Saramago. All other novelists in the Lusophone world should be placed, canonically considering, below them. (If we were just talking about greatest novels, *Grande sertão: veredas* by Guimarães Rosa would certainly be included in the conversation. But, as *Grande sertão* is the only novel written by Rosa, we usually don't see him as a novelist.)

Eça and Machado were contemporaries: Machado was six years Eça's senior. They never met, as Machado never traveled to Portugal and Eça never visited Brazil; but they were aware of each other, or, rather, they read each other's works. Machado wrote a harsh review of Eça's *O primo Basílio* in 1878; Eça was said to know and be able to recite by heart *Brás Cubas*'s famous Chapter VII, "The Delirium."[37] Stylistically and conceptually speaking, these two contemporary novelists, writing in the same language, couldn't be more different from one another. Eça's prose is solar, visual, synesthetic, symphonic; Machado's is microscopic, fleeting, fragmented, slippery. However, despite these and other differences, both are central pillars of Lusophone literature. Measuring their stature in order to conclude who stands the highest would be, in my view, a fruitless exercise. Both are titanic figures, period. Nevertheless, in terms of popularity, Eça and Machado cannot be put together. "Machado de Assis is virtually unknown in Portugal," writes Pedro Calheiros in 1993.[38] Machado's reception in Portugal has improved since then.[39] The efforts made by a few critics – with an emphasis on Abel Baptista Barros – to promote Machado's works in Portugal are undoubtedly praiseworthy. However, there is much still to be done in order actually to overturn Calheiros's assessment.

---

37 Heitor Lyra, *O Brasil na vida de Eça de Queirós* (Lisboa: Livros do Brasil, 1965), 199–200.
38 Pedro Calheiros, "A recepção de Machado de Assis em Portugal," *Travessia*, no. 27 (1993), 52.
39 See "Machado de Assis in Portugal," Arnaldo Saraiva, trans. Claire Williams, *The Author as a Plagiarist: The Case of Machado de Assis*, ed. João Cezar de Castro Rocha, *Portuguese Literary & Cultural Studies* 13/14 (Fall 2004/Spring 2005), 649–60.

As for Eça in Brazil, since the last quarter of the nineteenth century up until at least the first half of the twentieth century, three words can reliably describe the relationship between Brazilian readers and Eça de Queirós: worship, adoration, and devotion.[40] During that period, Eça monopolized critics and readers like no other Lusophone author in Brazil, including Brazilians. Eça was respected by critics and idolized by readers. If Machado was (and still is) a *succès d'estime*, Eça received both critical acclaim *and* readers' reverence. Machado surely deserves more recognition and readership outside of Brazil; however, we must admit that his fiction will never be a best-seller like Eça's was and Saramago's is. Why?

Lúcia Miguel-Pereira offered a reasonable answer to this question in a brief but enlightened article she wrote in 1939. In the article, she reflects on the contradiction involving the resounding success of Eça's novels in Brazil vis-à-vis the poor reception of Machado's works in Portugal. According to Miguel-Pereira, "one doesn't need to be an intellectual to feel the seduction [of Eça's writings]"; however, Machado's crafty style, full of subtleties and meticulousness, "requires initiation to be fully appreciated."[41] Bingo! Miguel-Pereira is among the cleverest scholars of Machado. And, here, she simply hit the nail on the head. That is to say, for good or for bad, Machado de Assis is definitely not for beginners. His stories demand a considerable effort from the reader to ensure they get the most out of them. If the complacent, distracted reader refuses the calling and the challenge to go beyond the surface of the text, the story is just ... *nice*. However, if they embrace the endeavor and descend into the subterranean passages of the plot and the characters, they will surely find hidden treasures. In this regard, Machado's novels and stories function much like maps. You can simply look at them, but you can (and should) also use them to find and explore charted and uncharted territories. An example?

A Personal Teaching Experience

I have been teaching Eça and Machado for over two decades in both Brazil and the U.S. Having witnessed the reactions of my students when they work with both writers, I can attest to the validity of Lúcia Miguel-Pereira's assessment. It's actually not that easy to fall in love with

---

40 See Clóvis Ramalhete, *Eça de Queiroz* (São Paulo: Livraria Martins, 1942).
41 Lúcia Miguel-Pereira, "Machado de Assis e Eça de Queiroz," *Revista de Portugal*, vol. 2, no. 8 (Jul. 1939), 474.

Machado, like it is with Eça (or Saramago). Love for the latter happens almost instantly. The obstacles that Machado's stories pose to readers reminds me of a French saying by Edmond Jabès: "*Dans le mot amour il y a le mot mur*" (In the word love [*amour*], there is the word wall [*mur*])[42]. For us to love Machado, we first need to overcome the intricacies ("the wall") of his narratives.[43]

Here's one example: after reading the story "Missa do galo" ("Midnight Mass"), my students invariably come to class with a huge question mark on their faces. They are intrigued by a narrative in which expectations were clearly frustrated. Where is the greatness in a story in which nothing happens beyond a dull, near one-hour conversation between a young man and a mature woman on the night of Christmas Eve, just before the Midnight Mass? What is the point? they ask. The point is that, underneath the whispering dialogue between these two characters, a miracle is happening, a Christmas miracle, as the title suggests. But it's not a miracle in a religious sense, contradicting, thus, the title. It's more like a revolution or an earthquake, or rather, a silent revolution, or a motionless earthquake. One needs to re-educate the senses in order to feel it. "Missa do galo" reminds me of another quote, now by Guimarães Rosa: "When nothing happens, there is a miracle we do not see."[44] Although the context of Rosa's story is entirely distinct, Machado's "Missa do galo" fits perfectly into the same premise: nothing happens, just a miracle.

For teachers, such as myself, the story offers the challenging task of guiding the students "through the forest of symbols"[45] towards the path that will eventually lead them to experience the miracle. For "Missa do galo" is a story which students do not usually *engage* with upon their first reading. They need a second, a third, a fourth reading ... The same is true for other stories and novels by Machado. Their fruition requires guidance and persistence. For readers fully to interact and engage with them, it's highly recommended to provide them with some sort of assistance.

---

42 Edmond Jabès, *The Book of Questions*, vol. II, trans. Rosmarie Waldrop (Hanover: Wesleyan UP, 1991), 385.

43 In 2001, Professor Daphne Patai stated, in a lecture at the Brazilian Academy of Letters, that her students have "great difficult in understanding [Machado de Assis]." And she continues: "Maybe this is a general sense." www.machadodeassis.org.br/abl_minisites/cgi/cgilua.exe/sys/starta272.html

44 The quote ends the first paragraph of the story "O espelho" ("The Mirror"), in the collection *Primeiras estórias* (*First Stories*), published in 1962.

45 "... à travers des forêts de symboles." Charles Baudelaire, "Correspondances / Correspondences," *Fleurs du mal / Flowers of Evil*.

Otherwise, the story will most likely seem loose and pointless, or, at most, *nice*. The process of unveiling the multiple layers and revealing the hidden meanings and messages of Machado's narratives may be onerous, even for experienced readers. See, in this respect, what the American writer Maya Angelou said in an interview with *The Paris Review* in the Fall of 1990:

> Years ago I read a man named Machado de Assis who wrote a book called *Dom Casmurro*. Machado de Assis is a South American writer – black father, Portuguese mother – writing in 1865, say. I thought the book was very nice. Then I went back and read the book and said, Hmm. I didn't realize all that was in that book. Then I read it again, and again, and I came to the conclusion that what Machado de Assis had done for me was almost a trick: he had beckoned me onto the beach to watch a sunset. And I had watched the sunset with pleasure. When I turned around to come back in I found that the tide had come in over my head.[46]

Now let's imagine for a moment that Maya Angelou, for whatever reason, had read *Dom Casmurro* only once. She still would have had the experience of reading a "very nice" book. In her words, she would still have seen "the sunset with pleasure." Nonetheless, by going through *Dom Casmurro* just once, Angelou would have missed a point of utmost importance. She would have missed out on the core element of the reading process: the tsunami moment. It is in this moment – which she describes in her interview ("I found that the tide had come in over my head") – that the book actually, and somewhat magically, overwhelms the reader's mind and heart.

Two people are responsible for *Dom Casmurro*'s being, from the reader's perspective, a literary *tsunami*: its author, Machado de Assis, and one of its interpreters, the American scholar Helen Caldwell (1904–1987). The novel *Dom Casmurro* produced two heroines: the main female character, Capitu, who is arguably *the* most notable female character of Brazilian literature; and Helen Caldwell, who is responsible for changing the way we read Machado's book. Few critics in literary history have been able to write a study that revolutionizes the understanding of one given work. Great critics usually contribute towards a gradual revolution that eventually ends up changing the perception of a story, a poem, a painting. That's not the case with Caldwell, who started and carried out a successful revolution all by herself. It's not an overstatement to say, therefore, that,

---

[46] www.theparisreview.org/interviews/2279/the-art-of-fiction-no-119-maya-angelou

in the history of the novel's critical reception, there are two "*Dom Casmurros*": one before and one after Caldwell's interpretation.

As if that was not enough, Caldwell also translated five of Machado's novels and a selection of his stories. Her translation of *Dom Casmurro* came out in 1953 and was the second novel by Machado to be published in English; the first was *Brás Cubas* rendered by William Grossman in 1951. This 1951 edition, however, was first published in Brazil by São Paulo Editora with the title *The Posthumous Memoirs of Braz Cubas*. The next year, it appeared in the U.S. from Noonday, and the following year in England from W. H. Allen. Both the American and the British editions received the questionable title *Epitaph of a Small Winner*. In terms of chronology, then, Machado finally set foot on American soil in 1952 and on British soil in 1953. Before that, only three stories of Machado's had appeared, in a 1921 anthology titled *Brazilian Tales* (Boston: Four Seas), edited and translated by Isaac Goldberg.

In the 1950s, Machado's trilogy (*Brás Cubas*, *Quincas Borba*, and *Dom Casmurro*) was available to English-language readers, both in the U.S. and England. I haven't mentioned *Quincas Borba* so far. I'll mention it now, along with a list of noteworthy translations of Machado's trilogy from this period:

1. *Brás Cubas*. English title: *Epitaph of a Small Winner*. Trans. William Grossman. New York, Noonday, 1952.
2. *Brás Cubas*. English title: *Epitaph of a Small Winner*. Trans. William Grossman. London, W. H. Allen, 1953.
3. *Dom Casmurro*. English title: *Dom Casmurro*. Trans. Helen Caldwell. New York, Noonday, 1953.[47]
4. *Dom Casmurro*. English title: *Dom Casmurro*. Trans. Helen Caldwell. London, W. H. Allen, 1953.
5. *Quincas Borba*. English title: *Philosopher or Dog?* Trans. Clotilde Wilson. New York, Noonday, 1954.
6. *Quincas Borba*. English title: *The Heritage of Quincas Borba*. Trans. Clotilde Wilson. London, W. H. Allen, 1954.

---

47 Some critics argue that Helen Caldwell's translation of *Dom Casmurro* arrived in the U.S. for the first time in 1966, published by the University of California Press. To the best of my knowledge, the 1953 Noonday edition of the novel was available for American readers the year it was out. That's the conclusion I drew from reading the reviews from that time. See, in this respect, *Washington Post*, May 10, 1953; *New York Times*, May 24 and Nov. 22, 1953; *Time*, May 18, 1953; and *New Yorker*, Jun. 6, 1953.

I did not include the 1951 *Brás Cubas* translated by William Grossman, nor the 1955 *Brás Cubas* translated by E. Percy Ellis in this list because both editions were published in Brazil and have been out of print since their release; therefore, they have had very little to no impact in the Anglo-American world. The point that I wish to underline with this list is that by 1954 the English-language reader, in both the U.S. and in England, had an eloquent sample of Machado's main works available. Moreover, the reviews were overall fairly positive, in both countries, by that time. However, despite these promising signs, Machado didn't gain traction as expected. Why? Maybe for the reasons we have already speculated on here.

But why focus on the 1950s? That's another good question. This decade marks the period when Brazil started to leave behind its image as an "exotic" country by embarking on a vigorous process of modernization. In this regard, it is emblematic that the decade begins with Brazil hosting the fourth World Cup and finishes on the verge of the inauguration of the new federal capital, Brasília, founded on April 21, 1960. Architecturally speaking, the majestic Maracanã stadium – the largest soccer stadium in the world, back in 1950 – and the futuristic city of Brasília – planned and constructed from scratch to be the Brazil's federal capital – constituted two symbols of the thriving new country. Moreover, between the 1950 World Cup and the 1960 foundation of Brasília, a quiet revolution occurred in Brazil: the creative musical fusion of American jazz with Afro-Brazilian samba which gave birth to the Bossa Nova style and movement. Music and modernity brought Brazil and the U.S. closer than ever before. In this context, not by accident, the modern and urban Machado de Assis arrived in the U.S. accompanied by three American translators: Caldwell, Grossman, and Wilson.

This does not imply, however, that tropical Brazil – in all its picturesque, exotic, and sensual glory – was dead or discarded. In 1958, while João Gilberto was recording the first Bossa Nova album, *Chega de Saudade*, which was released the next year, Jorge Amado wrote and published one of his biggest hits: *Gabriela, cravo e canela* (*Gabriela, Clove, and Cinnamon*). Jorge Amado's novel appeared in the U.S. in 1962, co-translated by William Grossman. This same year, the album *Jazz Samba* by Stan Getz and Charlie Byrd was released with both Bossa Nova songs and Bossa Nova-style songs. Both *Gabriela, Clove, and Cinnamon* and *Jazz Samba* took off in America. In 1963, Grossman and Caldwell translated a collection of Machado's twelve stories published by the University of California Press with the title *The Psychiatrist and Other Stories*. Also in the 1960s, Caldwell's translation of *Esaú e Jacó* was published in the U.S.

(1965, U of California P) and in England (1966, London, Owen). Moreover, Caldwell's rendition of *Dom Casmurro* was reprinted (1966, U of California P). Nonetheless, even though *Gabriela* and Bossa Nova took off, Machado didn't.

We won't go into every English translation of Machado as it would lead us *hors piste*. The point I want to make here is that Machado could have gained momentum in the 1950s and 1960s, particularly in the U.S., but it didn't occur. Another event that could have favored Machado was the publication, in 1960, of Caldwell's classic study of *Dom Casmurro* entitled *The Brazilian Othello of Machado de Assis*. As I mentioned before, with this study, Caldwell revolutionized the way readers view and interpret Machado's novel. We'll discuss this topic further in Chapter Six.

For now, let's jump to another "revolution" that happened ten years later: the publication in the U.S. of Gabriel García Márquez's *Cien años de soledad* (*One Hundred Years of Solitude*), translated into English by Gregory Rabassa. García Márquez's novel has been rightly considered the epicenter of a literary and editorial phenomenon called the Latin American Boom. This phenomenon was almost entirely centered around Hispanic American authors; so, truthfully, it would be more reasonable to name it the Hispanic American or Spanish American Boom. Some critics, though, squeeze Jorge Amado into the group of the Boom's authors so as not to leave Brazil out, perhaps for commercial reasons. Others mention Clarice Lispector and Guimarães Rosa as part of the Boom without presenting any convincing argument. The fact is that, due to the Boom, the circulation of Latin American writers greatly increased in the U.S. during this period. In this climate, Machado could have benefitted and gained ground. Did he? Yes and no.

In the 1970s and 1980s, novels from the so-called "first phase of Machado" appeared in English translations – *A mão e a luva* (*The Hand and the Glove*, 1970), *Iaiá Garcia* (1976; 1977); *Helena* (1984) – and editions from the 1950s were reprinted – *Brás Cubas* (1970; 1978; 1985) and *Quincas Borba* (1982). Also, in terms of academic production, the number of dissertations and theses on Machado presented in British and American universities doubled from five in the 1960s to ten in the 1970s. These numbers stayed stable until the 2000s when they doubled again: in 2000–09 period, graduate students submitted twenty dissertations/theses on Machado. Are these figures high or low? By Brazilian Studies standards in the Anglo-American academic world, they are about average. The point to be underlined here is the growth of interest in Machado over the years.

Yes, the interest has been growing since the Boom. But not as fast as it should be. What is missing? Well, setting a place for Machado to sit at the table of the world literature requires a long-term plan. And many should be involved: publishers, professors, critics, translators, cultural journalists, readers, and others. One figure, in particular, can play a crucial role in this game – and that's the public intellectual. Harkening back to the beginning of this chapter, Machado's ringing endorsement by Susan Sontag in 1990 paved the way for other heavyweight supporters to show up and join her. Sontag's article in *The New Yorker* was also followed by new translations of Machado's golden trio: *Brás Cubas* (Gregory Rabassa, 1997), *Dom Casmurro* (John Gledson, 1997), and *Quincas Borba* (Gregory Rabassa, 1998), all published by Oxford University Press.

Readers in the 1990s did know that García Márquez, following the advice of Julio Cortázar, waited three years for his novel *Cien años de soledad* to be translated into English by Gregory Rabassa. Readers in the 1990s also knew that García Márquez himself had once stated that Rabassa's translation improved upon the original; so, having Rabassa translate Machado's novels was a landmark in his reception into the English-speaking world. The British critic John Gledson, in his turn, is probably the best-equipped scholar of Machado outside Brazil. His critical works have been widely read and respected among Machado lovers. Harold Bloom praised both translators and classified the previous English translations of Machado as "inadequate" in comparison. As Bloom suggests, translation would have been an obstacle – one "now fully remedied by Gregory Rabassa ... and John Gledson"[48] – to Machado's flourishing in the Anglo-American lands.

So, problem solved – thanks to Rabassa and Gledson! Well, not so much. There is a complicating factor that we should not overlook. John Gledson, who has been actively and successfully publishing on Machado for over thirty-five years, holds a highly critical view of Rabassa's versions of Machado. For Gledson, the old translations of Grassman's *Brás Cubas* and Wilson's *Quincas Borba* are "much better" than those of Rabassa, whose "gaucherie and lack of feel for Machado's irony and his rhythms" make them, in Gledson's eyes, a huge "disappointment."[49]

---

48 Harold Bloom, *Genius: A Mosaic of One Hundred Exemplary Creative Minds* (New York, Warner Books, 2002), 675.
49 John Gledson, "Interview with John Gledson," Gustavo Althoff, *Sciencia Traductionis*, no. 14 (2013), 245.

Another drawback was the infamous 1992 version of *Dom Casmurro* by the Scottish-born Robert Scott-Buccleuch, which oddly abridges the novel by cutting, without comment, nine of its 148 original chapters. Scott-Buccleuch's rendition, first published by Peter Owen, was bought and distributed in 1994 by the Penguin Group. When the exclusion was discovered and revealed, the Brazilian writer Josué Montello immediately reacted in the press by advocating for the use of "diplomatic channels" to collect back and stop the distribution of the edition.[50] That, of course, never happened.

All in all, with highs and lows, it's fair to say that Machado gained momentum in the 1990s as he had done in the 1950s. In both periods, however, his star went up and then went down. Currently, that star is once again on the rise. The two new translations of *Brás Cubas* released almost simultaneously in June 2020 have set the skies back in motion. This process of regaining momentum did actually start two years earlier with the monumental edition of Machado's *Collected Stories*, translated by Margaret Jull Costa and Robin Patterson, and published by Liveright. It's now our duty – we who love Machado – to help maintain the height of his star in the sky, high up where it deserves to be. This is a complex task, far from easy to accomplish fully, but it is what has to be done. We'll continue relying on publishers, translators, critics, scholars, public intellectuals, teachers, cultural journalists, and readers. I commented a few lines ago on the role played by public intellectuals; now, I want to turn my commentary to another group: the World Literature teachers at both the secondary and higher-education levels. Why them?

In the context of American colleges and universities, the Spanish and Portuguese, or Luso-Hispanic, departments have been steadily offering fewer literature courses over the years. This is an irreversible trend, as far as I'm concerned, since the Spanish and Portuguese students' demand for a diversified offering of courses is here to stay. Based on this demand, these students have been learning less literature and more Latin American and Iberian cinema, cultural studies, gender studies, race and ethnicity studies, and so on. This does not mean, however, that we cannot rely on Portuguese professors in the U.S. to teach courses on literature and Machado. We can, and we do. But this is not enough, since the cultural and academic environments keep pushing against them. Thus, the main agents of change in helping to improve the reception of Machado in the realm

---

50 "Tradução inglesa altera livro de Machado de Assis," *O Globo*, Aug. 6, 1997, Segundo Caderno, 5.

of education, particularly in America (but also in other English-speaking countries), are the teachers of World Literature. They are able to map out a journey through Machado's territory of fiction in a way that their students will engage in and enjoy. These teachers are crucial figures for helping to change this game once and for all. As for this book, I hope to make it useful to teachers, students, readers, critics – everyone, in sum, who has an interest in powerful writers, crafty texts, and compelling stories.

Now, it's time to move on to discuss Machado's life and *ethos*. *Ethos*? you may ask. What is *ethos*? I shall tell you.

Chapter Two

Machado de Assis: Life and *Ethos*

What is *Ethos*?

IN HIS MEMOIRS, Brazilian writer Lêdo Ivo recalls a conversation he had over the phone with Guimarães Rosa: "Not too long before dying, Guimarães Rosa called me. He had had a formidable idea for one of my literary articles. He came to the conclusion that the real person does not exist – what does exist are versions of this person made by their close friends. He, thus, suggested that I should write a lengthy article on Guimarães Rosa, based on testimonials from his friends, whose names he then invoked."[1]

While reading this passage, years ago, one of its points stood out to me and drew my attention: what did Guimarães Rosa mean in claiming that "the real person does not exist"? Don't I, who write these lines, exist? Don't you, who read these lines, exist? Didn't Machado de Assis, who wrote thousands and thousands of pages, exist? Well, maybe Calderón de la Barca was right: life is just a dream. Or maybe Borges, in writing "The Circular Ruins," was right: every man is a dreamed man in a dreaming man's dream. Or maybe not.

Maybe we should start by breaking Rosa's statement down in order to get a better sense of it. Let's get to it. Let's begin with *existence*: what does it mean to exist? According to Idealists – and philosophical Idealism is a key concept here – reality, as we know and experience it, exists only as a projection within each of our own minds. In other words, when we see or feel something, or when we think of something, this *thing* comes to exist only within the limits of our mind. This suggests that, outside of the mind, things have no existence or, better yet, no *functionality* of existence.

---

[1] Lêdo Ivo, *Confissões de um poeta* (São Paulo: Difel, 1979), 206.

Let's translate this idea into a premise, the first of two: things are ideas. In order for things to exist – myself, you, trees, love, hope, God – they need to be either perceived and/or conceived by a rational mind. A tree in the middle of a forest, without any perceptive system *intentionally* targeting it, lives in a sort of limbo: this tree, say, anticipates being actualized by a decoding machine – i.e. the human mind – to enter existence. Existing, in this respect, entails the permanent and integrated act of perceiving and/or conceiving, decoding, interpreting, understanding. Without these actions being performed, no existence is possible.

Now, let's imagine two people who are standing in the middle of a forest and look at a tree, the same tree. Each perceptive system will decode (i.e. see and understand) a distinct tree. *Two* trees, thus, will exist in the end. Although the images will share commonalities, the image sustained by each mind will not be *exactly* the same. That is to say, two people looking at the same tree will decode two distinct objects. Why? Because, besides the sensory organs, the decoding process relies on experience, and, as no two people have two identical experiences, the results of the decoding process (i.e. the cultural image of the object) will not be identical either. The object, say, a tree or Mona Lisa, can be the same, but the object's "resolution" in one mind will never be repeated in another mind, because different experiences frame and conceptualize the object in different ways. My tree or *my* Mona Lisa are both unreachable by and untransferable to others. So here goes the second premise of our analysis as I keep on interpreting (and, for our purposes, somewhat simplifying) philosophical Idealism: a thing that comes to exist in the rational mind is not a thing-in-itself (for instance, "the real person") but rather a *conceptualized representation* of that thing (as in "versions of this person"). This second premise repeats and complements the first: things are not things, things are ideas.

These premises (again, here loosely expressed) were postulated by seventeenth- and eighteenth-century philosophers, such as George Berkley (1685–1753) – to stay in just one paradigmatic example. The notion of *ethos* has to do with them, but it was postulated well before. In his *Rhetoric*, Aristotle (384–322 BCE) identifies and comments on three modes of persuasion: *ethos*, *pathos*, and *logos*. Simply put, the first mode relates to the speaker; the second, to the audience; and the third, to the discourse. For persuasion to occur, the speaker must be trustworthy; the audience, receptive; and the discourse, organically and logically constructed. From these three modes, *ethos* constitutes, for Aristotle, "perhaps the most effective means of persuasion."[2]

---

2 Aristóteles, *Retórica*, 2nd edn., rev., trans. Manuel Alexandre Júnior, Paulo Farmhouse Alberto & Abel do Nascimento Pena (Lisboa: IN-CM, 2005), 96.

When we blend Aristotle's notion of *ethos* with the premises of philosophical Idealism to examine authorship in literary criticism, we may come to the following conclusion: real authors don't exist. When we say "Shakespeare," or "Borges," or "Machado de Assis," or any dead or living author, we do not refer to a person – the person who wrote *Macbeth*, or *Ficciones*, or *Brás Cubas* – instead, we refer to a concept. The concept of Shakespeare corresponds to the Shakespeare I'm able to determine in my mind with the data on him I have collected at a certain point of my life. Most importantly, my concept of Shakespeare is a contextual, critical category that interferes *a priori* in my process of understanding, interpreting, and evaluating his works. My concept of Shakespeare participates in my experience when I read his poems and plays. The lack of context in critical reading – as shown in the famous A. I. Richards experiment[3] – tends to mislead readers, just as the lack of a compass or a map (to revisit metaphors from Chapter One) tends to mislead travelers.

What's the bottom line? The bottom line is that, in this chapter, we will learn about Machado de Assis's *ethos*, that is to say, a collection of pictures, facets, concepts, and versions of him as depicted by some of his friends, readers, scholars, and, of course, Machado himself. These fragments of the historical Machado de Assis play an important part in the process of better understanding his works. Again, when I say, "the historical Machado," I'm referring to Machado as a character of himself – someone as a character of themself, by the way, is another definition of *ethos*. But you should bear in mind that behind the character there is no "real person"; the character overthrew it, and now solely the character exists. So let's start at the beginning: the adverse conditions whereby Machado de Assis became Machado de Assis.

Machado de Assis: The Miracle

As we learned in Chapter One, a few critics place Machado de Assis over Borges in the Latin American literary canon. This standing is far from unanimously agreed. However, there is one indisputable point in this canonical debate: Machado de Assis is undoubtedly deemed the greatest Latin American fictionist of the nineteenth century. Carlos Fuentes goes even further, to expand the radius of Machado's greatness into Iberian America: "Machado de Assis," he says, "is the brightest star in the nineteenth-century

---

3 See I. A. Richards, *Practical Criticism: A Study of Literary Judgement* (London: Kegan Paul, Trench, & Co. Ltd, 1930). Richards asked his students to evaluate and grade literary texts, without providing any indication of authorship.

novelist sky of Ibero-America."[4] With these words, Fuentes places Machado over the Portuguese Eça de Queirós and the Spanish Benito Pérez Galdós. Let's not go too far. Let's step on stable ground, instead, and assert loud and clear that Machado de Assis, at this point in history, has no rival in nineteenth-century Latin American fiction.

According to Fuentes, this is also a "miracle."[5] Why a miracle? To put it simply, it's because the overall conditions of Brazil in the nineteenth century did not prefigure the emergence of a writer with the stature of Machado de Assis. The appearance of Eça de Queirós in nineteenth-century Portugal is, from a social-historical viewpoint, and to a certain extent, rather predictable. The same could be said about Pérez Galdós and nineteenth-century Spain. But the advent of Machado de Assis constitutes a fact that defeats every possible expectation. Indeed, it's a miracle. Both the personal and the social-historical environments into which Machado was born were highly hostile to the emergence of a genius. For us to understand this argument, let's begin by commenting on the environment, i.e. Brazil, from a historical perspective. Into what Brazil was Machado de Assis born? I'll briefly tackle this question in the next section.

Brazil: Commerce and Faith

Brazil was colonized by the Portuguese, who first docked their caravels on the coast of the country on April 22, 1500, according to official reports. Upon arrival, the explorers took possession of the land, but a *de facto* process of colonization started a few decades later. Two dates may help us understand this period: 1532 and 1549. In 1532, São Vicente, in the current state of São Paulo, was the first village to be founded. Around this time, Brazil began to import the first enslaved individuals from Africa after a thwarted attempt to enslave the Indigenous peoples. Historians estimate that five million Africans were forced to cross the Atlantic and coerced to work on Brazilian properties from the 1530s to the 1880s. No country has imported more slave labor than Brazil in the history of humanity.

As for the Indigenous peoples, it is estimated that three million were living in the present Brazilian territory in 1500. In 2010, according to official figures, the total Indigenous population was 817,962.[6] These num-

---

4   Carlos Fuentes, *Machado de la Mancha* (México DF: Fondo de Cultura Económica, 2001), 5.
5   Ibid., 7.
6   www.funai.gov.br/index.php/indios-no-brasil/quem-sao

bers represented – back in 2010 – 0.26% of Brazil's entire population. In addition to using enslaved Africans as the workforce, the Portuguese also used Indigenous people as land guides, agricultural experts, and warrior allies against French, Dutch, and English invaders. We may sadly conclude, then, that Brazil, as a nation, was shamefully built from the blood, sweat, and tears of enslaved Africans and Indigenous peoples. The other side of this conclusion is that there wouldn't be a Brazil at all without the presence and, most importantly, the sacrifice of African and Indigenous peoples.

The Portuguese who arrived in Brazil at the turn of the sixteenth century had no agricultural expertise. They were traders, not farmers. Although the Portuguese had been farmers in medieval times, the Renaissance revolution had transformed them into astute traders; and, as such, they had to rely on the knowledge of the Indigenous peoples and on the labor of the Africans to cultivate the land and grow crops – particularly sugarcane, and later coffee – in order for the Portuguese Crown to make a profit. The Brazilian Gold Rush era, during the eighteenth century, also came out of this conjunction of Indigenous guidance and slave labor, and ended up extracting the largest amount of gold and precious stones in the history of Latin America.

In sum, all the goods produced in Brazil from 1500 to 1808 were basically sent to the metropolis to be either internally consumed or commercially (re-)exported. In 1808, the Portuguese royal family transferred the court from Lisbon to Rio de Janeiro due to a political crisis involving Napoleon's invasion of the Iberian Peninsula. The transfer of the Portuguese Court to Brazil – fourteen years before the country's independence and thirty-one years before Machado's birth – was a major turning point in Brazilian history. We'll elaborate on this topic later. Let's take a look, now, at our second date of focus.

In 1549, the first vessels bringing Jesuits to Brazil dropped anchor at the port of Salvador, located in the current state of Bahia. The city of Salvador was then the administrative center of the colony. Jesuits arrived there with a primary mission: to spread the Catholic faith among the Indigenous communities. For political reasons, the Portuguese enterprise in Brazil needed a spiritual initiative in order to justify the conquest of the colony in the face of other European nations. Conquering the New World could not be reduced solely to a trade adventure; it also required a non-materialistic, "unselfish," religious counterpoint to balance out the scale. This is the reason – or at least one of them – why the Jesuits were called in by the Portuguese Crown and by the Spanish Crown. And herein lie the roots of Catholicism in Latin America, which contrast in several ways with the Protestant foundation in Anglo-America (particularly in the New England area). Of all the possible contrasts, I want to single out one that plays a crucial role in our analysis: the notion of intermediation.

Catholic culture, broadly considered, is greatly determined by the notion of intermediation. The functionality of the Church ultimately depends on an authority figure who serves as an intermediary between God and the laity. The pope is the most authoritative figure to exert this power. Below the pope are the rest of the clergy (cardinals, archbishops, bishops, priests, and deacons), hierarchically structured; all positions in this hierarchy function to bridge the gap between the Divine and humanity. Historically, the laity must rely on members of the clergy to achieve salvation. The clergy's words are God's words. Their works are God's works. If the laity wish to find righteousness and truth, they should humbly hear and obey those who speak and work for God's will.

The main instrument for the pope and the rest of the clergy to act officially as intermediaries of God, the Creator, is the Bible, or rather *their* Bible. They are the ones interpreting the Holy Scripture and, most of all, they are seen as the sole reliable source of interpretation. In a Catholic community, the priest is the authority endowed with the responsibility of reading and revealing the Holy Word, in a sense that the priest is allegedly capable of understanding the spirit beyond the written letters, to translate the meaning behind the message. Thus, as a messenger of God, the priest conveys to his audience the truth, that is, what the Bible *truly* says. In this environment, and from this standpoint, the clergy owns and controls the information. This way, the Church effectively kept the believers in colonial Brazil amenable while preventing them from questioning, or even rebelling against, the religious rules and rulers.

In the sixteenth century, Protestants took a distinct path: they questioned and rebelled against the rules of the Catholic Church. Through their rebellion, they questioned the concept of ecclesiastical authority. For Protestants, Christ constitutes the only mediator between God and the people. This principle is called *solo Christo* ("Christ alone"), and it's one of the five Protestant *solae* (from the Latin *solo*, meaning "alone") doctrines – the other four are: *sola scriptura* ("by Scripture alone"), *sola fide* ("by faith alone"), *sola gratia* ("by grace alone"), and *soli Deo gloria* ("glory to God alone").

Sola scriptura teaches that God's truth emanates from the Bible coupled with the reader's consciousness without intermediation, for Scripture itself is the ultimate authority to speak. "I believe neither the Pope nor the councils alone, since it is clear that they have often erred and contradicted one another," says Martin Luther. He then continues: "I am convinced by the passages of Scripture, which I have cited, and my conscious is bound in the word of God."[7] Not the pope's word, not the priest's word, not the word of any intermediary who has interpreted the word of God, but the word of God itself is seen as *the* authority.

The five *solae* doctrine, in short, attests to how Protestantism is embedded in individualism, or individual consciousness, in contrast to the Catholic culture of authoritative intermediation. The consequences of this opposition are enormous, particularly in the field of education, which in Portugal and its colonies was controlled by the Jesuits for over two centuries, from 1555 to 1759. Just think: New Englanders in America were able to print in Massachusetts in 1638, that is to say, eighteen years after the *Mayflower*'s arrival with the Pilgrims on the east coast, and just eight years after the arrival of the English Puritans in the region. Printing activities in Brazil, by contrast, officially began in 1808, that is to say, 308 years(!) after the first Portuguese fleet dropped anchor on the northeast coast of the country. For over three centuries, printing was not just nonexistent in Brazil; it was officially forbidden by the Portuguese Crown in all colonial territory. There were a few isolated, clandestine prints before 1808, mainly pamphlets which, once discovered, were all immediately confiscated by commissioned officers.[8]

What's the point here? The point to be highlighted is that, from 1500 to 1808, Brazil was not exactly a (colonized) *country*. What was it, then? Brazil was made a huge slave-based estate, a trading post, and a church. No printing or media press, no public libraries, no museums, no secular schools – the latter until 1759, the year when the Marquis of Pombal expelled the Jesuits from Portugal and its empire. For the sake of comparison, the first public, community-based school in New England was founded in Boston in 1635. These assets and others came or developed with the arrival of the royal family in Brazil in 1808, when the country slowly started having a cultural (and social) life, following Western standards.[9]

---

7 *Apud* Henry Eyster Jacobs, *Martin Luther: The Hero of the Reformation* (New York: G. P. Putnam's Sons, 1906), 192.
8 See Laurence Hallewell, *Books in Brazil: A History of the Publishing Trade* (Metuchen, NJ: Scarecrow, 1982).
9 This does not mean that Brazil didn't have a rich cultural production during colonial times. It certainly did. However, the great names of Brazilian culture of this period were either Jesuits or priests (Father Antônio Vieira, Father

Let me give you another comparison to think on (it's not a fair one, but it can help us anyway): in 1829, the city of Rio de Janeiro had nine bookshops and seven printing firms; Paris, in the mid-1820s, had 480 bookshops and 850 printing presses. Perhaps the fairest comparison to draw would be between Rio de Janeiro and Buenos Aires, which, in 1826, had five booksellers and four printing firms.[10]

Now, let's focus more specifically on the literary scene. The first piece of Brazilian literature published in Brazil was the poetry book *Marília de Dirceu* by Tomás Antônio Gonzaga in 1810. This edition, however, was a reissue of previous Lisbon editions. The first Brazilian fiction of this post-1808 era was the novella *Statira e Zoroastes* by Lucas José de Alvarenga. This 58-page allegorical narrative was published in 1826, just four years after the independence of Brazil. Four years later, that is, in 1830, the first Brazilian fictional narrative in *feuilleton* form, which appeared anonymously, was released: *Olaia e Júlio, ou a Periquita*.

Now, it's time to call in Machado de Assis. Joaquim Maria Machado de Assis was born in Rio de Janeiro on June 21, 1839. His birth occurred 31 years after the arrival of the Portuguese royal family who brought "modernity" to Brazil; 29 years after the first Brazilian literary work was published in the country (*Marília de Dirceu*, 1810); 17 years after Brazil's independence was declared in 1822; 13 years after the first Brazilian fictional narrative was released (*Statira e Zoroastes*, 1826); and just nine years after the publication of the first Brazilian serialized fictional narrative (*Olaia e Júlio, ou a Periquita*; 1830). One more piece of data: in 1842, the city of Rio de Janeiro had twelve bookshops and twelve printing firms.[11]

So here's the point: if it's logical to think that the sociohistorical and cultural environments contribute to the emergence of ingenious minds (although it's not the sole factor, of course), it's not *that* surprising that, throughout the nineteenth century, New England and the state of New York "produced" Poe, Emerson, Hawthorne, Dickinson, Beecher Stowe, Thoreau, Melville, Whitman, and Henry James; that France gave birth to Hugo, Balzac, Flaubert, Zola, Rimbaud, George Sand, and Baudelaire; that Germany was the birthplace of Nietzsche, Heine, von Hahn-Hahn,

---

José Maurício Nunes Garcia), or intellectuals who had studied in Europe (Gregório de Matos, Tomás Antônio Gonzaga). One remarkable exception may be the sculptor Antônio Francisco Lisboa, better known as Aleijadinho, who most likely never left Brazil.

10 Laurence Hallewell, *Books in Brazil: A History of the Publishing Trade*, 36.
11 Ibid., 36.

Theodor Storm, and Marx; that from England came the voices of Elizabeth Browning, the Brontë sisters, Lewis Carroll, Hardy, and Dickens; not to mention Russia and Turgenev, Gogol, Chekhov, Dostoevsky, and Tolstoy. All these names are contemporaries of Machado de Assis. However, based on the same logic – the logic that claims some sort of interconnection between the environment as a cultivated land and the cultural production as the crops to be harvested – it's not just unpredictable, it's actually unbelievable that nineteenth-century Latin America, or, more specifically, Brazil, presented the world with an artist of Machado de Assis's caliber. This is indeed a mystery and a miracle.

Incredibly enough, the miracle continues ...

Machado de Assis: Family and Childhood

In 1839, when Machado de Assis was born, the top of the social pyramid was occupied by landowners who ruled Brazil's economy and politics *de facto*. Considering that Catholicism was the official religion of the state, the Catholic Church still had power through its members, albeit not as much as in colonial times. Brazil, then governed by Emperor Dom Pedro II, had a growing middle class, consisting of liberal professionals such as doctors, engineers, and lawyers. The lower-middle class was comprised of low-ranking public servants, small business owners, and sales clerks. Manufacturing was quite limited; so, factory workers did not play a relevant economic role at this time. Brazil's economy continued to be agriculture-based and, as such, fully hinged on slavery. Thus, enslaved persons made up the bottom of the social pyramid. There was, however, an unofficial class positioned between the lower-middle class and enslaved people. This group encompassed free men and free women who, without having a formal job, strove to make their living as informal workers for a landowner in exchange for board and lodging on his land. Sometimes, these dependent workers, called *agregados* in Portuguese, were invited to live in the main household; their job, in that case, solely consisted in offering good companionship to the homeowner. This nineteenth-century relationship resembled, to a degree, that of medieval feudalism and the serfdom system.[12]

---

12 In relation to enslaved individuals in Brazil, Marc Hertzman notes: "Some slaves were required to bow or kneel while kissing their master's hand each morning" – *Making Samba* (Durham, NC: Duke UP, 2013), 17. Although *agregados* and other dependents were not usually expected to make the same

Machado de Assis's parents were *agregados* at the Livramento estate in the city of Rio de Janeiro. This means that Machado's father, Francisco José de Assis, and Machado's mother, Maria Leopoldina Machado, lived and worked at the Livramento estate. Instead of living in the main house, though, they lived in a modest, single-family dwelling located in a small village where other *agregados* also resided. What did Machado's parents do as *agregados* on the estate? Both carried out tasks, particularly manual labor, not performed by the enslaved individuals. Documents suggest that Francisco José was a craftsman. The first biographers of Machado claimed that Francisco José had skills at restoration, gold plating, and wall and furniture painting. Other *agregado* jobs also included shoemaker, carpenter, blacksmith, and bricklayer. As for Maria Leopoldina, she probably carried out domestic tasks such as sewing or embroidery. It's not plausible, as some biographers maintain, that she was a washerwoman, as washing clothes was a task commonly assigned to enslaved women.[13] Maria Leopoldina may also have worked in children's education on the estate, since both she and Francisco José were educated people.

In 1839, the owner of the Livramento estate was Maria José Mendonça Barroso Pereira, a wealthy widow born in Portugal who had been married twice and had two children. Maria José was Machado's godmother, and all the evidence shows that she held Maria Leopoldina in high regard. It's also believed that Maria José had grown fond of Machado. If that's true – and it most likely is – then little Machado seems to have enjoyed a happy childhood between his parents' own house and Maria José's. This happiness lasted for six years, at least, because in 1845, the little Machado had to face two losses within a period of three months. First, his only sister and sibling, Maria, died at the age of four, and then his godmother at the age of 72 (or 75, depending on the source), both victims of a deadly measles outbreak. In 1849, when Machado wasn't even ten years old, his mother died of tuberculosis at the age of 36.

After Maria Leopoldina's passing, Francisco José found himself in trouble as a single father of a 9-year-old boy. Around this time, he met Maria Inês da Silva. For a while, Francisco José and Maria Inês lived together with Machado. The new couple eventually got married in 1854. By

---

gesture, the general attitude of obedience and respect towards their masters was expected to be that of an enslaved person.
13 See Jean-Michel Massa, *A juventude de Machado de Assis*, trans. Marco Aurélio de Moura Matos (Rio de Janeiro: Civilização Brasileira, 1971), 57–61.

this time, the new family had already moved from the Livramento estate to the neighborhood of São Cristóvão, within the city of Rio de Janeiro.

Maria Inês worked as a confectioner, and perhaps also as a cook, in an all-girls school in São Cristóvão. It remains unclear whether Machado attended a school at all. He was probably homeschooled first by his mother and later by his stepmother, since both had skills – most likely basic skills – in reading and math. It appears that Maria Inês was a good replacement for Maria Leopoldina. At the time of her marriage, Maria Inês was 33 years old and had no children. Presumably, she adopted Machado as her child, treating him with care and generosity. That being said, from 1849, when Maria Leopoldina died, until 1854 or 1855, when Machado left his home, most of what we know about him are inferences drawn from scattered and unreliable sources. From this period, it's also said, but not proven, that Machado sold sweets made by his stepmother at the school where she worked, and where he was allowed to watch some classes. Additionally, it's claimed that he learned rudiments of Latin and French with a priest in São Cristóvão, whom he served as an altar boy.

One Brief Conclusion

Machado, who was reserved in general, was particularly reticent about his childhood. However, despite all the unknowns in Machado's biography regarding this period, we can confidently make a few assertions based on the scarce factual data available. (1) Machado had a modest but happy childhood. Critics, at times, insist on drawing a picture worse than it appears to have been. In other words, they tend to romanticize Machado's early years. It's emotionally appealing, but it seems not to have been always the case. (2) Three women played a pivotal role in Machado's overall development as a child, the three "Marias": Maria Leopoldina, his mother; Maria José, his godmother; and Maria Inês, his stepmother. A fourth Maria should also be counted: his one and only sister, whom he lost when she was four and he was six. (3) As an *agregado* and as Maria José and her family's protégé, Machado had the opportunity to witness, from the inside, the daily lives of the wealthy, how they thought and behaved. While living at the Livramento estate, Machado had access to the enslaved people's quarters as well. He most likely played with children of enslaved families. These overarching experiences, which covered the whole social spectrum of the time, would be later reflected in his works as a fictionist.

Machado: The Stigmas

On October 3, 1854, the 15-year-old Machado de Assis made his debut as a writer. He published his first poem, simply entitled "Sonnet," in the pages of *Periódico dos Pobres* (*Periodical of the Poor*). Around this time – end of 1854, beginning of 1855 – Machado left the suburb of São Cristóvão daily, heading towards downtown Rio, to look for a job. In Rio, he met Francisco de Paula Brito, who went down in history as the first independent publisher in Brazil. Paula Brito owned a bookshop and a printing firm. In 1856, the young Machado got his first (or one of his first) job(s) – most likely through Paula Brito – as an apprentice typographer at *Tipografia Nacional* (National Press), formerly known as *Imprensa Régia* (Royal Press), which was founded in 1808 by Prince Regent Dom João VI as the first printing house of Brazil.

In 1858, Machado quit his job at *Tipografia Nacional* to work as a proofreader for two periodicals: *A Marmota Fluminense*, owned and directed by Paula Brito, and *Correio Mercantil*, which, along with *Jornal do Comércio* and *Diário do Rio de Janeiro*, was one of the most influential *carioca* (i.e. "from Rio de Janeiro") newspapers. The latter interrupted its activities in 1859 but returned in 1860 when Quintino Bocaiúva invited Machado to be one of its regular contributors. This was Machado's first appearance as a columnist in the big local press. The year before, 1859, he had written a regular column, every Sunday, as a theater critic, for the short-lived *O Espelho*. The theater reviews gave Machado visibility and opened up the opportunity for him to be hired by the prestigious *Diário de Rio de Janeiro*. Nonetheless, it's worth noting that it was in *A Marmota Fluminense* that Machado published his first writings, from 1855 to 1861, after his debut in 1854. These writings were mainly poetry, but also fiction, translation, drama, and essay.

This is all to say that Paula Brito was the first person in Rio to lend a helping hand to Machado. In his welcoming bookshop, the smart teenager from São Cristóvão had the opportunity to meet with the intellectual elite of the city. Machado soon began contributing to A *Marmota Fluminense*, under the auspices of Paula Brito (in January 1855, when he published his first text there, a poem, Machado was still only 15). Paula Brito was probably the one who connected the young writer with *Tipografia Nacional*, as mentioned above. In 1858, the publisher hired Machado as a proofreader for A *Marmota*.[14] Finally, in 1861, the year of his death,

---

14 Paula Brito's periodical A *Marmota Fluminense* shortened its name to A *Marmota* in July of 1857.

Paula Brito published the first two titles in book form by Machado: *Queda que as mulheres têm para os tolos* (*The Weakness Women Have for Fools*) and *Desencantos* (*Disenchantment*). The former is the 43-page satirical essay translated by Machado. For some reason, the original source is not indicated in the volume. The essay had been published in *feuilleton* form in *A Marmota* that same year, with the same omission. For decades, the authorship of *Queda* was ascribed to Machado himself, even though the title page of the booklet displays the words "Translation by Mr. Machado de Assis." A century later, Jean-Michel Massa eventually cleared this matter up by finding the original source: *De l'amour des femmes pour les sots* (*On the Love Women Feel for Fools*) by Victor Hénaux, first published in 1859.[15] The second title – *Desencantos* – is a two-part drama which appears in Machado's bibliography as the first work authored by him to be published in book form. We'll be commenting on the play in the next chapter.

Both Paula Brito and Machado de Assis were of Afro-European descent, living in a slaveholding society. In an ostentatious, imperial society, both were humbly born into low-income families. (Both, coincidently, also got their first paid jobs as typographers.) Being a biracial person, from a humble family, in mid-nineteenth-century Imperial Brazil, meant being burdened with strong social stigmas. Nevertheless, both Paula Brito and Machado thrived in this hostile milieu. They admirably succeeded in overcoming many systemic obstacles as they went on their way. In this regard, they were not alone.

Other notable names in Brazilian history of biracial (African and European) background include – just from the realm of letters and in the period from the mid-eighteenth to the beginning of twentieth century – Caldas Barbosa (1740–1800), Silva Alvarenga (1749–1814), Gonçalves Dias (1823–1864), Teixeira e Sousa (1812–1861), Gonçalves Crespo (1846–1883; Brazilian-born, Portuguese naturalized), José do Patrocínio (1853–1905), Coelho Neto (1864–1934), João do Rio (1881–1921), and Lima Barreto (1881–1922). Please note: this list is not intended to suggest that Brazil, as a nation, offered the same opportunities to all its citizens, regardless of their racial background. This isn't true currently, and it certainly wasn't during Machado's lifetime, when the country was outrageously pushing to keep slavery legal until 1888. Racial and social stigmas were (and still are, unfortunately) as real as their pernicious effects. Against all odds, though, underprivileged people, such as Paula Brito and

---

15 Jean-Michel Massa, *Machado de Assis tradutor*, trans. Oséias Silas Ferraz (Belo Horizonte: Crisálida, 2008), 25–26.

Machado, still succeeded in achieving their goals as well as receiving proper recognition for them.

In the case of Machado, however, stigmas went beyond those attached to his skin color and humble social origins. Health issues also stigmatized his life. At some point, perhaps shortly after or before his marriage in 1869, his epileptic episodes began. In the years following, he seems to have been haunted by the illness. The prospect of having a seizure in a public space terrified him. It happened a few times, though. On August 28, 1907, for instance, Machado went into convulsions at *Cais* Pharoux (Pharoux Dock), in Rio, while waiting for the French politician Paul Doumer to land. He was promptly assisted by friends and passers-by. The next day, to Machado's embarrassment, several newspapers reported the event. During the last years of his life, as his overall health gradually declined, the seizures became more frequent.

Possibly connected to his epilepsy, Machado developed a light but perceptible stutter. This also emerged, presumably, around the time of his marriage. It's well known that, during his youth, Machado had a pretty hectic social life. As a theater critic and member of the *Conservatório Dramático Brasileiro* (Brazilian Dramatic Conservatory), he attended performances every, or almost every, night; as a poet, he often participated in poetry recitals where he recited his own poems; as a member of literary societies, he was present at nearly all meetings and dinners. In addition to his frenetic social activities, Machado still held jobs at more than one periodical, to which he contributed regularly with *crônicas*, poems, plays, reviews, stories, translations ... Such a frenzied lifestyle could not be kept up by a person with serious health issues. The young Machado, however, lived fully in this social scene until at least 1868, when he met Carolina Augusta, whom he married the next year.

The couple then shared a quiet life. After his marriage, Machado became a reserved person, or rather, a less socially exposed person. The marriage itself may have caused this change. The fact that Machado had got a job in 1867 as assistant director of the *Diário Oficial* (the *Official Journal* of the Empire) may have also contributed. The appointment at the *Diário Oficial* provided Machado with career stability for the first time, although the pay wasn't sufficient for him to quit his other jobs at the presses. In addition to these events, the gradual decline of Machado's health, with the onset (or the worsening) of both his epilepsy and his stuttering, certainly influenced his decision to live a quieter social life, with Carolina by his side.

Social origins, skin color, heath issues – there were indeed many stigmas born from these factors. We should not feel sorry for Machado, though. That's not the point I'm trying to make here. Moreover, Machado surely would dismiss this sort of feeling towards him. We can, instead, stop for a moment and view this topic from another angle, one that you have already heard of …

Better than Borges, Again

For decades now, Borges has collectively been lauded as the national writer of Argentina. For over a century, Machado has been undisputedly hailed as the national writer of Brazil. Also, for over a century, Argentina and Brazil have been bitter rivals in soccer. By comparing Borges and Machado in terms of canonical placement, some critics, whether consciously or not, may have intended to recreate this rivalry between Argentina and Brazil in the literary field, too. In Chapter One, I firmly promised that I would not play this game. But I am about to break my promise.

There is one realm in which Machado far surpasses Borges: adversity. The conditions under which he, Machado, was born were significantly worse than Borges's. Borges was born in his father's library – well, not literally, but, say, metaphorically. Borges repeatedly declared that the most remarkable image from his childhood was his father's personal library, a collection of thousands of fine books in Spanish as well as English. The shy little Borges spent hours reading there. Machado, who was also a more introverted person, spent hours of reading in one library as well: the *Real Gabinete Português de Leitura* (Royal Portuguese Cabinet of Reading). Whether living at the Livramento estate or in São Cristóvão, Machado travelled miles to this public library to read. Borges was 38 when he started his first regular job as an assistant librarian at the Miguel Cané Municipal Library. Machado got his first paid job at the age of 17, maybe 16, at *Tipografia Nacional*. Borges lived and studied in Europe. Machado barely left his hometown and never travelled abroad. But Borges – you may want to remind me – did have a degenerative eye disease that eventually made him go blind in his early 50s. Machado had eye problems, too, although not as serious. In his late thirties, he developed a type of eye inflammation – retinitis – that led his doctors to prohibit him from reading and writing for certain periods. Carolina, then, stepped in as his private reader and scribe. The first chapters of *Brás Cubas*, for instance, were dictated by Machado to Carolina.

In sum, if we metaphorically think of, say, a steeplechase, we can conclude fairly that Borges and Machado, in being regarded as today's national writers of their respective countries, have crossed the finish line together. However – and this is a big *however* – based on their biographies, or based on how they got there, we can also impartially argue that Borges started the race a long way ahead of Machado. In other words, Machado had to face and overcome many more social obstacles than Borges did. Eventually, this may lead us to the following conclusion: given the overall circumstances under which both wrote their works, the fact that Borges and Machado were tied upon crossing the finish line represents a clear victory for Machado.

Machado: Racial Identity

Racial identity is a complex concept, sometimes difficult to grasp in Brazilian culture. Why is this? For numerous reasons, one being the regular occurrence of interracial unions between colonizers and Indigenous and enslaved peoples. (This is, by the way, another point that sets the Anglo and Iberian modes of colonization apart. Broadly speaking, English settlers refused to have physical contact with the native peoples in Australia, New Zealand, or the U.S., for instance. Iberian settlers, on the other hand, did quite the opposite in Latin America. Ultimately, these practices in Brazil resulted in a very complex notion of race. The root causes of distinct attitudes towards native communities can be traced further back to the very formation of Great Britain [less ethnically diverse] versus that of Iberian Peninsula [more ethnically diverse] – for those who are interested in or just curious about exploring this topic, there is a fine book by Lilia Schwarcz, already translated into English.[16])

One practical consequence of this complexity is that, throughout the twentieth and twenty-first centuries, Machado has been categorized on nearly every part of the racial spectrum, from Caucasian white to African black. Racially speaking, he was certainly neither one nor the other. However, the issue here involves not science but politics – or less science than politics. In other words, due to political motivations, Machado's image (or *ethos*) went through a process of whitening in the past, and,

---

16 Lilia Schwarcz, *The Spectacle of the Races: Scientists, Institutions, and the Race Question in Brazil, 1870–1930*, trans. Leland Guyer (New York: Hill and Wang, 1999). The Brazilian edition was first published in 1993.

for different reasons, but still political ones, Machado has recently been portrayed as a black writer. All the political implications render the topic quite slippery and dangerously explosive. Let's handle it with care. And let's start from the beginning.

What do we know for sure? We do know that, on his father's side, Machado's grandparents were freed enslaved people. We do know that both grandparents were children of an enslaved mother and a white or biracial father. Machado's grandparents were described in documents by the Portuguese term *pardo*. In the nineteenth century, *pardo* was (and to a certain degree still is) an ambiguous racial category. Enslaved individuals were categorized as black, but freed enslaved individuals could be identified as *pardos*. Thus, an enslaved person who was considered black could see his/her racial status changed overnight to *pardo/a* once he/she obtained freedom from his/her owner. Francisco de Assis, Machado's father, was identified, or self-identified, as *pardo* in documents, just like his parents. This doesn't clarify much, beyond the fact that he wasn't white. Machado's mother, for her turn, was a Portuguese white woman from the Azores. Machado, as a result, was a biracial man of African and European descent.

Nevertheless, in terms of racial identity, perception may take precedence over nature itself. In this regard, this issue is not exactly about *what* or *who you are*, it's instead much about *how people see you*. And how people have seen Machado has greatly differed over the years. On September 29, 1908, when Machado dies, his death certificate, filled out and signed by the official Olympio da Silva Pereira, states: "skin color: white."[17] In his obituary, the critic and close friend José Veríssimo refers to Machado as "mulato."[18] In a letter to Veríssimo dated November 25, 1908, Joaquim

---

17 https://pt.wikipedia.org/wiki/Certidão_de_óbito#/media/Ficheiro:Certidão_de_óbito_de_Machado_de_Assis.tif
18 The recent debate over Portuguese terms such as "mulato/a" and "escravo/a" is still going on, and it seems far from being over. In the specific case of "mulato," the controversy has much to do with one of its possible etymologies claiming that the word derives from *mule*, or *mulus* in Latin. There is, however, another interpretation that argues that "mulato" originated from the Arabic term *muwallad*, which means "person of mixed ancestry," that is, Arabic and non-Arabic (see, in this respect, Jack D. Forbes, *Africans and Native Americans: The Language of Race and the Evolution of Red-Black Peoples*, 2nd edn. [Urbana: U of Illinois P, 1993], 131–50). As we can see in this paragraph, Joaquim Nabuco viewed as derogatory Veríssimo's reference to Machado as "mulato." Veríssimo, for his turn, while praising his friend, was just attesting to a fact: Machado was a biracial man of African and European descent. The

Nabuco protests by claiming that the word *mulato* "is not literary and is derogatory." For Nabuco, who was also Machado's friend, "Machado was white, and ... he took himself as such."[19]

Machado's iconography, or the way it was manipulated, has indeed whitewashed his image. Machado himself seems to have contributed to this whitening process by straightening his hair and beard with cream, as did Brazilian soccer players, like Arthur Friedenreich, and American jazz musicians, like Duke Ellington, at the beginning of the twentieth century. So, did Machado want to look whiter? I would argue that this is the wrong question to ask when approaching this topic. I would ask, instead, did Machado hope to climb the social ladder? Oh, yes – definitely and fiercely he did. It's even possible to say, obsessively. Since his teenage years, or perhaps before, Machado seemed to be well aware of the choices he had to make in order to reach the top of the mountain, which he surely did. Success, for Machado, however, didn't come randomly: it was meticulously planned and restlessly pursued. In this regard, Machado personified the American concept of a self-made man: Machado did make himself. How? One possible answer is: by choosing the Western side. In other words, by fully embracing Western culture, Western rhetoric, Western dress, Western manners, the Western way of living, Western aspirations, Western *appearance* – and herein lies the topic of looking whiter. Facing the bifurcated path that would lead him to either a Western or a non-Western destination, Machado took the former. As for his humble and African origins, he let them drift towards oblivion.

The *ethos* of Machado as a writer of humble and, especially, African origins did indeed fade during his lifetime and after his death in 1908 up until the advent of the Estado Novo in 1937. Getúlio Vargas's populist regime, better known as Estado Novo, worked tirelessly to launch a national mythology that could be used to unify the then divided nation. Ultimately, from this mythology emerges Brazil *as we now know it*; that is, the country of samba, *feijoada, malandro* (a lower-class street guy, clever,

---

problem, in that context was not the term itself, but rather the concept to which it refers. In the 1930s, however, this scenario greatly changed, and Ary Barroso called Brazil a "mulato inzoneiro" (*an intriguing mulatto*) in the song which is considered to be the unofficial national anthem of Brazil: "Aquarela do Brasil." Three decades later, Caetano Veloso praised the "mulata" in "Tropicália," the song which is a sort of manifesto for the Tropicalismo movement. It was roughly in the 1990s, under the aegis of political correctness ideas, that the term "mulato" started to be systematically questioned.

19 *Apud* Jean-Michel Massa, *A juventude de Machado de Assis*, 46.

charismatic, seducer, whose personal style may include walking with a swagger), *jeitinho* (a spontaneous or improvised astuteness used to deceive the established order for taking personal advantage), *capoeira*, and Carnival. Interracial unions were celebrated under the Vargas regime. The African and Indigenous heritages came to be officially acknowledged. In this context, the Brazilian multiracial woman, as a conceptual image, was appointed to the post of national muse.

Also in this context, the country organized, in 1939, the festivities to celebrate the 100th anniversary of Machado's birth. On the one hand, the country exalted the biracial writer, the genius of Afro-Brazilian descent. The government sponsored a short movie based on a popular story by Machado – "Um apólogo" ("An Apologue") – and directed by the acclaimed filmmaker Humberto Mauro.[20] Other public events were scheduled to honor the date. On the other hand, during the Estado Novo – which lasted until 1945 – Machado suffered bitter attacks from intellectuals aligned with the regime, such as Cassiano Ricardo and José Lins do Rego.[21] The reasons for these harsh criticisms? Machado's anti-nationalism. According to his detractors, his fiction lacks the local color, the sentiment of Brazilianess, seen in the works by José de Alencar and Gonçalves Dias, for instance; Machado's style is immaculate, it disregards the richness of the language by overlooking its multiple social layers and focusing solely on the upper-class variant; lastly, Machado's elitist characters and plots blatantly pass over the urgent social-political issues of his time, such as slavery, for example.

The Estado Novo ultimately created two conflicting images of Machado: the Afro-Brazilian genius and the Europeanized absentee. As for the latter, it's worth noting that somewhat similar accusations had already been brought against Machado by Sílvio Romero, one of the most influential literary critics of the nineteenth century. These accusations, however, did not carry much weight during Machado's lifetime. They grew stronger decades later, under the nationalist propaganda of Vargas's Estado Novo regime.

Let's go back to the topic of this section: Machado's racial identity, or rather, racial identities. Machado died as a white man. During Vargas's era, he was celebrated as well as criticized as a biracial writer; then, finally,

---

20 Link to the short movie *Um apólogo* (*An Apologue*): www.youtube.com/watch?v=TLMhPpoBEwM
21 See Cassiano Ricardo, *Marcha para o Oeste* (Rio de Janeiro: José Olympio, 1940), 548–50; and José Lins do Rego, "Um escritor sem raízes," *A Manhã*, ano 2, Sept. 28, 1941.

in 2002, his racial status changed again. That year, in a bold and oft-quoted statement, the American scholar Harold Bloom praises Machado as "the supreme black literary artist to date."[22] Bloom naturally referred to Machado as a black writer for, under the one-drop rule in America's racial culture, people of biracial descent are black. In Brazil, however, a reversed version of the American one-drop rule prevailed for over a century. In a predominantly interracial Brazilian society, if you had one drop of white blood, you were considered white, or you were allowed to consider yourself white. Only a few decades ago, Brazilians unofficially embraced – to a great extent, at least – the American version of the one-drop rule as a way to show support for and pride in black communities. Through this perspective – that of people being identified, racially speaking, as either black or white – Machado became black in Brazil as well. An article which appeared in *The New York Times* in 2019 broadly discusses how this change has been occurring.[23] More recently, in 2020, another article, in *Le Monde*, examined the new rendering of Machado's racial identity; in the French newspaper, Machado was also referred to as a black writer.[24]

This racial transformation of Machado reached an important and decisive chapter in 2011, however. That year, one unbelievable event took place and, in practical terms, changed, or helped change, the course of how Machado had been historically represented.

2011: It Happened, Believe It or Not...

In 1898, Machado made his last will and testament. In the document, he named Carolina (then still alive)[25] as the beneficiary to receive the balance of his savings account at *Caixa Econômica* (today *Caixa Econômica Federal* [Federal Savings Bank]). Every month, while going to or coming back from work, Machado stopped by the bank and made small deposits into his savings account.

Founded in 1861, the *Caixa Econômica Federal* celebrated its 150th anniversary in 2011. As part of the celebrations, the bank ran a TV

---

22 Harold Bloom, *Genius: A Mosaic of One Hundred Exemplary Creative Minds* (New York: Warner Books, 2002), 674.
23 www.nytimes.com/2019/06/14/books/brazil-machado-de-assis.html?searchResultPosition=7
24 www.lemonde.fr/international/article/2020/06/25/au-bresil-la-redecouverte-des-grandes-figures-noires-blanchisees_6044082_3210.html
25 Carolina died in 1904 and Machado made another will in 1906.

commercial in which Machado de Assis, back in 1908, walks down the streets of old Rio, greets people, enters the doors of *Caixa*, approaches the bank teller, and pays some money into his account. The one-minute ad, in sum, paid tribute to Machado by featuring him as one of the bank's most illustrious account holders in its 150-year history. That's lovely, except for one fact: the actor who played Machado was white! A resounding reaction came out on social media. Readers and fans of Machado spoke out and up in protest against the commercial. The president of *Caixa* rapidly released an official notice in which he acknowledged and apologized for the mistake. The commercial broadcast was immediately suspended. One month later, *Caixa* produced a second version of the ad. In this new version, Machado was played by a black actor. (You can find the links for both versions in the footnotes.)[26]

What conclusions, then, can we draw from this episode? Here are a few possible ones. (1) The perception of Machado as a white writer was so engrained and naturalized in Brazilian culture that no one seems to have realized the blatant error in the ad piece – neither the president of *Caixa*, who had to approve the commercial before it was broadcast, nor the entire production crew, which includes directors, cast members, camera operators, costume designers, make-up artists, hairstylists, screenwriters, film editors, and so forth. (2) The feelings of shock, discontent, and dissent provoked by the commercial ultimately gave birth to a civil movement which has now been fighting for the recognition of Machado as a Brazilian writer of African descent. This movement has achieved successful results so far, both nationally and internationally. The articles in *The New York Times* and *Le Monde*, referred to a few lines above, attest to this fact. (3) For the sake of historical accuracy, both "Machados" in the *Caixa* commercial appear inaccurate, for Machado was neither white nor black. However, historical accuracy does not appear to be the main point in this debate. The point, it seems to me, is to restore the Africanness of Machado which faded into oblivion after the Estado Novo. (4) For the sake of historical accuracy, Machado was of both African and European descent. This conclusion doesn't solve the puzzle, though. On the contrary, it creates a permeable boundary where ambivalence can prevail over certainty. That's the reason why Machado could be seen as whiter in the past and can been seen as blacker in the present. (5) Lastly, another reason to explain why Machado has suffered a process of whitewashing

---

26 White Machado: www.youtube.com/watch?v=1oP8fZ5I1Wk / Black Machado: www.youtube.com/watch?v=XX71Z_7p-As

is, obviously, racism. Anti-racist groups in Brazil have been emphasizing the blackness of Machado as a way ultimately to combat institutionalized racism, which, unfortunately, still permeates the country. This opposition is coherently possible under the American one-drop rule, which Brazilian society has on the whole embraced. Under the American one-drop rule, Machado de Assis *is* black. And herein lies the irony of this story: the racist American one-drop rule has been used in Brazil to protect Machado against racism!

Machado: The Conventional Man

Machado spent most of his lifetime reading and writing. Apart from these silent and solitary activities, he was an exemplary public servant, an active member of literary clubs, and a caring husband. As a public servant, Machado started his career at the *Diário Oficial* in 1867, as we have already mentioned. In December of 1873 (to begin in January of 1874), he was appointed as First Official in the *Secretaria da Agricultura* (Agriculture Department). Two years later, Machado was promoted to Head of his division; he was then 37. His earnings were sufficient to provide him and Carolina with a simple but comfortable life. He continued contributing regularly to the press with articles, *crônicas*, stories, reviews, etc., but not primarily for the pay anymore. In 1880, Machado got a new promotion as Cabinet Official. Nine years later, he was offered the position of Director of the Commerce Office in the Agriculture, Commerce, and Public Works Department. It was the pinnacle of Machado's career in public service. He still occupied other positions, but all of them comparable in terms of level or rank. Machado retired in 1908, just months before he died. Not counting the period at the *Diário Oficial*, he served the Agriculture Department and its branches, almost continuously, or with few interruptions, for thirty-four years, from 1874 until 1908. During this time, the very dedicated Machado reportedly fulfilled his duties with impeccable professionalism, by which he earned the respect and admiration of his co-workers.

As for the literary societies, Machado participated in several and is widely recognized as one of the founders and the first president of the *Academia Brasileira de Letras* (Brazilian Academy of Letters), a non-profit institution dedicated to fostering and diffusing "the culture of language and national literature."[27] In its inaugural session, on July 20, 1897, speaking

---

27 www.academia.org.br/academia/estatuto

as president of the Academy, Machado declared: "Your [the Academy's] desire is to preserve literary unity in the midst of the political federation."[28] Despite its ups and downs, it's fair to affirm that, for over a century, the House of Machado de Assis, as the Academy is also known, has accomplished its noble mission.

Two years after the inauguration of the Brazilian Academy of Letters, that is, in 1899, Machado and Carolina celebrated thirty years of happy marriage. Carolina Augusta Xavier de Novais had arrived in Rio in June of 1868 from Portugal. The reason for her travel to Brazil was allegedly because her brother, the Portuguese poet Faustino Xavier de Novais, was sick and needed someone to take care of him. Machado and Faustino Xavier were mutual acquaintances, and Machado met Carolina sometime after her arrival. The couple soon got engaged and eventually married on November 12, 1869. Machado was then 30, and Carolina was 34. Faustino Xavier died a few months before the wedding.

Carolina was a cultured woman whose family's house in Porto was frequented by eminent Portuguese writers, such as Camilo Castelo Branco, the Brazilian-born Gonçalves Crespo, and Guerra Junqueiro. Beyond being a zealous and loving wife, Carolina was Machado's first reader and his unofficial literary counselor for thirty-five years, from 1869 until her death in 1904. It's known that Machado submitted all his manuscripts to Carolina before publishing. One month after her passing, Machado said to Joaquim Nabuco in a letter: "The best part of me is gone, and here I am, alone in the world."[29] To Carolina, Machado wrote a moving Camões-style sonnet, published in 1906, which is among the best of his poetic productions and one of the most esteemed in the Portuguese language. Here it is in translation by Frederick G. Williams:

To Carolina

My sweet, here at the foot of your last bed
In which you're resting now from your long life,
I've come and always will, poor dearest wife,
To bring you the companion's heart you wed.

It pulses from affection tried and true
And which, despite all human drudgery,

---

28 Machado de Assis, *Obra Completa*, vol. III, ed. Afrânio Coutinho (Rio de Janeiro: Nova Aguilar, 1997), 926.
29 Ibid., 1071.

Had made our life's existence ecstasy
And brought our home a world for me and you.

I bring you flowers, remnants plucked now faded
From earth that saw us jointly walk this way
And now has left us dead and separated.

If I, within my wounded eyes today
Still carry thoughts of life I'd formulated,
Those thoughts once lived, but now they've gone away.[30]

As mentioned in Chapter One, it was quite uncommon for a non-widowed woman in the nineteenth century to get married at the age of 34. Carolina most likely didn't expect such a late nuptial. Did she have suitors in Portugal? How was her romantic life there? As a young woman, she was attractive, educated, and raised in a middle-class family – her father worked as a goldsmith. There was nothing apparently preventing her from getting married. The environment where Carolina brought up prepared young women for marriage. And that was what young women did: they got married. So why didn't Carolina?

It was the French researcher Jean-Michel Massa, whom I introduced in Chapter One, who took up the challenge of answering these questions. What did he find out? Massa learnt that Carolina had been courted by at least three suitors, who wrote poems to her. Another piece of the puzzle that Massa discovered was a passage in a 1906 text that outlines the history of the Novais family. In this passage, the author, Viscount Sanches de Frias, mentions that Carolina left Porto on her way to Rio, "by virtue of a grave occurrence,"[31] in the company of Artur Napoleão, a renowned pianist and a close friend of her family. It's not clear which *occurrence* Frias was referring to; it may be Faustino Xavier's debilitating health condition, but it may not be. In Artur Napoleão's memoirs – unpublished but whose manuscripts Massa had access to – Napoleão declares he would cut a chapter about Carolina for the sake of her privacy. He went on to justify his action by bringing up the fact that Carolina avoided an "intimate family drama"[32] when she traveled to Brazil. To put it another way, Carolina

---

30 Machado de Assis, "To Carolina," *Poets of Brazil: A Bilingual Selection*, trans. Frederick G. Williams (Provo-UT; Salvador; New York: Brigham Young Universities Studies; Editora da UFBA; Luso-Brazilian Books, 2004), 149.
31 *Apud* Jean-Michel Massa, *A juventude de Machado de Assis*, 582.
32 Ibid., 582.

would have been the victim of a local scandal had she stayed in Portugal. What scandal? Napoleão didn't provide any specifics.

And what about Machado? Carolina and Machado exchanged letters for quite some time before they got married. How much time? How many letters? We don't know and most likely never will because, before dying, Machado gave strict instructions that all their letters should be burned – and it was done. For some reason, though, two were preserved: two letters from Machado to Carolina. What did they reveal about Carolina's mysterious past? Not much. Machado does mention, though, that Carolina suffered: "Besides," he says, "you have one quality that enhances all the others: you have suffered." In the same letter, written in March of 1869, Machado also suggests feelings of jealousy on his part: "You accuse me of not confiding in you. It is true and yet it is not true."[33]

Connecting the Dots (or Trying to ...)

As the documents presented by Jean-Michel Massa suggest, Faustino Xavier's illness was not the only reason for Carolina's travelling to Brazil. It's plausible that her brother's health condition was, in fact, a pretext for Carolina to flee Portugal in order to elude a family scandal involving some sort of romantic imbroglio. As a young woman, Carolina apparently flirted with her admirers. Three of them wrote poems to her. What happened next? We don't know. Did she do something reprehensible according to the moral framework of the time? This remains unknown, too. Was Machado aware of her whole story? He likely was. Did this awareness trigger his feelings of jealousy? It probably did, even though Machado doesn't seem to have been a jealous husband.

In the midst of so many slippery speculations, we can finally step on more solid ground. Literarily speaking, jealousy and its ramifications – adultery, envy, deception, procrastination – constitute major themes within Machado's fictional works. His first novel, *Ressurreição* (*Resurrection*), released in 1872, for instance, presents a protagonist, Félix, who is undermined by feelings of jealousy and distrust. The plot of *Dom Casmurro*, one of Machado's masterpieces, published in 1899, orbits around the narrator, Bento Santiago, whose discourse aims to convince the reader

---

[33] Machado de Assis, *apud* Helen Caldwell, *Machado de Assis: The Brazilian Master and His Novels* (Berkeley: U of California P, 1970), 28–29. Trans. Helen Caldwell.

that he was betrayed by his wife, Capitolina (commonly referred to as Capitu), and his best friend, Escobar. Moreover, it's worth noting that Machado was obsessed with Shakespeare's *Othello*, which had an enormous impact on his fictional works. In sum, the exercise of knowing the Other as a practice of self-entrapment and self-deception is a theme developed by Machado in his fiction, to which Carolina and her past may or may not have contributed. We'll never know. From a strictly critical standpoint, knowing may not be relevant. From a biographical point of view, however, these possible connections keep us speculating. So here goes one more speculation.

Bento and Capitolina are the central characters in *Dom Casmurro*. The names of characters in Machado's works often carry suggestive meanings with implications, more or less fruitful, for critical understanding of the narrative. In *Dom Casmurro*, one of these possible meanings correlates Bento with Machado and Capitolina with Carolina. For the latter, the relationship is at first sonic: Ca(pi)*tolina*/Carolina. As for Machado as Bento, it's a bit more complicated. In the name Joaquim Maria Machado de Assis, *Joaquim* comes from Machado's godfather Joaquim Alberto de Sousa da Silveira, and *Maria*, from his godmother Maria José de Mendonça Barroso Pereira. Joaquim Alberto was Maria José's son-in-law. Who was Maria José's husband? It was Bento Barroso Pereira, a prominent politician of his time, who died in 1837 – that is, two years before Machado's birth. So here is the point: if Bento Barroso had still been alive in 1839, he would naturally have been Machado's godfather. And Machado, therefore, would be named *Bento*, instead of *Joaquim*, Maria Machado de Assis ...

Speculating beyond this point, from a critical perspective, would be not recommended. From a biographical viewpoint, it wouldn't be either. The key point is that, from a biographical standpoint, there is as much mystery surrounding Carolina's past as, from a fictional standpoint, there is surrounding Capitu's. The burning of the letters exchanged between Carolina and Machado, for instance, reinforces the first thesis. As for Capitu, we'll be discussing her enigma further in Chapter Six. Now, it's time to advance to the last, big mystery.

Machado: The Big Mystery

First, a brief recap before we continue. Machado de Assis was born into unfavorable conditions. Notwithstanding the adversities he had to face – poverty, skin color, loss of his mother at 9 years old, health issues, etc. – Machado *miraculously* became, still in his lifetime, the major figure of Brazilian letters. This remarkable achievement, however, didn't occur overnight, or by chance. It happened after a long period of continuous practice with a clear watershed moment: the publication of the novel *Memórias Póstumas de Brás Cubas*, which first appeared in *feuilleton* form in 1880, when Machado was 41, and was then released in book form the following year. Machado himself recognized the publication of *Brás Cubas* as a turning point is his career. There are, thus, two very distinct "Machados": one before and one after *Brás Cubas*. The problem here is that the first Machado, broadly speaking, did not prefigure the second. That is to say, if Machado had, for any reason, decided to abandon writing at the beginning of 1880, he would have gone down in history as simply a mediocre author.

In 1878, Machado published *Iaiá Garcia*, a good and, to a certain degree, sophisticated novel which indeed represents an improvement when compared with his previous novels (*Ressurreição*, 1872; *A mão e a luva*, 1874; and *Helena*, 1876). However, the leap in quality between the conventional *Iaiá Garcia* and the radical *Brás Cubas* is so extreme, so impressively unexpected, that it makes Machado's readers wonder, even today, how this leap was possible. How could a second-rate author, who generally conformed to the literary system of his epoch, emerge, in a short period, as the most brilliantly unorthodox writer who had ever appeared – up to that point – in Brazil and Latin America? Something must have happened for Machado to leave behind his ordinary style and – somewhat out of the blue – develop an astonishing and extraordinary one, thereby reinventing himself. What happened?

We don't know exactly. However, we do know some context. Before revealing it, let me first resume the brief recapitulation I started two paragraphs above. Beyond the drawbacks Machado had to confront, there isn't much else to add biographically, in terms of pivotal events. As already mentioned, Machado spent most of his lifetime reading and writing whenever he wasn't cooped up in a public office carrying out bureaucratic tasks, or in a bookshop chatting with friends, or inside his house in the company of his beloved wife, Carolina. In this regard, Machado's life could be summarized as *perfectly unadventurous*. Being unadventurous, though, doesn't mean being idle. Machado was obsessively dedicated, whether it be as a reader, writer, bureaucrat, friend, or husband. His work at the Agriculture Department was particularly exhausting for its high demand of duties and tight deadlines. On top of that, Machado consistently refused to go on vacation, and, for years in a row, kept himself committed to working hard for the government, the press, literary societies, his family, and his publisher.

In 1878, for the first time, Machado was forced to take a break. He had exhausted his physical and mental limits. As a consequence, he grew sick and his doctor somehow obliged him to take leave from work, which he eventually agreed to do. It happened that Carolina was somewhat unwell at the time, too. The couple, thus, took a vacation to the quiet neighboring town of Nova Friburgo, which lies in a mountainous region with an excellent climate. Machado and Carolina stayed there, in a hotel, from December 1878 to March 1879. It's widely believed that the "transformation" of Machado occurred while he was in Nova Friburgo. Or, the writer who came back from Nova Friburgo was another Machado, renewed and updated. It was as if the mountains of Nova Friburgo magically orchestrated the change. The fact is that exactly one year later, in March 1880, Machado sent the first chapters of *Brás Cubas* to *Revista Brasileira* (*Brazilian Magazine*), where the novel was published, in installments, through to December. A revised version, as already mentioned, came out in book form the following year.

Indeed, something happened in Nova Friburgo, but what might it have been? As I've said, we don't know. However, even if we don't know the *cause*, we do know quite well the *effects*. Starting with the outlandish and disconcerting *Brás Cubas*, Machado's novels and stories redefined the literary scene in Brazil. In fact, from *Brás Cubas* onward, Machado occupied – with no interruption or dispute – the center of Brazilian cultural and intellectual life. Brazil, of course, has produced other world-class writers: Euclides da Cunha, Carlos Drummond de Andrade, João Guimarães Rosa, Clarice Lispector. Still, none have mobilized the critics quite like Machado. Brazil, of course, has also produced other geniuses: Tom Jobim and João Gilberto, in music; Pelé, in sports; Santos-Dumont, in science. Machado predates them all. Machado initiated the noble lineage of world-class Brazilian writers and geniuses. Starting with *Brás Cubas* in 1880, Machado changed the game for both Brazil and Latin America. The region that encompasses Portuguese and Spanish America finally yielded a fictionist whose works could be compared on an equal basis, qualitatively speaking, with those of major European and North American novelists and storywriters.

Was this revolution fully conceived during the three-month stay in Nova Friburgo? Of course not! It all began with Machado's first readings and writings. It was, therefore, a long-term process. Nonetheless, there was a major turning point between March 1878, when *Iaiá Garcia*'s last chapter appeared in *feuilleton* form, and March 1880, when the first, serialized chapters of *Brás Cubas* were published. During this two-year period, *something happened* for Machado to start anew, reinvent himself, burn all the ships in his harbor, and reestablish his style on fresh, radical premises. During this two-year period, two events seem to have connections with the emergence of the second, post-1880 Machado: the vacation in Nova Friburgo and, a few months before, in March 1878, the arrival in Rio of Eça de Queirós's novel O *primo Basílio*, which we'll discuss later, in Chapter Four.

During the last years of Machado's life, particularly after Carolina's death in 1904, a close friendship developed between him and Mário de Alencar, José de Alencar's son. Intrigued by the existence of two so different "Machados," two authors so distant from one another, Mário once asked Machado how he could possibly conceive *Brás Cubas* after creating *Helena*. Machado allegedly said in response to Mário: "The novelist (i.e. Machado himself) became disillusioned with humanity."[34]

Ultimately, from a biographical standpoint, the mystery involving the turnaround in Machado's fiction became one of the main "events" of his life. This ultimately underlines two points in Machado's biography. First, it shows how regular, discreet, and devoid of alluring facts Machado's life was. Second, it exhibits how Machado's personal history is linked to his activities as a writer. It wouldn't be far-fetched to assert, therefore, that the main occurrence in Machado's biography was indeed his writings. In other words, if you want to know Machado, the best sources are his novels, stories, *crônicas*, reviews, articles, plays, poems, letters, and translations. Beyond his works, everything nearly falls into either speculation or bare facts. We know for sure, in brief, that Machado preserved his privacy as much as he possibly could. The public figure assiduously hid the private one. On top of that, Machado lived, as already said, a *perfectly unadventurous* life that, in essence, defines itself through the literary act. In this regard, Machado's biography bears a resemblance to those of other major Luso-Hispanic authors, such as Fernando Pessoa and Jorge Luis Borges.

Borges Again ...

Speaking of Borges and of similarities in biographies, I offer you just one curious and brief remark. One crucial episode in Borges's biography is that of an accident he suffered on Christmas Eve, 1938. This accident – later fictionalized in his story "The South" – is deemed to be *the* turning point

---

34 *Apud* Lúcia Miguel-Pereira, *Machado de Assis (Estudo crítico e biográfico)* (São Paulo: Companhia Editora Nacional, 1936), 217.

in his literary career. While struggling for his life in a hospital bed, Borges reconfigured his fiction into the parameters that define his style as we know it. After recovering, he wrote "Pierre Menard, autor del Quijote" ("Pierre Menard, Author of the Quixote") which was published in May 1939. With "Pierre Menard," the 39-year-old Borges created a new avenue for his fiction to explore. From this exploration, he harvested fame and glory. Had Borges died from the accident, or had the accident in some way impaired his ability to write, he would have gone down in history as simply one more Argentinian writer among many others. Not dying turned out to be a rebirth for Borges, not just as a person (obviously) but also as a creator.

In sum, in May 1939, at the age of 39, a renewed Borges made history with his strangely enticing, hardly definable, and powerfully provocative fiction. Likewise, in March 1880, at the age of 41, a renewed Machado de Assis made history with his strangely enticing, hardly definable, and powerfully provocative fiction. In contrast to Borges, though, we don't know exactly what (if anything in particular) catalyzed the change from which the definitive Machado emerged. So long as the mystery remains (and it will likely never be solved), we'll continue speculating as to the possible factors that not only enabled but specifically drove Machado to run the risk of revolutionizing his style. We'll return to this topic in the next chapters as it connects with other facets of Machado's life.

Filling In the Final Gaps (... But Not All of Them)

Before we advance to the next chapter, just a final note about Machado. For us to pick up the threads, let me return to some dates and facts. In January 1855, at the age of 15, Machado started contributing to Paula Brito's *A Marmota Fluminense*. At this point, Machado's daily routine consisted of going back and forth between São Cristóvão, where he lived with his father and stepmother, and downtown Rio, where everything, from a cultural standpoint, was happening. From 1856 to 1858, Machado reportedly worked at *Tipografia Nacional*. In 1859, he allegedly got two jobs at two different presses, *A Marmota Fluminense* and *Correio Mercantil*, as a proofreader. We don't know for sure, but it's likely around that year that he left São Cristóvão to move downtown, where he rented a small room. Machado never returned to live at his father's house. In 1864, his father, Francisco José, died; his stepmother, Maria Inês, lived longer, until 1891. At the time of her death, Machado was a well-established, well-respected 52-year-old writer.

When Machado abandoned São Cristóvão, he apparently left behind not just his father's house but all his past. In order to assert himself literarily, Machado seems to have silenced his origins. Apart from a poem on his mother, and another on his sister, Machado's writings barely touch on his childhood and youth at the Livramento estate and São Cristóvão. With friends, Machado seemingly never talked about his past. For a while, at the beginning of his career, he signed his texts Machado d'Assis. The prepositional contraction – as in d'Assis – was a recurrent linguistic trait in the European variant of Portuguese. The use of this contraction may be evidence that Machado, at that point, was trying to embrace and exhibit his Portuguese roots. Does this mean that he denied his Afro-Brazilian heritage? *Denying, refusing, concealing, neglecting* – they are all *negative* terms with an aura of culpability around them. As I stated before, I would rather frame this matter by affirming that Machado *chose* to follow the Western route, even though, from *Brás Cubas* on, he uses Western tools to dismantle Western values. Machado should not be blamed for making the choices he made. This does not suggest, however, that he was faultless. He wasn't. At least, not to Hemetério dos Santos ...

Machado de Assis died of an ulcerated tumor in his mouth on September 29, 1908. That day, as the news spread, the entire city of Rio de Janeiro mourned the loss of its greatest writer. As press photos of that day attest, his funeral procession was a public event attended by thousands of mourners. Brazil had never seen such a widespread demonstration of sorrow and respect at the passing of a national artist. Machado ended his days glorified. One voice, however, tried to stain this glory with an open letter published in the *Gazeta de Notícias* on November 29, 1908.

In this letter, the grammarian and Portuguese language teacher Hemetério dos Santos severely criticized Machado the writer and the man. He criticized Machado the writer for overlooking issues of race in his works, despite "his own color and provenance." He blasted Machado the man for abandoning his stepmother when he left São Cristóvão. According to Hemetério, who personally knew the "good old mulatta" Maria Inês, she supported and helped Machado in pursuing his dream of becoming a writer, against the will of Machado's father, who wished his son had focused on seeking a stable career. However, despite her crucial encouragement and assistance, Machado selfishly turned his back on Maria Inês, who died in poverty, living as an *agregada* (i.e. allowed to live as a favor) in a modest family house.[35]

---

35 Hemetério dos Santos, "Machado de Assis – Carta ao Sr. Fabio Luz," *Gazeta de Notícias*, Nov. 29, 1908, 2.

Not all biographers have seconded Hemetério's accusations. Nevertheless, as commonly happens regarding Machado's biography, shade prevails over light. As a result, the topic is open to speculation. Did Machado actually abandon Maria Inês? Did Maria Inês attend Machado and Carolina's wedding ceremony in 1869? Did Carolina meet Maria Inês at any time? Did Maria Inês visit her stepson and his wife in their house at least once? It would be quite helpful if we knew the answer to at least one of these questions, but we don't. We do know, however, that Machado attended Maria Inês's funeral. According to the report, Machado was going to the funeral by himself when he bumped into a friend, the writer Coelho Neto, who spontaneously accompanied him.[36]

The pieces of information we have, particularly the episode of Machado intentionally going to say his last farewell to Maria Inês alone, may lead us to the conclusion that he did hide his past from his circle of friends and acquaintances in Rio. In order to climb the social ladder, as he did, Machado opted to embrace his Western European roots, while, say, diverting people's attention away from his African origins. What does this strategy mean in practical terms? There is a myriad of implications in it, of course. Let me put it this way to make it simpler.

For Machado, the embrace of Western culture translated into the kind of unflinching discipline and work that was seen by many as emblematic of that culture.[37] From his early years onwards, Machado learned to be disciplined to the extreme. His extensive productivity, and his high quality of writing, came from his meticulous and restless self-discipline. The genius of Machado did not appear all of a sudden on a whim; it was developed little by little, step by step, page by page, as he went on and on studying and absorbing and interacting and negotiating with the major works of Western literature.

On a literary level, Machado did nothing but emulate and parody the major writers of Western literature. Machado set himself the highest expectations possible based on parameters established by Shakespeare,

---

[36] Lúcia Miguel-Pereira, *Machado de Assis (Estudo crítico e biográfico)*, 135–36.
[37] In the dialectics that characterizes Brazilian culture, there isn't necessarily a hierarchy imposed on what are commonly considered to be Western and non-Western values. That is to say, the non-Western forms of discipline and what some see as a focus on immediate sensory pleasure (food, dance, music) are not considered morally, nor even axiologically, less valuable than the traditional Western emphasis on systematic discipline and work. We'll be back to this topic in Chapter Three while discussing Machado's last play, *Lição de botânica*.

Cervantes, Hugo, Goethe, Dante, and, immediately thereafter, went tenaciously after them. By emulating and parodying these writers, Machado gradually became one of them. Is it fair to assert, then, that Machado is a European-like author who created European-like characters, ambience, and plots? To a certain degree, yes, it is. Or, better yet, on the surface that is correct. What actually matters in regard to Machado's style, though, lies, instead, beneath the surface. That's the problem. One must learn how to see what is out of sight, in order to catch, let's say, the *real* Machado, or rather, the *other* Machado. And here's the point: beneath the European-like surface, readers will find deep layers of Brazilianess with Brazilian characters, ambience, and plots. We'll expand on this topic, for its centrality, in the next chapters.

Conclusion: Machado and Nietzsche

Let's go back to the concept of *ethos* that opened this chapter and loosely apply it to a German thinker who was five years younger than Machado: Friedrich Nietzsche. Machado and Nietzsche converge on several points. They were both devoted readers of Schopenhauer, for instance. Through Schopenhauer, they came to share a number of similar views on human nature and the nature of history. The title of this book – *The World Keeps Changing to Remain the Same* – has a dash of Machado and a dash of Nietzsche. We'll come back to the topic of Machado vis-à-vis Nietzsche in Chapter Seven. For now, I just want to single out one aspect of Nietzsche's style that, despite all the possible differences, could be fairly compared to Machado's.

Nietzsche's style is so self-contradictory and so self-conscious, so slippery and so solid; Nietzsche scrutinizes ideas so distinct from one another, in such distinct ways; his approach is so experimental, so allegorical; he corrects and re-corrects himself so many times; his postulations are so assertive and so provisional, that it's eventually too risky to reach any conclusive assertion about Nietzsche and what he stands for. His works have ultimately created a number of "Nietzsches." Not just different ones but also opposing and even totally antinomic "Nietzsches." There is a right-wing and a left-wing Nietzsche; there is a Nazi and a Communist Nietzsche; there is a democratic, an anarchist, and a totalitarian Nietzsche; there is an atheist and a theologian Nietzsche; there is a misogynist and a libertarian Nietzsche. And all of them are equally as true as incoherent. In the long run, Nietzsche's style allows us to approach it from different angles and thus arrive at different conclusions. That's how the game works when it comes to Nietzsche – and that's why his works are so powerfully seductive.

That's how the game works when we read Machado, too. From reading his pages, several "Machados" jump out. There is a European-like and a Brazilian Machado. There is a Machado who barely cares about the pressing political issues of the country and another one whose penetrating eyes see and reveal the internal structure of Brazilian society like no other fictional writer before or after him. There is a reactionary and a revolutionary Machado. There is one Machado who overlooks the tropical landscape and another who looks deeply into the psychological landscape of his characters. There is a misogynistic and a feminist Machado.[38] You can pick your favorite among these many "Machados" available. Sometimes they complement one another, sometimes they collide with and contradict one another. In dealing with them, just try not to nail Machado or his works down. That'd be a waste of time.

In this chapter, we tackled some of the facets of Machado the man – his humble social origins, his African-European descent, his health issues, his professionalism as a public servant, his dedication to the press, his affection as a husband, his vacation with Carolina in Nova Friburgo, his change as a writer in 1880, his participation in establishing the Brazilian Academy of Letters, to which he was elected the first president, his death as the towering figure of Brazilian literature, his supposed ingratitude towards his stepmother. In the next chapter, we will focus more on Machado the writer and some of the *ethe* (plural form of *ethos*) derived from his literary works.

---

38 Maria Manuel Lisboa, *Machado de Assis and Feminism* (Lewiston, NY: Edwin Mellen Press, 1996), 7–13.

Chapter Three

Translation, Poetry, and Drama: The Quest for Greatness

The Modern Renaissance Man

IN THE LAST chapter, we learned that Machado made his debut as a writer by publishing a poem in a local periodical when he was 15 years old. From then until his death at the age of 69, he never refrained from writing and publishing. Along with poetry, Machado wrote articles, essays, reviews, *crônicas*, plays, stories, novellas, novels, forewords, speeches, letters, reports, and translations. As a translator, he translated into Portuguese texts originally written in French, English, Italian, Spanish, and German. During the last period of his life, while old and retired, he spent his time learning ancient Greek (much like Borges, by the way, who took Arabic lessons during the last months of his life). Machado never stopped learning. Beyond literature, his many writings drew from multiple areas of knowledge, such as art, music, philosophy, religion, politics, economics, and history. Machado's curiosity had no bounds. His capacity to absorb knowledge was unrestrained. His continuous ability to articulate his vast repertoire with clarity and wit constitutes a hallmark of his impeccable style. In this respect, Machado admirably embodies the superior ideal of the Renaissance man: a type of intellectual who seeks to develop his capacities as fully as possible by studying and achieving accomplishments in varying disciplines.

With the triumph of the modern division of labor, and the consequent segmentation of knowledge, the figure of the polymath (a person who has accumulated great knowledge on a variety of subjects) and the polygraph (a person who is able to write across genres on different subjects) became rarer with each generation that passed. This idea of an encyclopedic knowledge was, perhaps, last celebrated by the eighteenth-century thinkers during the Age of Enlightenment. From the nineteenth century on, specialization has prevailed over breadth. Similarly, nationalism has ruled – at times perversely – over universalism. In more than one aspect, Machado epitomizes the spirit of the *homo universalis*, that is, the modern Renaissance man who strives to understand the world in a holistic manner, particularly by availing himself of every possible tool of analysis.

Machado worked across every literary genre available in his time. Nonetheless, he is considered to be a master of the short story (novella included) and the novel. To a certain degree, it's logical to affirm that Machado the translator, the poet, the playwright, the *cronista*, and the critic prepared the ground for Machado the notable short-story writer and the novelist to emerge. In this chapter, we'll be focusing on Machado the translator, the poet, and the playwright. In the next, we'll tackle Machado the critic and the *cronista*. By examining these facets separately, we'll see how each distinct but interrelated facet of Machado as a writer contributed to the major turning point in his career, which occurred in 1880, when *Brás Cubas* first came to light in *feuilleton* form.

Machado as a Literary Translator

As mentioned in the last chapter, it is as a translator that the name of Machado de Assis appears for the first time on the cover of a book: *Queda que as mulheres têm para os tolos*, published by Paula Brito in 1861. It's a French satirical essay by Victor Hénaux – whose name, for some reason, is omitted from the edition – translated by Machado. One year prior to *Queda*, in 1860, Machado had published the play *Hoje avental, amanhã luva* (*Today an Apron, Tomorrow a Glove*) in the pages of Paula Brito's *A Marmota*. Like *Queda*, *Hoje avental* is not an original work. But it's not a translation in the traditional sense either. *Hoje avental* is a "transladaption" (i.e. a translation-adaptation) of Gustave Vattier and Émile de Najac's comic play *Chasse au lion* (*The Lion Hunt*), which was performed in Paris in 1852. In *Hoje avental*, Machado transposes the original setting of the play to 1859 Rio de Janeiro. This change of setting allows several more changes to occur in Machado's version. One character, for instance, reads the *Jornal do Comércio*. In one of the final scenes, this same character, named Bento, pretends to be a Spanish nobleman; whereas, in the original play, the character, named François, poses as a Russian prince.

Despite these adjustments, Machado's plot closely follows the original French source. It's inaccurate, thus, to attribute the authorship of *Hoje avental, amanhã luva*, as some critics do, to Machado.

As a translator then, we can initially assert that Machado performed two types of translation: one remaining very close to the original source (as in *Queda*) and the other taking greater liberties with the source text (as in *Hoje avental*). It wouldn't be off target, however, to affirm that Machado also performed a third form of translation in his fiction. In other words, the fictionist can also be viewed a translator, a creative translator. When Helen Caldwell, for instance, entitled her groundbreaking 1960 study on *Dom Casmurro* as *The Brazilian Othello of Machado de Assis*, she hit the mark. Despite its ethnocentric nature and effects – as already discussed in Chapter One – Caldwell's title shows what *Dom Casmurro* is, in essence: a creative translation, re-elaboration, idiosyncratic reading (or misreading, according to Harold Bloom's concept[1]) of Shakespeare's *Othello*, which, in its turn, is a creative translation, re-elaboration, idiosyncratic reading (or misreading) of Giovanni Battista Giraldi's *Un capitano moro* (*A Moorish Captain*). In this regard, both Machado and Shakespeare, as creators, are fundamentally translators, or rather, a particular type of "translator."

One may fairly argue that, from this perspective, every creator is a "translator"; no writer does anything but rewrite (or "miswrite") other writers; or, still, every text is a metatext. That's true. One should also recognize, though, that this process of metaliterature or intertextuality in fiction turns out to be more explicit and decisive with some authors – such as Shakespeare, Cervantes, and Machado de Assis – than with others. From Hispanic America, we could also mention Borges and Roberto Bolaño as notable members of this club, too. All of them, ultimately, write about literature; or, better yet, we could say that literature constitutes the raw material of their fictional works. In the case of Machado, the examples abound. Let me comment on one of them, one already mentioned in this chapter, to illustrate this idea.

Hoje avental, amanhã luva presents a heroine, Rosinha, who works as a maid in a rich house where Ms. Sofia de Melo, her mistress, lives. The play begins with Durval, a middle-aged dandy, coming back after being absent for two years. He is looking for Sofia, who, in the past, had a weakness for him. Back then, Durval took advantage of his power and position and seduced the innocent Rosinha while also flirting with Sofia. For

---

[1] Harold Bloom, "The Necessity of Misreading," *The Georgia Review*, vol. 55–56, nos. 4/1 (Winter 2001/Spring 2002), 69–87.

revenge, Rosinha now crafts a plan to catch Durval and use his power and position to benefit herself, to strip her of her "apron" (*avental*) and get her the "gloves" (*luvas*), or, said literally, to leave the maid's life behind and enter high society. To put it another way, two years after being seduced by Durval, the naïve Rosinha eventually becomes an ambitious and clever social climber. With the help of Bento, another domestic servant, she carries out her plan and finally steals Durval's heart after getting Sofia out of her way.

The clever social climber Rosinha – originally named Florette in Gustave Vattier and Émile de Najac's play – ends up becoming a model from which Machado develops his subsequent heroines in three of the four novels written during his so-called first or Romantic phase. Guiomar, from *A mão e a luva* (1874); Helena, from *Helena* (1876); and Iaiá Garcia, from *Iaiá Garcia* (1878), are all characters from low social echelons, endowed with cunning and charismatic spirits, and they act deliberately to climb the social ladder by marrying a man from the ruling class. In her biography on Machado, Lúcia Miguel-Pereira famously argues that these three characters can be viewed as their author in disguise.[2] Like Guiomar, Helena, and Lina (Iaiá) Garcia, Machado was also a member of the lower-middle class struggling to thrive in a social milieu to which, hierarchically considering, he didn't belong. Machado, then, would have created these ambitious heroines, in Miguel-Pereira's view, in order psychologically to justify and ethically to legitimize his own ambition to himself. In any case, Guiomar, Helena, and Iaiá Garcia all have a literary predecessor and an artistic source in Rosinha/Florette. In other words, all of them are "translations" of Rosinha/Florette (with Rosinha as the original translation of Florette).

Aside from Guiomar, Helena, and Iaiá Garcia, Lalau, the heroine of *Casa velha* (*The Old House*) – a novella published in *feuilleton* form in 1885–86 – shares the same basic traits of the characters previously cited. Throughout the years, Machado seems to have practiced by drawing sketches of the same character before he finally created the ultimate version of the one he idealized. And that ultimate version has a name; she is arguably the greatest female character in Brazilian literature. Her name is Capitu. In *Dom Casmurro*, Capitu is depicted as a bright, lively, and poor girl, who seduces and happens to marry Bento, the heir of a wealthy family and the narrator of his own story. In the last chapter of the novel, the

---

2 Lúcia Miguel-Pereira, *Machado de Assis (Estudo crítico e biográfico)* (São Paulo: Companhia Editora Nacional, 1936), 180.

old, solitary, and taciturn Bento asks himself (and the reader) whether or not the malicious Capitu, whom he accuses of betraying him, was already *inside* the beautiful, young girl, who initially enchanted him. From a strict literary perspective, we could say that a portion of Capitu was *inside* Lalau, Iaiá Garcia, Helena, Guiomar, and Rosinha/Florette. Likewise, a portion of *Othello* is inside *Dom Casmurro*. These transfigurations, from one element into another, have their roots in the very exercise of translation as a creative process.

One last note about this process. Machado made his debut as a novelist in 1872 with *Ressurreição (Resurrection)*. In the prologue, the author explains that the novel aims to put into action a passage from Shakespeare's *Measure for Measure* (Act I, Scene 4) that reads: "Our doubts are traitors, / And make us lose the good we oft might win, / By fearing to attempt." The novel's plot, thus, evolves from this textual point of departure. Why did Machado decide to indicate the literary source of his novel, when he simply could have omitted it? Perhaps, to make it clear that the main source of his fiction is ultimately of fictional nature; to make it clear that the process of his creation has a rational basis; to make it clear, at last, that his story stems from another story, that his text originates from another text, that his readings *translate* into his writings.

Literary Translations *Stricto Sensu*

Machado performed literary translations *stricto sensu* as well. From 1857 to 1894, he penned forty-six translations, among them opera *libretti*, essays, plays, poems, and novels, from authors such as Shakespeare, Heine, Hugo, Dante, and Poe. It's worth noting, though, that by 1876, forty-two of Machado's renditions (i.e. 90% of the total amount) were completed.[3] This fact indicates that Machado applied himself to the art of translation mostly in the first phase of his career, the years prior to *Brás Cubas*.

It's also important to mention that, although Machado had a clear knack for literary translation, and his versions were sober and faithful, he is probably not among the most artful translators of his generation (I'm thinking of Odorico Mendes, João Cardoso de Menezes e Sousa, and Francisco Otaviano). To give just one example, his translation of the classic "The Raven" by Edgar Allan Poe – especially when compared

---

3 Jean-Michel Massa, *Machado de Assis tradutor*, trans. Oséias Silas Ferraz (Belo Horizonte: Crisálida, 2008), 115–17.

with Fernando Pessoa's magnificent rendition of the same poem – exposes a translator who didn't take risks, and, when he did, his choices were, in most cases, questionable. Jean-Michel Massa suggests that Machado's version of "The Raven" was based on Baudelaire's. That's not an issue, in principle. The problem, as Massa demonstrates, is that Machado replicates in his version Baudelaire's own mistakes.[4]

In sum, the art of translation definitely plays a central role in the development of Machado as a writer. During his career, Machado performed two types of translation: one that renders texts from other languages into Portuguese, sometimes acclimatizing the original to Brazilian circumstances (as in *Hoje avental, amanhã luva*); and another that "translates" other authors' texts into his – the "translator's" – own. In the case of the latter, translation appears as a practice close to notions such as parody, intertextuality, metaliterature, appropriation, hypertext, misreading, rewriting, emulation, imitation, and even plagiarism.[5]

Machado as a Poet: Why Poetry?

Machado started off his career as poet. After his debut in 1854, his first writings, published the next year in *A Marmota Fluminense*, were all poems. Why poetry? Even though there is no definitive answer, we can reflect on this question. One possible response could be found in the culture of poetry. During the nineteenth century, when educated male teenagers started practicing writing in the intimacy of their rooms, they usually wrote poetry. Why poetry? The cultural environment somehow compelled these teenagers to try writing in verse. In this environment, poetry carried greater prestige than, say, prose fiction. Poetry was the suitable channel through which a personal voice could convey its intimate message. If the spirits of these teenagers tended towards romantic dreams, they tried verses of love; if their spirits tended towards communicating social reforms, they tried verses of revolution. Contemplative spirits would try poetry of

---

4   Ibid., 55–56. On Machado's version of "The Raven" in comparison with Fernando Pessoa's, see Edgar Allan Poe, *O corvo*, trans. Machado de Assis and Fernando Pessoa, ed. Paulo Henriques Brito (São Paulo: Companhia das Letras, 2018).

5   See João Cezar de Castro Rocha, "Introduction: Machado de Assis: The Location of an Author," *The Author as Plagiarist: The Case of Machado de Assis*, ed. João Cezar de Castro Rocha, *Portuguese Literary & Cultural Studies* 13/14 (Fall 2004/Spring 2005), ix–xxxix.

nature; devotional spirits, poetry of religion; and so on. Writing poetry, then, was more akin to a social habit, one practiced with no necessary intention of being published. Machado, however, published his teenage verses. Why?

In the mid-1850s, Machado was an educated (most likely homeschooled and self-taught) teenager who, despite his humble origins and dark skin color, dreamed of participating in the cultural life of Rio de Janeiro. He then met Paula Brito, who opened the pages of his periodical *A Marmota Fluminense* for Machado to publish his first poems. This decision to publish suggests Machado wanted to be read, commented on, admired, and respected. And, in 1855, the best way for him to achieve this was through poetry. In other words, it would have been harder for Machado to find readership and respect had he first divulged his name publicly through novels or plays. Poetry, in this case, was the most socially sound choice.

As the nineteenth century progressed, however, the cultural capital of poetry went down whereas that of the prose fiction went up. The historical reasons that informed this move were complex and had most of their roots in the social-cultural changes provoked by the Industrial Revolution, particularly the process of secularization of Western societies during this period. Ultimately, prose fiction triumphed over poetry; or, in Hegelian terms, the prosaic (logical-scientific) mind prevailed over the poetic (magical-metaphysical) consciousness in modern culture and art.[6] As a consequence, novels and novelists were pulled towards the center of the literary system while poetry and poets were gradually pushed towards the edge. We should not forget, in this respect, that the novel itself as a genre evolved directly from the epic poem when the latter could no longer fulfill the expectations of the new, bourgeois society and readership, as it had done previously.[7]

By and large, Machado's career develops in parallel with these nineteenth-century changes; that is to say, he starts with poetry, when poetry could lend him cultural capital, and ends with fictional prose, when fictional prose became hegemonic in the realm of letters. Whether these moves were deliberately planned or not isn't under consideration. I'm

---

6 See G. W. F. Hegel, *Aesthetics: Lectures on Fine Art*, vol. II, trans. T. M. Knox (London: Oxford UP, 1975). Particularly the section "Poetic and Prosaic Treatment," 972–78.
7 See Georg Lukács, *The Theory of the Novel*, trans. Anna Bostock (Cambridge, MA: MIT Press, 1971), 56–69.

just putting some pieces of the puzzle together so we can see whether they fit, or to what extent they fit. In this respect, I want to advance a final hypothesis about why Machado took the first steps in his career as a poet.

Machado's first book of poetry, *Crisálidas* (*Chrysalises*), was released in 1864. That same year, Gonçalves Dias died tragically by drowning in a shipwreck off the coast of Northeast Brazil. Gonçalves Dias was the major figure of Indianist poetry, which came into vogue in Brazil in the 1840s and 1850s. Another major name in Brazilian poetry at the time was Álvares de Azevedo, who had died in 1852 at the age of just 20. The last remarkable poet of that time was Castro Alves, whom Machado met in 1868, and whose first book, *Espumas flutuantes* (*Floating Foam*), came out in 1870. So, this is the picture: in 1864, Gonçalves Dias dies; Álvares de Azevedo is dead; and Castro Alves has not yet emerged. Conclusion: there was a gap to be filled in Brazilian poetry. Machado might have perceived that when he entered the stage as a poet, perhaps with the intention of filling this gap with his own poetry. He might have envisioned himself occupying the seat left available by the deaths of Álvares de Azevedo and Gonçalves Dias.

Machado's second collection of poems, *Falenas* (*Moths*), came out in 1870. The release of both *Crisálidas* and *Falenas* along with the poems that Machado had been regularly publishing in the press since 1855 eventually drew a remarkably positive response in 1873. On January 30 of that year, the periodical *Arquivo Contemporâneo* (*Contemporary Archive*) printed a portrait of José de Alencar on its cover, side by side with that of Machado de Assis. José de Alencar was, at that time, the most highly regarded figure in Brazilian literature. Machado deeply admired Alencar and was likely euphoric when he got his hands on this periodical. The article inside presented Alencar as a "refined novelist," Machado as a "delightful lyrical poet," and the "two of [them as] the most splendid minds of [Brazil's] Literary Pantheon."[8] These words ultimately reveal that in the first half of the 1870s, Machado was primarily esteemed as a poet. Here, one may ask what happened to cause Machado the poet to be later devoured by Machado the prose writer? Or, as Manuel Bandeira puts it: how did Machado the poet become "victim" to Machado the fictionist?[9]

---

8   *Apud* Raimundo Magalhães Jr., *Vida e obra de Machado de Assis*, vol. II (Rio de Janeiro: Civilização Brasileira, 1981), 130.
9   Manuel Bandeira, "O poeta," *Obra completa*, Machado de Assis, vol. III, ed. Afrânio Coutinho (Rio de Janeiro: Nova Aguilar, 1997), 11.

As I have been suggesting, ambition maybe played a part in this story. After all, Machado was intellectually ambitious, that is to say, he wanted to climb the social ladder through his writings – which he eventually did. He thus used poetry when poetry was useful to him. He moved towards prose fiction when prose fiction became more advantageous. In between, he simultaneously tried theater, criticism, *crônica* … In the end, Machado's prose fiction gathered steam and brought him praise and glory, while he was still alive. Nonetheless, this fact has at times unjustly overshadowed some segments of Machado's oeuvre, such as his last poetry. Machado's last poems stand out among the best ever written in Portuguese. The problem, beyond his prose fiction overshadowing them, lies in the matter of quantity, or proportionality. Let me explain with some figures.

Throughout his life, Machado penned 278 poems, amounting to nearly 21,000 verses.[10] That's certainly not a small output. Nevertheless, just a handful of this number were written by the *second* Machado. That's the crux of the matter. We have already learned that there exist two "Machados": the mediocre and the ingenious one, the pre- and the post-1880, the pre- and the post-*Brás Cubas*. Similarly, in poetry, we find these two very distinct artists, one each side of the 1880 turning point. Whenever approaching Machado's poetry, one should bear this distinction in mind.

Machado's Poetry Before 1880

Before 1880, Machado published three volumes of poetry. The first two were *Crisálidas* and *Falenas*, as we have seen. Both titles allude to butterflies – insects with which Machado had a sort of fascination. Like butterflies, the poems in these collections evince lightness, delicacy, elegance, and beauty. Their emotions are restrained and sober, and their language and style are polished and primarily committed to correctness. Technically considered, Machado's poetry comes close to perfection; and, in terms of sentiment, it is just regular and morally fine. That way, his poems glow but don't shine. Or, to use a butterfly metaphor, they fly but not too high.

In *Crisálidas*, the opening poem, "Musa consolatrix" ("Consolatrix Muse"), and the closing poem, "Última folha" ("Last Leaf"), are both metapoems, or poems about poetry. This literary self-referentiality and

---

10 Cláudio Murilo Leal, "A vocação narrativa da poesia de Machado de Assis," www.machadodeassis.org.br/abl_minisites/cgi/cgilua.exe/sys/start8686.html?UserActiveTemplate=machadodeassis&from_info_index=1&infoid=265&sid=37

self-consciousness constitutes a hallmark of Machado's style that permeates all his works, particularly those of the post-1880 period. One composition from *Crisálidas* has always been evoked whenever critics comment on the book: "Versos a Corina" ("Verses to Corina"), a love poem divided into six parts, and whose muse's name – Corina – was actually a pseudonym for a woman Machado loved before he was introduced to Carolina – a fact confirmed by Machado in a letter to Carolina.[11]

Beyond the semantic proximity that links *Crisálidas* and *Falenas* to the butterfly imagery, these titles also suggest a sense of sequential development (i.e. *falenas* [moths] are developed from, or developed forms of, *crisálidas* [chrysalises]). In *Falenas*, indeed, Machado expands his style by including in the collection a play written in French alexandrine verses and set in Ancient Greece entitled "Uma ode de Anacreonte" ("An Ode by Anacreon"); a set of poems by Chinese contemporary authors, which Machado translated from a French version, entitled "Lira chinesa" ("Chinese Lire"); a 97-stanza narrative poem in *ottava rima* based on the legend of Don Juan entitled "Pálida Elvira" ("Pale Elvira"); and a poem originally composed in French, entitled "Un vieux pays" ("An Old Country").

The old country in the beautiful "Un vieux pays" is an allegory of the poet's heart. Another allegorical poem about hearts is the short piece "O verme" ("The Worm"). If "Versos a Corina" is the composition that metonymically represents *Crisálidas*, the same can be said about "O verme" in relation to *Falenas*. Here it is:

The Worm

There exists a flower that holds
Heavenly dew and perfume.
She was planted in a fertile land
By the merciful hand of a goddess.

A hideous and repulsive worm,
Engendered in a mortal sludge,
Seeks this virginal flower
To lie and rest on her bosom.

He bites, bleeds, tears, and saps,
He sucks her life and spirit up;
The flower bends her calyx over,
Her leaves stripped off by the wind.

---

[11] Machado de Assis, *Obra Completa*, vol. III, 1029. The letter has an English translation by Helen Caldwell. See Helen Caldwell, *Machado de Assis: The Brazilian Master and His Novels* (Berkeley: U of California P, 1970), 27–29.

Not even the perfume lingers,
Thereafter, in the loneliness breeze ...
This flower is the heart,
Jealousy is that worm.[12]

Following one of the dominant threads of thought in Romantic lyricism, "O verme" combines allegory and didacticism with moral intent. The post-1880 Machado, by the way, maintains an allegorical approach in his works but discards the didactic message. In 1872, though, two years after publishing *Falenas*, Machado released his first novel, *Ressurreição*. The plot of this novel involves a protagonist, Félix, whose heart is destroyed by jealousy. In this respect, "O verme" can be viewed as a miniature version of *Ressurreição*, which, in turn, has been read as a sort of first draft of *Dom Casmurro*, another work about jealousy.

As mentioned before, both novels, *Ressurreição* and *Dom Casmurro* have direct connections to Shakespearian plays. Machado was an avid reader of British and American literature: Poe, Shakespeare, Swift, Sterne ... but not William Blake. He most likely had no contact with the works of Blake, who remained largely unrecognized, even in his own hometown of London, until nearly half a century after his death in 1827. So, the striking similarities between "O verme" and a brief poem by Blake entitled "The Sick Rose,"[13] which is transcribed below, might be just a curious coincidence:

The Sick Rose

O Rose thou art sick.
The invisible worm,
That flies in the night
In the howling storm:

Has found out thy bed
Of crimson joy:
And his dark secret love
Does thy life destroy.[14]

---

12 Machado de Assis, *Obra Completa*, vol. III, 52.
13 The critic and translator Ivo Barroso drew attention to the similarities between Machado and Blake. See https://gavetadoivo.wordpress.com/2010/09/04/ainda-blake-e-machado-uma-curiosa-coincidencia/
14 William Blake, *The Complete Poetry and Prose of William Blake*, ed. David Erdman (Berkeley: U California P, 1982), 23.

With its contrasting imagery of the rose and the worm, the bed (bosom, in Machado's poem) and destruction, "The Sick Rose" could be read as a compact version of "O verme." However, while the latter didactically names jealousy as the cause of the flower's death, the former refers ambiguously to "dark secret love," which may be another "name" for jealousy given how the sentiment can live in *darkness* and *secrecy* inside one's heart.

The third volume of poetry published by Machado in his first phase was *Americanas* (*From America*), which came out in 1875. In *Americanas*, Machado shifts his focus radically from sentimental to nationalistic Romanticism. Following Romantic (José de Alencar and Gonçalves Dias) and pre-Romantic (Basílio da Gama) models, Machado made his first and last attempt to create a national mythology based on non-Western, Indigenous roots.

Romantic Indianism gained its momentum beginning in the 1840s, but mainly in the 1850s and 1860s, when authors such as José de Alencar and Gonçalves Dias along with João Cardoso de Menezes e Sousa ("Cântico do tupi"), Gonçalves de Magalhães (*Confederação dos Tamoios*), Araripe Júnior ("Jaguaraçu e Saí"), and Bernardo Guimarães (*A voz do Pajé*, "Jupira"), strove to lay the foundation for a Brazilian national identity, then in the course of being established. Broadly speaking, these Romantic authors achieved their goal by following the Rousseauian path of idealization of Native Americans and their "primitive" culture. Brazil was, then, in need of a heroic mythology or a foundational discourse to use as a mirror to reflect the reinvented and idealized past into the future.

When Machado embarked on this project with *Americanas*, in 1875, the peak of the movement had already passed. In other words, Romantic nationalism had already taken another direction – so much so that *Americanas* has long been viewed as an outlier in Machado's oeuvre. Machado himself advocated for renewed forms of nationalism, away from Indianism and regionalism, in a famous article entitled "Instinto de nacionalidade" ("Instinct of Nationality"), which will be discussed in the next chapter. Strangely enough, "Instinto de nacionalidade" was written in 1873, two years prior to *Americanas*, making that collection a foreign body that's even more out of place within Machado's work.

Ultimately, Machado wrote the poems of *Americanas* to pay tribute to his literary heroes Basílio da Gama, Gonçalves Dias, and José de Alencar. Beyond that point, it's difficult to provide any reasonable explanation as to why he decided to venture upon a project of writing Indianist and colonial poems in the mid-1870s. The fact, however, is that he did – and completed it. At this point, *Americanas* is basically forgotten. Not totally forgotten, though, thanks to two pieces in it: "Última jornada" ("The Last Journey") and "Sabina."

In 1939, Mário de Andrade praised "Última jornada" as "one of the most beautiful creations of Machado as well as of [Brazilian] poetry."[15] Before that, in 1910, José Veríssimo hailed "Última jornada" as "admirable" and "superb," and even comparable to Gonçalves Dias's Indianist poems.[16] Written in *terza rima*, in the most Dantean tradition, "Última jornada" narrates a love and revenge story. The main narrator is an Indian warrior who murdered his (apparently pregnant[17]) wife in revenge for her having abandoned him. He was then mysteriously killed by forces of nature, as a revenge for the revenge, or as a natural punishment for his crime. In the poem, both characters, the Indian and his wife, are depicted as spirits traveling to their ultimate destination: she towards infinite light, he towards eternal darkness.

"Sabina" is another remarkable poem but for other reasons. If Machado made attempts at writing Indianist poems, he didn't make the same effort – except for a few pieces – in relation to abolitionist literature. This cause was taken up by Castro Alves, who won the epithet "The Poet of the Slaves." In Machado's fiction, whenever enslaved persons appear, they commonly play a secondary role in the plot, such as Lucrécia, from the story "O caso da vara" ("The Case of the Stick"), and Arminda, from "Pai contra mãe" ("Father Against Mother"). There are two enslaved women, however, who played central roles: Mariana, the heroine of the homonymous 1871 story,[18] and Sabina, the heroine of the homonymous poem. Thus, Mariana and Sabina share a unique place in Machado's oeuvre.

The poem tells a story of a young enslaved woman named Sabina. Her master, Otávio, seduces and later abandons her when she becomes pregnant. In despair, Sabina decides to commit suicide but changes her mind at the last minute: "The mother's instinct prevails," says the lyrical

---

15 Mário de Andrade, "Machado de Assis," *Aspectos da literatura brasileira* (São Paulo: Martins, 1967), 94.
16 José Veríssimo, "O Sr. Machado de Assis, poeta," *Estudos de literatura brasileira*, 4th series (Belo Horizonte: Itatiaia, 1977), 56.
17 See verses 50–51 from the second part of the poem: "Lágrimas de *materno* amado seio; / Viu somente morrer a flor das *vidas*" ("Tears of beloved *maternal* bosom; / [a cedar tree] Just saw the flower of *lives* dying"). Emphasis added. Machado de Assis, *Obra Completa*, vol. III, 144.
18 Machado wrote two stories entitled "Mariana." The second was published in 1891 and included in the 1896 volume *Várias histórias* (*Assorted Stories*).

narrator.[19] Sabina is depicted as a black heroine whose sad story denounces a common colonial practice of white masters attracting, enticing, and sexually abusing young enslaved women, who were then discarded by their abusers. This practice was widespread and somewhat normalized in colonial Brazil and unfortunately continued during the imperial era. The empire eventually abolished slavery on May 13, 1888. On that day, Machado wrote a one-stanza, one-page civic poem entitled "13 de maio" ("May 13th"), which circulated in pamphlet form in Rio. This was the second and the last poem by Machado addressing the topic of slavery. As "13 de maio" was never collected in a volume, "Sabina" remains the only poem by Machado on the topic of slavery published in book form.

Machado's Poetry After 1880

After twenty years of intense poetic production – from 1855, when Machado began publishing in A Marmota Fluminense, to 1875, the year of Americanas' release – Machado's poetry went into hibernation. During those two decades, the lepidopterans inside their hard shells (Crisálidas) metamorphosed into moths (Falenas) and eventually migrated and flew high over America (Americanas). In 1901, Machado collected his poetry in a single volume entitled Poesias completas (Complete Poetry). The title, however, doesn't reflect its contents: while reviewing his poetic work for this volume, Machado excluded 16 poems (out of 28) from the original edition of Crisálidas; 9 poems (out of 35) from Falenas; and 1 (out of 13) from Americanas. The volume also includes a collection of 23 compositions and four translations, either not published before or previously appearing in periodicals. This new collection inside Poesias completas goes by the name Ocidentais (Occidentals).

In Ocidentais, readers will find some of the finest poems ever written in the Portuguese language. They are few in number, but all are guileless gems. Poetic language continues to provide the thought with formal stability, but the thought itself develops with less conventional ties and more ironic views. Some pieces – as is a common occurrence in Machado's works – intersect directly with other texts from the Western tradition. That is the case, for instance, of the metapoem "No alto" ("At the Top"), which is the closing composition of Ocidentais. "No alto" beautifully engages in a dialogue with Shakespeare's The Tempest. The poem features

---

19 Machado de Assis, Obra Completa, vol. III, 142.

the characters Ariel, Prospero, and Caliban, although only Ariel is outright named in the text. The setting is a mountain depicted as a space of transition for the character of the poet, who, after reaching the top, is about to go down the other side. Here it is:

At the Top

The poet had reached the top of the mountain,
And, when he was going to descend the west slope,
> He saw an odd thing,
> A wicked creature.

He, then, turning his sight back to the delicate, celestial,
Gracious Ariel, who follows him from below,
> In a fearful and rough tone,
> Questions what it shall be.

As a sweet and joyful sound vanishes into thin air,
> Or as if it were
> A useless thought,

Ariel faded away without giving him any answer.
> In order to go down the slope,
> The other offered his hand.[20]

Three geographical spaces on the mountain are identifiable: the east slope, the top, and the west slope. The poet goes up by the east side, reaches the top, and then is about to go down by the west slope. While going up the mountain, his traveling companion is Ariel, the airy spirit from *The Tempest*. At the top of the mountain, the poet sees a "wicked creature," looks back at Ariel, and questions what the future will bring. At this point, the reader can infer that the poet embodies the character of Prospero since he is the only character in Shakespeare's play able to see Ariel. Similarly, the reader can conclude that "the other," who offers his hand to the poet, is the dark, earthly, and ambiguous Caliban. The poem, therefore, narrates a rite of passage, the precise moment whereby the poet switches allegiance from Ariel to Caliban. Under the aegis of Caliban, the poet will abandon the "delicate, celestial, gracious" aura and rhetoric to eventually incorporate the spirit of darkness, earthiness, and ambiguity.

---

20 Ibid., 179.

Ambiguity, by the way, plays a key role in this context. Despite his prevalent, monstrous appearance and brutal demeanor, Caliban may, at times, be as sensitive as he is eloquent. In *The Tempest*, he describes the eerie beauty of the island, providing the audience with some of the most moving imagery in the play. Also, Caliban can be viewed as noble as Prospero for he owns the island before Prospero arrives. Caliban maintains his dignity in the times, few as they are, when he refuses to bow before Prospero. This ambiguity between coarseness and sensitivity, monstrosity and nobility, is both exhibited and concealed in Shakespeare's play. The characters never acknowledge it. Instead, they insist on characterizing Caliban as a dirty brute. The task of unveiling Caliban's ambiguity and dealing with it, in terms of moral meaning, is up to the audience. Machado, in his turn, was perfectly aware of this ambiguous dynamic of proposing meaning to and concealing meaning from the reader as he masterfully developed it in his mature fictional works. Indeed – and curiously enough – Machado began ambiguously playing with meaning just pages after "No alto." Pages after "No alto"? Yes, let me explain.

"No alto" was first published in 1880, in *Revista Brasileira*, along with other poems later included in *Ocidentais*. In the periodical, as well as in the volume *Poesias completas*, "No alto" is placed as the closing poem. In *Revista Brasileira*, it appears on page 140 of the January–March issue, released in March 1880. Later, on page 353, in that very same issue, readers came across the first chapters of *Brás Cubas* (Chapters I to IX).[21] In other words, after symbolically holding the hand of Caliban, and leaving Ariel behind, Machado – 213 pages later – introduces the readers to his first Calibanesque work: *Brás Cubas*. To put it another way, it's quite emblematic – though not necessarily deliberate – that *Brás Cubas* comes into being separated from "No alto" by only a number of pages in the same periodical: the poem signals a change that the novel, pages later, ultimately substantiates.

Moreover, in "No alto," Ariel and Caliban may also represent poetry and fictional prose, respectively, for after March 1880, Machado set poetry aside and put nearly all his creative energy into fictional prose. At that point, he had likely perceived that Caliban, or rather *his* Caliban, had a bold message to convey, and the best way to convey it would be through fictional prose, and not poetry or drama.

---

21 *Revista Brasileira*, Primeiro Ano, Tomo III (Rio de Janeiro: N. Midosi Editor, Janeiro-Março, 1880), 135–40 (poems); 353–89 (*Brás Cubas*).

Machado as a Playwright; or, Machado and the Theater

In 1857, at the age of 18, Machado had initiated his relationship with theater by translating the French libretto A ópera das janelas (*The Opera of the Windows*), unfortunately now lost. From 1857 to 1869, whether it was as a translator, playwright, or critic, Machado was seriously committed to theater. During this period, he either penned or translated an impressive number of plays: twenty-five in total, thirteen of which are lost.[22] He also wrote theater criticism. In 1859, he joined the periodical O *Espelho* (*The Mirror*), for which he wrote a weekly column entitled "Revista do teatro" ("Theater's Journal"). This was the first regular column of theater criticism to appear in the Brazilian press. Every Sunday, from September 1859 to January 1860, Machado reviewed plays that were being performed in Rio. The critic commented on every aspect of the spectacles: plot, performance, setting, costume, style ... In total, he wrote eighteen columns for the nineteen issues during which the short-lived O *Espelho* existed.

"Ideas on Theater"

For O *Espelho*, Machado also wrote a series of three articles entitled "Ideias sobre o teatro" ("Ideas on Theater"). A fourth article, which completes the series, appeared in A *Marmota* in March 1860. What were Machado's ideas about theater?[23] For Machado, theater played a pivotal role in the process of building up a nation that had recently become independent, such as Brazil. Along with politics and the press, theater was seen as an effective tool to promote civilized values. Thereby, theater, in its noble mission of civilizing the country, could not be reduced to mere entertainment: the dramatic arts could, and should, both entertain and educate the audience. Machado's mentality was that a strong theater sets the stage for a stronger community in the days to come.

Unfortunately, the status of the dramatic arts in Brazil, according to Machado, left much to be desired. There was no such thing as national

---

22 Jean-Michel Massa, "Reabilitação de Machado de Assis," *Machado de Assis e a crítica internacional*, eds. Benedito Antunes & Sérgio Vicente Motta (São Paulo: Unesp, 2009), 47.
23 In the following lines, I will be paraphrasing Machado's arguments as expressed in "Ideias sobre o teatro." Machado de Assis, *Obra completa*, vol. III, 789–98.

theater. There were efforts, here and there, to create a theater that could foster a sense of community, that could propose a concept of collective identity. But those efforts were isolated, unsatisfactory, and insufficient for achieving such a complex goal. The public, for their part, enjoyed watching frivolous dramas, most of them in translation. Audiences weren't interest in educating themselves. In its liveliness, the spoken word in theater is potentially transformative, says Machado. But the masses didn't want to be transformed. They wanted to be amused by lightweight, foolish tales and spectacles.

It's like a tug of war between the public and the conscious artist. In this battle, the will of the public usually outweighs the work of a few dramatists committed to a thoughtful art. As a nation taking its first steps towards civilization, Brazil needed a theater imbued with a civilizing spirit. But, for Machado, the masses got in the way of this progress due to their self-satisfied lack of consciousness. Ultimately, in a vicious circle, the public demanded second-rate shows, and the entertainment industry, by feeding into the public's desire, maintained their second-rate taste. In "Ideias sobre o teatro" and other writings on theater, Machado tackles this complicated issue involving the market and art, or rather the market and the massification of art.

The Brazilian Dramatic Conservatory and Machado as a Censor of Theater

The last two articles of the series "Ideias sobre o teatro" address the topic of the *Conservatório Dramático Brasileiro* (Brazilian Dramatic Conservatory) and its role in overseeing dramatic productions. In these articles, Machado advocates for the Brazilian Dramatic Conservatory and its social function as an agent of theatrical censorship. Machado's main argument is that the Conservatory's interventions could stop some of the effects caused by the massification of theater. What was the Brazilian Dramatic Conservatory, then?

It was a private association made up of invited *littérateurs*, who were in charge of overseeing dramatic productions before they went on stage, among other duties. Whenever these productions were considered to be offensive by religious or moral standards, the examiners could legally veto the performance from showing on stage. The Empire of Brazil supported the Conservatory by subsidizing its activities during the first period of its existence, from 1843 to 1864. In 1871, the Conservatory reopened as a public institution and operated as such until 1897.

In 1857, Machado submitted to the Conservatory his translation of *Ópera das janelas*, which was granted approval. From 1862 to 1864, Machado served the Conservatory as one of its members. During this period, he wrote seventeen evaluation reports. By reading these reports, one may find a clear, albeit fragmented, picture of the state of dramatic literature in Brazil: poor translations and even worse original dramas, with a few exceptions. By reading these reports, one can also see how strict and accomplished Machado was as a critical reader of plays. Besides recommending – or not – the play under evaluation, Machado usually went further, commenting on general aspects of the dramas.

In one noteworthy case, dated July 30, 1862, Machado would grant his recommendation on the condition that the author make a change to the plot. The play is *Os mistérios sociais* (*The Social Mysteries*) by the Portuguese writer Augusto César de Lacerda. The drama's action involves a protagonist, Frederico de Lucena, who, as a child, was sold as an enslaved person in Mexico, along with his mother, by his father. Years went by and, by tortuous paths, Lucena became a wealthy, free man. He then traveled to Portugal in search of his father and ended up marrying a Portuguese baroness to whom Lucena eventually reveals his enslaved past. In love with him, the baroness shows no concerns about her beloved's origins.

In his report, Machado urges the playwright to alter the closing scene. Either Lucena should not marry the baroness, or, through some artifice, Lucena should find out at some point that he was sold in Mexico as a free person; that is to say, he never actually was an enslaved man. In Machado's view, a former enslaved person could not marry a baroness. Why? Machado justified his position with the following argument: "Philosophical theory does not acknowledge the distinction between two individuals who, like [Lucena and the baroness], are equally virtuous; however, taking into account the conditions of our society, this way of ending the play [by them marrying each other] should be altered."[24] Machado found the dramatization of a marriage between a former enslaved man and a member of the ruling class too daring.

This is not the only moment in which Machado exhibits his conservative values. Also, we should bear in mind that, in 1862, the Brazilian

---

24 Machado de Assis, "Parecer sobre o drama *Mistérios sociais*, original português de César de Lacerda," www.literaturabrasileira.ufsc.br/documentos/?action=download&id=8175

Dramatic Conservatory was a conservative institution working on behalf of the empire. Were Machado not an intellectual aligned with conservatism, he would never be invited to join the Conservatory's group of *littérateurs*, a position that the young writer certainly craved, and of which he actually took great advantage. After *Brás Cubas*, though, Machado the conservative makes room for Machado the liberal and the two work together like twin brothers who are both opposite and complementary – like Paulo and Pedro, the identical twin brothers in the novel *Esaú e Jacó*, in which Pedro is conservative and Paulo is liberal.

At this point in his life, though, only the conservative Machado had put his head above the parapet. For him, "philosophical theory," or modern ideas, although valid, should not be practiced on stage, for the "conditions of [Brazilian] society" would not benefit from them. On the contrary, the notion that there is no "distinction between two individuals who … are equally virtuous," no matter their social origins, could be a seed from which bitter fruits might grow. Theater, for Machado, could, and should, instead sow seeds of Western tradition and civilization among the audience. In this respect, as Machado indicates in "Ideias sobre o teatro," the Conservatory's role in separating the wheat from the chaff was crucial for the steady and righteous development of the country.

Contemporary Eyes

Looking at these events through our contemporary eyes, we may conclude that Machado adopted an objectionable stance in his advocacy for Western values. Machado took other reprehensible stands during his life, indeed. But he was a man of his time – obviously. And it's our duty as readers from our own time to try to understand his choices and decisions within the cultural-historical context in which he lived. The young Empire of Brazil dreamed about joining, as a transatlantic "peer," the club of modern European countries, whose cultural and moral patterns Brazil had actually inherited. The United States was advancing rapidly towards achieving that goal. The same could be said about Argentina. Brazil, the giant of South America, could not be left behind. Brazilian intellectual elites thought, in fact, that the country should lead this process.

But should Brazil have wanted to embrace modernity while still being a slaveholding society? Wasn't it hypocritical of a country with a fully operational system of slavery to desire modernity? After the beginning of the nineteenth century, modernity and slavery no longer corresponded as they once had. In 1862, when Machado advised that the plot of *Os mistérios sociais* ought to be changed, Argentina marked nine years since the abolition of slavery, and the U.S. was fighting a bloody civil war over the status of slavery. Meanwhile, the Brazilian elites, with sheer hypocrisy, continued to insist upon trying to reconcile the irreconcilable: modernity and slavery.

In 1862, the young Machado wasn't sharp enough to figure this out. It would take eighteen years until he finally caught on. The character of Brás Cubas, as we shall see, embodies these hypocritical elites that enjoyed showing off modern ideas – like the "philosophical theory" mentioned by Machado – while their social practices revealed just how obsolete, ambitious, and pernicious the ruling class actually was. Moreover, these social practices also exposed how resolutely the upper class protected the status quo in order to preserve, in Machado's words, the "conditions of [Brazilian] society."

These conditions presupposed two key factors: slavery and censorship. If progress on slavery was regrettably slow, however, the outlook as regards censorship was rather brighter.

The Popularity of Theater

Imperial Brazil during the Second Reign – that is, from 1841 to 1889 – developed under the auspices of a free press and free speech. There was no censorship of any kind – except for theater performances. Why just theater performances? Because Brazilian theater during the nineteenth century was by far the most popular art form of the day. Since tickets were affordable for the most part, basically every free person in Rio de Janeiro could attend plays. This accessibility made the dramatic arts as attractive as they were "potentially dangerous." By watching dramas, the masses could be easily infused with "bad ideas." Hence the perceived necessity for regulatory practice, of which the Brazilian Dramatic Conservatory was in charge.[25]

This regulation, though, was applied to only staged plays. A play whose performance had been vetoed by the Conservatory could yet be published in book form. (This happened a few times, by the way.) Why was it possible? Because there was no censorship of any kind over books, the press, or

---

25 Alex Castro, "O escravo que Machado de Assis censurou e outros pareceres do Conservatório Dramático Brasileiro," *Afro-Hispanic Review*, vol. 29, no. 2 (Fall 2010), 25–38.

political groups, just theatrical spectacles performed on stage. This reveals just how popular and appreciated, and thereby controlled and monitored, the art of theater was during Machado's lifetime.

The First Book(s)

As mentioned earlier, in 1861, Paula Brito published the first two books that display the name of Machado de Assis on their covers. The translation *Queda que a mulheres têm para os tolos* was the first. *Queda* came out in June. In September, Paula Brito's printing house released the first book authored by Machado: the play *Desencantos* (*Disenchantment*). Its plot revolves around a young widow, Clara, and her two neighbors, Luis and Pedro, who are both in love with her. Luis is a 22-year-old poet (just like Machado). He is a noble spirit full of romantic ideals. Pedro, on the contrary, is a practical and self-righteous man who prides himself on his physical body and his courage in confronting his opponents. Between the two, Clara allows herself to be lured by Pedro. In other words, between the delicate poet and the crude fool, she leans towards the latter. In this respect, Machado's play *Desencantos* dramatizes the central argument of the essay *Queda que as mulheres têm para os tolos* (*The Weakness Women Have for Fools*).

Queda and *Desencantos*, therefore, corroborate the argument that the creative process in Machado has one of its roots, perhaps the deepest one, in "translation." Machado's *Desencantos*, in other words, "translates" into the language of theater, or theatrical form, Victor Hénaux's essay *Queda que a mulheres têm para os tolos*. Besides introducing the fundamental idea that literary creation, for Machado, entails intertextual relationship, these two books also signaled that theater would occupy a central position in Machado's interests in the following years.

The 1860s; or, the "Theater Decade"

As mentioned above, from 1857 to 1869, Machado either authored or translated an impressive twenty-five plays. This shows how committed he was to theater in the 1860s. Yet, in the next decade, his productivity in terms of dramatic literature fell off sharply, from twenty-five to just three original plays – *Uma ode de Anacreonte* (1870), *Antes da missa* (*Before Mass*, 1878), and *O bote de rapé* (*The Snuff Box*, 1878) – and one translation – *Os demandistas* (*The Litigants*, 1876) by Jean Racine – which is now lost. In the 1880s, 1890s, and 1900s, this productivity dropped even further to one single play per decade: *Tu, só tu, puro amor ...* (*Thou, Only Thou, Pure Love ...*, 1880), *Não consultes médico* (*Don't Consult a Doctor*, 1896), and *Lição de botânica* (*A Botany Lesson*, 1906).

Here, a question emerges: what happened to cause Machado's activity as a dramatist to decrease considerably following the 1860s? Let's begin with two undeniable facts. First, Machado loved the dramatic art; he always loved it. Moved by this sentiment, he made every effort to help create a national theater in the 1860s. Second, after the so-called "theater decade," Machado gave up drama, despite still loving the art of the stage. Again, why? Two reasons could be put forward. First, a letter from Quintino Bocaiúva written in 1863. Second, an insightful understanding of the theatrical situation in Brazil that Machado expressed in the article "Instinto de nacionalidade," published in 1873. Let's start with Bocaiúva's letter.

In 1863, the second of Machado's authored books came out: *Teatro* (*Theater*). The volume comprised two plays that had been performed on stage the year before: *O caminho da porta* (*The Path to the Door*) and *O protocolo* (*Protocol*). The volume also presented, as an introductory section, two short letters: one from Machado to Bocaiúva and the other from Bocaiúva to Machado. In the first letter, Machado asks for advice. He mentions that both plays received good responses from the public when they were staged, but now that they are about to appear as printed works, he wishes to hear an authoritative opinion on them.

In his response, Bocaiúva praises Machado's talent as a playwright, offers him advice, but also points out his deficiencies. In a blunt and rough passage, he states: "[Your plays] are praiseworthy as literary artifacts. However, insofar as my vain critical presumption may be tolerated, I might say that they are cold and insensitive, like every person without a soul." By "praiseworthy as literary artifacts," Bocaiúva means that Machado's plays are essentially "written to be read, not staged."[26] These words obviously contradict the very nature of theater, whose ultimate goal as a *performing* art is to be ... performed. It's as if Bocaiúva were saying to a composer that their music is highly commendable but is not to be played in public. In the case of Machado, Bocaiúva seems to indicate that Machado's dramas are more literary than theatrical. Time has proven that Bocaiúva was correct in his evaluation. In fact, Machado's dramatic works, in terms of performance, never took off.

---

26 Quintino Bocaiúva, "Carta ao autor," *Teatro*, Machado de Assis (Rio de Janeiro: Tipografia do Diário do Rio de Janeiro, 1863) n.p. [iv].

Bocaiúva's words certainly had a deep and lasting impact on the young dramatist's spirit. Three years Machado's senior, Bocaiúva was an influential journalist who had, in 1860, invited Machado to join the team of reporters on *Diário do Rio de Janeiro*, one of the three major *carioca* newspapers along with *Correio Mercantil* and *Jornal do Comércio* at the time. Machado thus owned to Bocaiúva his first opportunity to work for the big press. Three years later, Bocaiúva examined Machado's first plays with sharp eyes. The playwright would have to agree with him at some point. This point seems to have been the beginning of the 1870s.

In 1873, in "Instinto de nacionalidade" – which will be commented on in the next chapter – Machado dedicated a section to examining the status of Brazilian theater at the time. His evaluation could not be worse: "This section could be reduced to a *dotted line*. At present there is no Brazilian theater. No national productions are being written, and it's very rare that a national production is staged." Who should be blamed for this dreadful situation? According to Machado, the public: "Now, with the public taste having descended to the lowest degree of decadence and perversion, those inclined to compose serious works of art are left without hope." What, in fact, dominated the stage at that time were "the burlesque or obscene songs, the can-can, and showy magic tricks, all of which appeal to the baser senses and instincts."[27]

Machado's decision to push his career as a dramatist backwards might have been influenced by these two factors: Bocaiúva's letter, with its strong but accurate words of criticism, and the whole unfavorable context in which national theater was developing. Still in "Instinto de nacionalidade," Machado indicates that poetry and the novel had – with the works of Gonçalves Dias and José de Alencar, respectively – a basis from which they could expand in Brazil. The same could not be said regarding the dramatic arts. In line with these arguments, Machado published in the 1870s two volumes of poetry (*Falenas* and *Americanas*), four novels (*Ressurreição*, *A mão e a luva*, *Helena*, and *Iaiá Garcia*), and two collections of stories (*Contos fluminenses* [Rio Tales] and *Histórias da meia-noite*

---

27 Machado de Assis, "Reflections on Brazilian Literature at the Present Moment – The National Instinct," trans. Robert Newcomb, *Journal of World Literature* 3 (2018), 414. Newcomb rendered the original "linha de reticência" as "single reservation." I choose "dotted line" instead, set here in italics. This is the only amendment I would propose to Newcomb's excellent and more than welcome translation.

[*Midnight Tales*]), not counting poems and stories that appeared in periodicals but were not collected in book form during this period.

One Play: *A Botany Lesson*

For more than a century, Machado has been hailed as the master of the Brazilian novel and short story. His *crônicas* have been published in annotated editions; some of his poems are fixtures in anthologies; and a few pages of his critical writings are simply inescapable for those who study literature. At least one of his translations, Poe's "The Raven," is often reproduced in collections of translated poems. But what about Machado's theater? The dramatic genre in Machado's oeuvre occupies the lowest position in terms of critical reception. Why? For several reasons, of which I will underline two.

First, Machado's plays are "molded by the spirit of French proverbs," as Bocaiúva rightly claims in his famous letter.[28] That is to say, they are light comedies that convey a common moralizing message with elegance and charm. Or rather, they shine for their elegant form, but the form itself accommodates a content that is mostly predictable and didactic. Second, of the twelve plays by Machado whose texts are not lost,[29] only three were written by the post-1880 Machado. This is a fact that mustn't be disregard since – as we already learned – the first Machado prepares the advent of the second, whose works brought him fame. And second Machado wrote at least one remarkable play: *Lição de botânica*, published in 1906, as part of the volume *Relíquias de casa velha* (*Relics from an Old House*).

In recent years, with Machado drawing more international attention, American scholars have revisited his final play. In a 2016 essay, Earl Fitz underscores *Lição*'s "social, political, and artistic achievement" in order to undo the image, put forward by Alfredo Bosi, of the play as a "mere *divertissement*." For Fitz, *Lição* "merits more critical attention than it has

---

28 Quintino Bocaiúva, "Carta ao autor," n.p. [p. iii].
29 The twelve plays by Machado I refer to are: *Desencantos* (1861), *O caminho da porta* (1863), *O protocolo* (1863), *Quase ministro* (1864), *As forcas caudinas* (1865), *Os deuses de casaca* (1866), *Uma ode de Anacreonte* (1870), *Antes da missa* (1878), *O bote de rapé* (1878), *Tu, só tu, puro amor …* (1880), *Não consultes médico* (1896), and *Lição de botânica* (1906). As mentioned in this chapter, *Hoje avental, amanhã luva* (1860) is not an original work bur rather a translation-adaptation of Gustave Vattier and Émile de Najac's *Chasse au lion*.

received."[30] Fitz's, say, "call for articles" brought responses from two other scholars: Paul Dixon and Anna-Lisa Halling, both in 2019. Dixon's essay explores, from a historical standpoint, the metaphor of organism/organic in the play. Dixon traces the metaphor back to seventeenth-century discourses on the notion of "vegetable love," particularly in the works of Robert Burton and Andrew Marvell. From the concept of the organic as associated with structural malleability, flexibility, or elasticity, Dixon goes to Henri Bergon's theory of humor, and from here to the Brazilian social practice of *jeitinho*, which Dixon defines as "the lateral maneuver that attempts to solve problems through indirect means, and often through bending the usual rules."[31]

Anna-Lisa Halling, for her turn, reads *Lição* through the lenses of feminism and intertextuality. Halling suggests that Machado's play contains echoes of and responds to Shakespeare's *Taming of the Shrew*. However, while Shakespeare in his work conveys a glaringly misogynistic message, Machado in *Lição* skillfully transforms, or "translates," misogyny into female agency. Or, to repeat Halling's pun, while Shakespeare depicts Katherine, *Taming*'s foul-tempered protagonist, as *shrew*, Machado portrays Helena, Katherine's counterpart and *Lição*'s heroine, as *shrewd*.[32] Halling's feminist approach to *Lição* follows and complements Fitz's 2016 arguments.

To some degree, Fitz's essay continues his 2014 study on Machado and feminism entitled *Machado de Assis and Female Characterization: The Novels*. In this study, Fitz sees Machado's female characters, particularly those created by the mature writer, as "embodying a number of new, progressive ideas about how to respond to a deeply entrenched patriarchal society."[33] For Fitz, Machado advocates for gender equality through his heroines, or behind their masks, as a way to undermine and overcome systemic patriarchalism. Egalitarianism, for Machado, was both a racial and a gender issue in Brazil. In other words, egalitarianism should constitute a social achievement among black and white people as well as men and women.

---

30 Earl Fitz, "Writing Womanhood in the New Brazil: Machado's *Lição de Botânica*," *Emerging Dialogues on Machado de Assis*, eds. Daniel F. Silva & Lamonte Aidoo (New York: Palgrave Macmillan, 2016), 125.

31 Paul Dixon, "Machado's Organic Sense: An Outline of Approaches to *Lição de Botânica*," *Machado de Assis em Linha*, vol. 12, no. 26 (April 2019), 75. The concept of *jeitinho* was briefly commented on in Chapter Two.

32 Anna-Lisa Halling, "The Shrew and the Shrewd: Machado de Assis' *Lição de Botânica*," *Machado de Assis em Linha*, vol. 12, no. 26 (April 2019), 77–89.

33 Earl Fitz, *Machado de Assis and Female Characterization: The Novels* (Lanham, MD: Bucknell UP, 2015), 8.

However, despite being an egalitarian, Machado's fiction tends to focus more on gender than on racial themes (and I'll offer a reason for this tendency in Chapter Five). In this respect, the heroines of his novels are witty, articulate, determined, and strong female characters who, each in their own way, stand for forms of emancipation from an oppressive, male-driven society.

As Fitz rightly claims in his 2016 essay, Helena, the protagonist of *Lição*, upholds the tradition of Machadian heroines. Her cleverness and attitude establish a balance of power that somewhat puts her on the same footing as the male character, Baron Segismundo de Kernoberg, who in the play epitomizes the patriarchal system. In the comedy, the baron wishes to teach Helena botany lessons; however, in the end, it's she who ends up "teaching" him an unexpected lesson. What is it? How does she do it?

To answer to these questions, we first need to examine a summary of the plot. Let me draw on Dixon's straight-to-the-point outline of the action, which is indeed quite simple:

> Leonor and her two nieces – Cecília and Helena (a widow) – live together in the same household. A neighbor, the Swedish botanist Baron Segismundo de Kernoberg, requests a meeting with D. Leonor. Cecília has been seeing the botanist's nephew Henrique, and the ladies' first guess is that the Swedish gentleman wants to ask for Cecília's hand in marriage on behalf of the young man. But the women are mistaken; instead, the professor requests that there be no further meeting between Cecília and Henrique. His nephew, he explains, is destined to follow his same vocation, and for several generations in the family, a succession of botanists (all uncles and nephews) have wisely chosen celibacy, or rather, to be married to their research. The demands of serious scientific inquiry are such that no other devotion, such as family, can be considered. At first Cecília is crestfallen, but by feigning an interest in botany and an openness to lessons from the professor, Helena begins to exercise her feminine charms upon the man. Before long, Kernoberg has decided that perhaps a botanist can be married after all. He consents to the marriage of Cecília and Henrique, and even begs to have the same privilege with Helena.[34]

The ambiguous and open-ended ending of *Lição* is probably the most Machadian part of the play. In it, Helena asks the baron to give her ninety days to decide whether she will marry him. Discontented, the baron asks

---

34 Paul Dixon, "Machado's Organic Sense: An Outline of Approaches to *Lição de Botânica*," 64.

her whether after this period he will get "happiness or despair." Enigmatically, she says, "The choice is in *your* hand." And, even more enigmatic, she tells the baffled D. Leonor, who witnesses the odd dialogue, "Don't be so surprised, aunt; this is all applied botany."[35]

Machado, therefore, leaves both marriages – Cecília and Henrique's and Helena and Segismundo's – up in the air at the conclusion of the play. We don't know either will actually transpire. It depends, according to Fitz, on whether the baron and his nephew treat Helena and Cecília as equals or as second-rate individuals. At the turn of the twentieth century, after the Republican regime had been implemented in 1889, Brazil was a country undergoing deep transformations and seeking modernity. Machado's views on modernity and progress in society were, to a large extent, morally based. For him, modernity and progress entailed, among other values, women's emancipation from the oppressive patriarchal system. For Fitz, Helena and Machado's other heroines embody this egalitarian message.

Now, let me offer two additional approaches to *Lição*: a possible intertextuality with José de Alencar's *Iracema* (1865) and a note on the concept of "Westerness." With that in mind, let's recall a few points of the action: a foreigner from the West (a Swedish botanist) enters a Brazilian house (in Scene 7, we read a reference to the house and its residents as "Brazilian"). The foreigner comes in with the intention to "rule" Brazilian territory by saying what should and should not be done (i.e. Cecília and Henrique should not meet each other anymore). Behind this "regulation," there is a blatant Western, rational value: Science (both the Swede and his nephew are scientists). The European foreigner, then, is unexpectedly enchanted by the grace and beauty of a Brazilian woman (Helena). While seduced by this strange but charming woman, he advances, as a powerful man, to join her clan and take possession of her body and …

Up until this point, Machado's play closely follows the narrative structure of the Brazilian canonical novel *Iracema* by José de Alencar. In *Iracema*, the Portuguese Martim Soares comes to colonize (i.e. "civilize," Westernize) sixteenth-century Brazil, and, without expecting it, falls in love with an Indigenous woman named Iracema. The difference, though, is that Iracema *gives herself* to the foreigner whereas Helena *withholds herself* for three months. Helena is undecided as to whether or not she will marry the foreigner. Iracema, for her part, decides to follow Martim, and this unfortunate choice brings her only frustration and pain and, eventually,

---

35 Machado de Assis, *Lição de botânica*, *Obra Completa*, vol. III, 1187. Emphasis added.

death. Iracema is an allegorical character whose name is an anagram of *America*. Her unhappy and deceitful marriage to Martim thereby allegorically represents the marriage of America to Western civilization: a deal profitable for Europeans but not at all for Native Americans.

By the beginning of the twentieth century, when the action of *Lição* is set, America's marriage to Western civilization was a *fait accompli*. Brazil had long been part of the Western world; for centuries, the country had adopted a Western language, political system, economic structure, social organization, religion, and the belief in reason and science. But the beginning of the twentieth century was also, as already mentioned, a period of transformation, a time of change for Brazil. Should the country, in this crucial historical context, deepen its relationship with the West? Should Helena marry the stiff, methodical, authoritarian, utilitarian, technical, and rational Baron Segismundo de Kernoberg? Or, should Helena (and Cecília, and Brazil) reject the proffered partnership? In Scene 4 of Machado's play, Helena lists a series of benefits that a wise man will enjoy by having a wife; but, what benefits would an independent woman, like Helena, secure by marring a wise man? Or, what benefits would an independent country, like Brazil, derive from strengthening its ties with the powerful West?

At the beginning of his career, as discussed in Chapter Two, Machado strategically aligned himself with the West in order to achieve his goal of socially ascent through writing. His fiction, thus, is conventionally Western in every basic aspect. By manipulating these conventions, Machado sought to please his readers, who expected to experience Western moral and aesthetic standards through the narrative, characters, and style. From *Brás Cubas* on, as we shall see, this perfect alignment between Machado and the "good" West becomes highly nuanced. The uncertainty around Helena and the baron's marriage in *Lição* may be viewed in this light as a symbolic suspension that may indicate feelings of doubt on Machado's part. Doubt about what?

Brazilian culture is deeply rooted in a complex dialectics of conflicting forces between Western and non-Western (i.e. African and Indigenous) values. In *Lição*, the Swedish baron embodies Western values: reason, science, formality, pragmatism. The Brazilian Helena, in contrast, typifies non-Western features: improvisation, versatility, adaptability, humor. If this argument is coherent, it relates to Dixon's reading of the vegetable malleability and elasticity metaphor associated with Helena and Brazilian culture. In this regard, Machado creates in *Lição* a game of power whereby Helena's tropical malleability contrasts with the baron's European stiffness. In this game, the baron eventually succumbs to Helena's charms. But will he be able to *bend* his values for Helena? Or will she have to *straighten out* her features for the baron? In the first case, Helena will likely accept the baron's proposal; in the second case, she will not. That's why Helena asks the baron for three months before giving him her final decision. The ultimate *lesson* of the play seems to suggest that, in the context of Brazil and Brazilian culture, it is possible to harmonize (or marry) malleability with stiffness, that is, non-Western with Western values. However, in terms of creating and defining a national identity, the former should prevail over the latter.

A Lateral Comment ...

In *Lição*, the concepts of malleability, flexibility, and elasticity that Helena seems to personify, in opposition to the rigid pragmatism of the prim baron, have close links to notions or practices usually associated with the idea of Brazil or Brazilianess, such as *jeitinho*, *ginga* (swing, swagger), and *malandragem* (urban roguery). When historically considered, some of these concepts and practices can be traced back to Western roots. The figure of *malandro*, for instance, can be viewed as a social, modern variation of the trickster archetype and the Spanish picaresque hero. In the Brazilian context, Manuel Antônio de Almeida's 1852–53 satirical novel *Memórias de um sargento de milícias* (*Memoirs of a Police Sergeant*) is a prototypical example of this type of literature, i.e. one that makes use of Western roots – the trickster archetype, the Spanish picaresque hero – to draw local characters – the Brazilian *malandro*. In Almeida's novel, Brazilian society and its main characters are depicted as morally permissive and behaviorally indulgent. This flexible morality and behavior also might have stemmed from Catholic forms of wielding power, creating moral values, and imposing them on devout believers in Brazil. If we compare the moral standards in *Memórias de um sargento de milícias* with those, for instance, of Nathaniel Hawthorne's 1850 *The Scarlet Letter*, we might argue that Protestants in New England ruled their society by holding the moral reins firmly, whereas Catholics in Brazil held the same reins slackly, for the most part.

I have to admit that, to make such an argument, the corpus of works presented above (just two novels) is – aside from being fictional – too limited. Nevertheless, as frames of reference, I'm convinced that those novels give us a fair historical sense of the consequences of how, in terms of moral principles, Anglo-Protestantism and Luso-Hispanic Catholicism built their societies in the Americas. The reasons I am making this point are, firstly, to continue the discussion initiated in Chapter Two about the structural differences between the processes of colonization and how the

European colonizers took distinct paths in Protestant New England and Catholic Brazil; and, secondly, to demonstrate how, in Brazil, the Catholic Church related to non-Western cultures and how both in conjunction ultimately created a society more prone to bending the prevailing moral values than its Northern, Protestant counterpart.

Machado's *Lição de botânica* heroine, Helena, and her virtues can be seen as a cultural product of this non-Western and Catholic Brazil, which, in the play, confronts the virtues and values of the Western and Protestant baron (as a Swede, the baron is implicitly Protestant). In this regard, Helena and Machado's other heroines bear resemblance *to some extent* to characters from the trickster and picaresque tradition. (If I'm not mistaken, this is one of the points Dixon makes in his essay on Machado's last play.) However, one important distinction between Helena and the trickster-picaresque tradition lies in the fact that the trickster-picaresque hero is conventionally male, while the majority of Machado's cleverly daring and ambiguous protagonists are female. By turning the gender of the hero on its head, Machado subtly undermines misogyny and patriarchalism, then prevalent in Brazilian society. This is one important argument that both Fitz and Halling discuss in their essays when examining Machado's feminism.

Recapping and Concluding

In the critical studies of Machado's works, the theater genre has attracted the least attention from scholars over the years. Departing from this fact, we may conclude that Machado was better, or more efficient, as literary translator, poet, critic, *cronista*, short-story writer, and novelist than as playwright. Most recently, though, American researchers have been revisiting Machado's dramatic literature. In the three studies mentioned above, Machado's final play, *Lição de botânica*, was the piece selected for critical scrutiny. This may not be a coincidence. Without exhibiting the same level of artful dexterity and depth as is exhibited in his mature stories and novels, *Lição* unquestionably displays a great degree of *representativeness* within Machado's oeuvre. Helena, for instance, definitely deserves a place in Machado's gallery of heroines. Fitz, by the way, compares her to the other Helena, the protagonist of the 1876 homonymous novel.[36] It's also worth noting how Machado successfully manipulates irony and

---

36 Fitz, "Writing Womanhood in the New Brazil: Machado's *Lição de Botânica*," 126.

ambiguity – two hallmarks of his style – in his last play. Thus, the first conclusion about Machado as a dramatist goes as follows: it appears safe to argue that *Lição de botânica* stands out among the dramas Machado wrote. In other words, if you have to read just one play by Machado, you should definitely consider *Lição de botânica*. However ...

As of yet, there is only one play by Machado translated into another language. Not *Lição*. The play is the 1880 *Tu, só tu, puro amor ...*, which was rendered into English by Edgar Knowlton Jr. in 1972 (see Appendix One).[37] The second conclusion thus takes the form of a "call for translation." If you are reading this, and you are a Portuguese–English translator, please consider translating *Lição de botânica*. It would be an enormous contribution towards Machado's (growing) reception into the Anglophone world.

Whenever addressing the topic of Machado de Assis and theater, one has to consider the existence of four "Machados": the critic of theater, the censor for the Brazilian Dramatic Conservatory, the translator of plays, and the playwright. Although interrelated, these four are autonomous. Each has his own history. And nearly all are associated with the young Machado, or rather, the Machado of the 1860s, the period also known as Machado's "theater decade." The mature Machado invested most of his creative energy in genres other than drama, particularly the novel and the short story.

Whenever addressing, from a historical standpoint, the theater of Machado de Assis, one has to comment on Quintino Bocaiúva's 1863 preface-letter. Written with surgical precision, Bocaiúva's critical remarks on Machado's theater, albeit short, have defined some still valid lines of approach to Machado's plays. Moreover, Bocaiúva's criticism appears to have influenced Machado's decision gradually to abandon his ambitions of becoming a successful dramatist. Nevertheless, if Machado gave up theater, theater didn't give up Machado. As David Jackson rightly puts it, "Machado's early involvement in the theater and opera, his own original plays and translations, may not have left a lasting influence in Brazilian theater ... yet the theater and opera, their atmosphere, characters, and conventions were a constant and profound presence that left an indelible mark on his fiction, visible in every major work throughout his career."[38]

---

37 Machado de Assis, *You, Love, and Love Alone*, trans. Edgar C. Knowlton Jr., *Boletim do Instituto Luis de Camões*, vol. 6, nos. 3–4 (Macau, 1972), 143–75.
38 David Jackson, *Machado de Assis: A Literary Life* (New Haven, CT: Yale UP, 2015), 151.

Chapter Four

Criticism and *Crônica*: The Quest for Greatness Continues

The "First Brazilian Critic" and "The Critic's Ideal"

LAST CHAPTER, WE speculated about Machado's feeling of exultation when he saw his portrait side by side with that of José de Alencar on the cover of the January 30, 1873, issue of *Arquivo Contemporâneo*. Around this time, Machado was best known and most praised for his poetry. Five years earlier, another publication should also have brought him joy. It was an open letter written by the same José de Alencar, appearing in the pages of *Correio Mercantil*, on February 22, 1868. In this letter, Alencar enthusiastically introduces a young poet named Castro Alves to Machado. In Alencar's view, Castro Alves was a promising talent in need of guidance through the "impassable path of the literary life." Who could be the "Virgil to the young Dante"? In Alencar's mind, it had to be Machado, whom he called the "first Brazilian critic."[1] And by "first," Alencar meant both *precursor* and *unrivaled*.

Looking back on these events, we can easily come to a twofold conclusion: first, that in 1868 Machado stood out as a critic; and second that, five years later, in 1873, Machado was celebrated as a poet. The documents that support these conclusions are, respectively, Alencar's letter published in *Correio Mercatil* on February 22, 1868; and *Arquivo Contemporâneo*'s issue of January 30, 1873. This is one way to read history. Nevertheless,

---

1 José de Alencar, "Literatura: um poeta," *Correio Mercantil*, Feb. 22, 1868, 2.

there's another way, also valid, which we should call in here: a way based on how the echoes of the past reverberate in the present.

When we look back at the year 1873 and feel the vibrations that have travelled to us across the years, it's Machado the critic who still stands out, not the poet. Why? Because in 1873, Machado wrote an article that eventually became a cornerstone of Brazilian criticism: "Notícia da atual literatura brasileira" ("News of the Present Brazilian Literature"), which went down in history through the title of the first of its five sections, "Instinto de nacionalidade" ("Instinct of Nationality"). Had Machado written only this article, and no other critical piece, still he would have left his mark on the history of Brazilian criticism. But Machado did much more. Was he, then, actually the "first Brazilian critic" in 1868, at the age of 29? Well, it depends on how we look at this issue. Let's examine a few historical points.

In literary criticism, Machado was preceded by José de Alencar, who in 1856 had severely criticized Gonçalves de Magalhães's epic and Indianist poem *A confederação dos Tamoios* (*Tamoios Confederation*) in a series of eight open letters that were published in *Diário do Rio de Janeiro*. The letters provoked an immediate reaction from key figures of the time, such as Manuel Araújo de Porto-Alegre and friar Francisco de Monte-Alverne, as well as from several anonymous writers, one presumably the Emperor Dom Pedro II himself. The teenage Machado no doubt followed this debate attentively and learned a great deal from it.

In fact, the first piece of criticism written by 17-year-old Machado was a series of three articles appropriately entitled "Ideias Vagas" ("Vague Ideas"), which were published in *A Marmota Fluminense* in 1856 amid the public controversy over Gonçalves de Magalhães's poem.[2] Nevertheless, although Alencar acted as a critic and a polemicist, he didn't engage regularly in criticism. In the second half of the 1850s, there wasn't a well-established literary critic in Brazil. Among those practicing in the then-incipient critical language, the most established name was, perhaps, that of Antônio Joaquim de Macedo Soares. Machado referred to him in the prologue to the third edition of *Brás Cubas*. Machado and Macedo Soares knew each other, and they can be viewed as precursory figures to Brazilian *modern* literary criticism.

---

2   When the first article of the series was published, on June 10, 1856, Machado was still 16. The first open letter written by Alencar, under the pseudonym Ig., on Gonçalves de Magalhães's poem appeared on June 18 of that year.

Modern, in this context, indicates a type of critical analysis and appraisal that went beyond purely subjective impression, beyond snobbishness and camaraderie. Back then, those factors permeated the act of examining a work of art. Machado, for his part, advocated for independent and judicious forms of evaluation. For him, the writing of discerning criticism was as important as the writing of laws. The interventions of critics and legislators were responsible for promoting the common good of society; the words of both were able to encourage and guide individuals towards progress. Similarly, the actions of both could prevent errors from spreading through the social body. Both critics and legislators, in short, worked as guardians of the community, to which they lent their knowledge and wisdom through thoughtful rules and judgments. These informed actions played a particularly relevant role in the context of a young nation like Brazil, which was, at that time, in search of a collective identity.

Machado compares critics and legislators in an 1865 article entitled "O ideal do crítico" ("The Critic's Ideal"). In various respects, this article can be viewed as a landmark in the history of Brazilian criticism, as it establishes some of the basic principles for the critical act. There wasn't, for instance, at that point, a clear boundary separating critical thought from review. At times, in the spirit of Romanticism, both were blended together. Also, in the same spirit, intuition tended to weigh more heavily than reflection in the critique of an artwork. In "O ideal do crítico," Machado lays down a strong foundation for the practice of thoughtful criticism. What are, then, the main principles of this foundation? Or, what principles should the *modern* critic follow?

"Science and consciousness, these are the two principal requirements to practice criticism," says Machado.[3] With this assertion, he prudently places himself and his praxis between the premises of the emerging Realism (science) and the waning Romanticism (individual consciousness). Study and sensibility are, for him, the two central pillars necessary for a rigorous and fruitful critique. In addition to them, or derived from them, Machado also addresses *coherence*, or avoiding contradiction; *impartiality*, or being dispassionate while appraising distinct styles; and *politeness*, or correcting and advising with tact and respect.

When we read "O ideal do crítico" with our present-day eyes, though, two other points stand out for their definitive connection with the future Machado: *perseverance* and *independence*. For perseverance, Machado

---

3 Machado de Assis, "O ideal do crítico," *Obra completa*, vol. III, ed. Afrânio Coutinho (Rio de Janeiro: Nova Aguilar, 1997), 798–99.

refers to a mode of scrutinizing the literary text that goes beyond its surface. Critics should base their evaluations on deep knowledge of the work under analysis. The critical act presupposes a tenacious reader who seeks "truth" with steely determination. This is, after all, an accurate picture of Machado as a reader. His tenacity and perceptive ability in terms of readership eventually paved the road for the emergence of the mature Machado and his masterpieces. The critic, in this regard, prepared and created the fictionist.

The second point, independence, sheds light on the post-1880 fictionist, too. As a creator, Machado strove to forge a style that could grant him a unique place in Brazilian literature. From *Brás Cubas* on, this style fights not to be reduced to any literary school, not to be attached to any aesthetic dogma, not to adhere to any set of preconceived ideas. From *Brás Cubas* on, Machado's style clamors for independence. It is as a critic that Machado first advocates for an autonomous stance on literature, but it is the mature fictionist who admirably converts autonomy, or independence, into a literary asset.

Following the publication of "O ideal do crítico" on October 8, 1865, in *Diário do Rio de Janeiro*, Machado wrote for the same periodical a weekly column called "Semana literária" ("The Literary Week"), from January 9 to July 31, 1866. In the thirty columns he produced, he mostly reviewed works that were recently released by Brazilian writers. Whenever there wasn't a new, important release to review, the critic commented on titles from the recent past, as was the case of the columns on writers and works such as Junqueira Freire's *Inspirações do claustro* (*Cloister Inspirations*, 1855) and Álvares de Azevedo's *Lira dos vinte anos* (*Twenty-Year-Old Lyre*, 1853). Eventually, through the articles and reviews of "Semana literária," Machado put into practice the elements of criticism he had addressed in "O ideal do crítico."

When in 1868 José de Alencar called Machado the "first Brazilian critic," most of this endorsement stemmed from the columns of "Semana literária." And I say "most" because Machado had a previous career as a critic, specifically a theater critic, in the late 1850s and early 1860s. In the 1870s, however, he gradually reduced the intensity of his critical activity while progressively increasing the production of his fictional prose. Also, during the 1870s, the major triad of nineteenth-century Brazilian criticism emerged: Araripe Júnior, Sílvio Romero, and José Veríssimo. This triangle of critics could have been a square had Machado not decided to channel his intellectual and creative energies into prose fiction; or it can still be viewed as a square if we consider, as several critics do, that the post-1880 Machado continued to write criticism, albeit in fictional form.

Without speculating, though, the two undisputable facts concerning this topic are as follows: first, Araripe Júnior, Sílvio Romero, and José Veríssimo were the most influential voices of literary criticism in nineteenth-century Brazil, and second, despite the prior proposition, it was Machado who wrote the most read, studied, and quoted piece of criticism of the same period, the article "Instinto de nacionalidade" ("Instinct of Nationality").

"Instinct of Nationality"

Let's start with some context. In September 1872, José Carlos Rodrigues, a Brazilian journalist then living in New York, commissioned Machado to write an article on the current state of Brazilian literature.[4] The article would appear in Rodrigues's periodical, *O Novo Mundo: Periódico Ilustrado do Progresso da Idade* (*The New World: Illustrated Periodical on the Progress of the Era*), which was founded in 1870 and printed in New York but published entirely in Portuguese. *O Novo Mundo* had a branch office in Rio de Janeiro from which the monthly issues were distributed. Machado accepted the commission and sent the article "Notícia da atual literatura brasileira" to Rodrigues in New York.

It may be a minor detail, but, in fact, the most read, studied, and quoted piece of nineteenth-century Brazilian criticism was originally just entitled "Notícia da atual literatura brasileira." "Instinto de nacionalidade" is the title of its introductory section. Usage, though, made the article widely known as "Notícia da atual literatura brasileira – Instinto de nacionalidade," which is not one-hundred-percent accurate, or simply "Instinto de nacionalidade," which is not accurate at all. In the end, usage won over accuracy, or the main idea prevailed over the general thought. Either way, we'll follow here the customary use and refer to Machado's famous article as "Instinto de nacionalidade."

The article appeared in the final two pages of *O Novo Mundo*'s March 24, 1873 issue. It was preceded by news on Portuguese literature provided by Augusto Ernesto de Castilho e Mello. However, while Castilho e Mello chose to make an extensive list of authors and works accompanied

---

4   The commissioning letter can be read in *Correspondência de Machado de Assis*, vol. II, ed. Sergio Paulo Rouanet (Rio de Janeiro: ABL, 2009), 78–79.

by brief notes, Machado took this opportunity not only to comment on recent writers and titles but also to address Brazilian literature from a historical and critical standpoint. In other words, while Castilho e Mello did his job by writing something close to a report, Machado preferred, instead, to carry out his task with an article that also functioned as a brief essay, whereby he reflected on the subject reported. Different from his Portuguese counterpart, Machado dove into the matter he presented and tried to come up with arguments that could contribute to the cultural debate on the topic and push it to the next level, that is, the level of imperative achievements. What arguments were these, after all?

Machado begins "Instinto de nacionalidade" by repeating an idea he had stated several times in past articles: Brazil had already achieved its political independence; now, in order to complete the process of becoming independent, the country needed to forge and assume a national identity. Or, as Machado put it in 1858, fifteen years before: "After the political *fiat* [i.e. Brazil's independence from Portugal in 1822], there should be a literary *fiat*."[5] However, the "literary *fiat*" wouldn't come overnight. The "other independence," as Machado asserts in "Instinto de nacionalidade," "lacks a Seventh of September and a field of Ipiranga" (referring to the day and site on which the proclamation of Brazil's independence occurred).[6] The "other independence" would require the continuous work of multiple generations. In this regard, what was Machado's generation doing?

Machado affirms in the first sentence of his article that the main tenet of Brazilian literature was a "certain national instinct."[7] Through this concept, he alludes to the consistent and recurrent attempts by Brazilian writers to impart a national character to poems and fictional narratives by focusing on the local culture. For the national character to manifest itself, it should draw on the local culture, traditions, customs, and landscape. This process of nationalizing Brazilian literature focused on the countryside, in opposition to the Europeanized cities, and the Indigenous cultures, in opposition to "civilized" paradigms. In "Instinto de nacionalidade," Machado points out the coherence of these focal points and choices but refutes their imposition and delimitation: "I should add

---

5 Machado de Assis, "O passado, o presente e o futuro da literatura," *Obra completa*, vol. III, 787.
6 Machado de Assis, "Reflections on Brazilian Literature at the Present Moment – The National Instinct," trans. Robert Newcomb, *Journal of World Literature* 3 (2018), 405.
7 Ibid., 404.

that one sometimes hears an opinion regarding this topic that I consider erroneous. This is that the only works of true national spirit are those that describe local subjects; a belief that if correct, would greatly limit the resources available to our literature."[8]

For Machado, in brief, equating national to local (or local color) wasn't wrong in principle. The issue lay in the fact that every attempt that fell outside of this equation would automatically be discarded and delegitimized as not national. In response to this argument, Machado reminds his readers that *Hamlet*, *Othello*, *Julius Cesar*, and *Romeo and Juliet* have no direct link to English history or British territory. Nevertheless, "in addition to being a universal genius," asks Machado, isn't Shakespeare a quintessential English poet? And he concludes: "What we should expect of the writer above all is a certain intimate feeling that renders him a man of his time and country, even when he addresses topics that are remote in time or space."[9]

With "Instinto de nacionalidade," in short, Machado redefines the concept of *national* in literature. For him, it's perfectly feasible to create a national work that doesn't rely on local traditions, characters, or landscape. In this case, the national component would lie underneath the text in hidden – but not locked – compartments. Nationalism based on external factors can also be seen as too simplistic. An author should not be viewed as national just because they cite a plethora of names of plants and birds of their country in a poem or a story; by doing so, they would simply produce a "nationhood of vocabulary," one that is limited to the lexical level.[10] Shakespeare's *Hamlet*, for instance, is a Danish story only at the referential level. Behind its superficial appearance, there is an English sentiment and thought pulsing through the veins of the narrative.

In making these points, Machado holds the view that the literary text mobilizes a twofold structure with an outer and an inner dimension, like a shell and a seed, or a stage and a backstage. This claim wasn't original, for sure. It simply manifests a dialectical thought that permeated the nineteenth century, influenced by such thinkers as Hegel and Marx. But the way Machado manipulates dialectics regarding literature and nationalism, or fiction and national identity – whether it's original or not – had a decisive impact on Brazilian criticism as well as the way in which we read Machado's fiction. His argument basically sets up the idea that, from a

---

8 Ibid., 408.
9 Ibid., 408.
10 Ibid., 414.

critical perspective, the seed defines the shell, or the backstage determines the stage. Thus, reading critically means reading beyond, reading through, and reading further. Otherwise, by staying on the surface, or just in one dimension, readers may miss pivotal points and, consequently, have their reading misled. The history of the reception of Machado's works shows that he himself came under attack on account of being read superficially.

In March 1873, when "Instinto de nacionalidade" came out, Machado had published one novel, *Ressurreição*, and one short-story collection, *Contos fluminenses*. Later, when he became widely recognized as a fictionist, both during his lifetime and posthumously, his detractors repeatedly accused his fictional works of lacking the national spirit and approach. For them, the country that appears in Machado's novels and stories is an elitist, Europeanized Brazil, depicted with French elegance and English humor. Most of Machado's stories are set in Rio; if they were in Paris or Berlin, little if anything would change. Most of Machado's characters are native *cariocas*; if they were born in London or New York, that wouldn't change much either. According to his opponents, there were hardly any Brazilian roots to Machado's fictional works. On top of this, his detachment from the pressing social issues of his time, such as slavery, was also publicly held against him. All this criticism ended up creating the *ethos* of Machado as a "foreign-ish," Europeanized, and socially uncommitted writer.

As with other *ethe* discussed in Chapter Two, these are not true or false in principle. The "foreign-ish" and uncommitted Machado emerges from one specific mode of reading his works – that of focusing on the outward signs of the texts. From these signs, it's possible to identify marks of Europeanization and disengagement in Machado's fiction concerning Brazil's traditions and social-political issues. But, if it's right, it's also shallow. This is what Machado indirectly argues in "Instinto de nacionalidade," while somehow anticipating a debate over his own works that took place mainly after 1880. Before 1880 – more specifically in 1878 – Machado wrote a text that the critic Agripino Grieco considered to be "the highest page of Brazilian criticism": the review of Eça de Queirós's *O primo Basílio* (*The Cousin Basílio*).

The Cousin Basílio

1878 was a key year in Machado's career. It was possibly more than that, it was perhaps *the* key year of Machado's career, as it has direct connections to the unexpected qualitative leap that resulted in *Brás Cubas* and the titles that followed. That said, it surely was not an easy year. In December, at the age of 39, Machado suffered his first breakdown due to excessive and strenuous work. For the first time in his life, he interrupted his multiple activities and, compelled by his doctors, took a vacation and recovery time. From December 1878 to March 1879, Machado and Carolina rested in the mountainous city of Nova Friburgo. After this period of rest and reflection, a new Machado emerged, totally transformed, almost unrecognizable: the one who, in March 1880, presented the revolutionary *Brás Cubas* to his readers.

Thus, the revolution called *Brás Cubas* likely has one of its origins in Carolina and Machado's three-month stay in Nova Friburgo. Another possible genesis of *Brás Cubas* is the peculiar review of Eça de Queirós's *O primo Basílio* that appeared in the pages of *O Cruzeiro* in April 1878. Why this review and why peculiar? Before commenting on the peculiarities of Machado's critical review, let's take a quick look at two events that preceded it: the death of José de Alencar and the appearance of the serialized version of *Iaiá Garcia*.

For Machado, the hardships of 1878 started on December 12, 1877. On this date, José de Alencar passed away. Machado attended the funeral the following day as Alencar's admirer and acquaintance but also officially on behalf of *Diário Oficial* where Machado held one of his two appointments at that time (the other was at the Agriculture Department). With novels such as *O Guarani* (1857), *Iracema* (1865), and *Senhora* (1875), Alencar succeeded in earning both critical acclaim and popular esteem. His death left vacant the high seat of Brazilian literature. Ten years Alencar's junior, it's reasonable to assume that the ambitious and determined Machado would undertake the task of working, from then on, to occupy Alencar's seat.

On January 1, 1878, the periodical *O Cruzeiro* published the first installment of *Iaiá Garcia*, the fourth and – up to that point – the most daring and well-structured novel by Machado. From January to March, *Iaiá Garcia* occupied the *feuilleton* section of *O Cruzeiro* on an almost daily basis. Also, in March, the second novel by Eça de Queirós, *O primo Basílio*, arrived in Rio and instantly became a sensation. In a few days, all the copies flew from the twenty-seven bookstores scattered across the city. Almost overnight, nearly every reader in Rio was commenting on the story of Luísa, Jorge, Basílio, and Juliana. Eça wasn't an obscure author in Brazil. Since 1871, Brazilians followed the cultural and political events in Portugal through the *crônicas* by Eça and Ramalho Ortigão published monthly under the general title *As farpas* (*The Barbs*). In 1875, Eça released his first novel, the anticlerical O crime do padre Amaro (*The Crime of Father Amaro*). Despite its controversial content, the novel didn't cause a stir in Brazil, as O primo Basílio, three years later, definitely did.

Machado's *Iaiá Garcia*, for its part, provoked a few mixed, mostly mild reviews. In 1878, the writer's reputation stemmed, for the most part, from his poetry, *crônicas*, and criticism. And it was as a critic that, in April 1878, Machado decided to go against the flow and fight an uphill battle by examining O primo Basílio through a rigorous lens. The result was a stout disapproval of Eça's novel, or rather, the literary movement Eça had embraced: Naturalism.[11] Machado indeed acknowledged and praised Eça's talent, but he also concluded that the Portuguese writer wasted his talent by adhering to the Naturalist doctrine. By advocating that literary fiction should copy reality, or mirror it in a scientific, impersonal way, Naturalism, or even Realism, falsified the very nature of art. For Machado, art should primarily rely not on reality, but instead on art itself in order to recreate reality in its own artistic way and within its own artistic limits. In other words, in accepting the premises of Naturalism, art and literature would be reduced and restricted in their arc of possibilities to the straitjacket of reality.

This is just one point that made O primo Basílio vulnerable in Machado's view, one point that the critic ascribed to Émile Zola's influence. Zola was the chief and active proponent of Naturalism in France, and Eça, according to Machado, followed in Zola's footsteps in Portugal. Ultimately, Machado's review tried to dissuade Eça from writing under the premises of Zola's Naturalism and persuade him to employ his talent in another direction. Machado's attempt, we may conclude, eventually succeeded; the next two fictional works by Eça – the novella O mandarim (*The Mandarin*, 1880) and the novel A relíquia (*The Relic*, 1887) – both present magical components interwoven with reality. Both came closer to the territory of Realism (i.e. social analysis and criticism) and moved away from Zola's Naturalism (i.e. *roman à thèse*). Whether Machado's critique had any bearing on Eça's decision to modify his style, we'll never know. Although it's unlikely, it's not impossible, for Eça did read the review and responded to Machado in a letter written with elegance and cordiality.[12]

---

11 Machado uses the terms Naturalism and Realism interchangeably. His main target, though, is Zola's style, which he vehemently opposes.
12 Eça's letter, dated June 29, 1878, can be read in *Correspondência de Machado de Assis*, vol. II, 141–42.

Recapping: Eça's style took a slight turn from Naturalism to a type of Realism that integrates fantastic elements during the period from 1878 to 1880, when he published O primo Basílio and O mandarim, respectively. Similarly, Machado's style also took a turn from Romanticism to a peculiar form of Realism, in the same period – from 1878 to 1880 – during which he published Iaiá Garcia and Brás Cubas, respectively. Nevertheless, in the case of Machado, the turn wasn't a slight one at all – it was, instead, a complete reversal. And herein lies an important point: while it's unlikely that Machado's review had any impact on Eça's new approach to Realism, it's quite likely that the same review had a decisive influence on Machado's decision to take the radical turn that resulted in Brás Cubas. It's fair to affirm, albeit not possible to prove, that Machado found his path towards his new and definitive phase after reviewing O primo Basílio. It's plausible that he developed an insight – one that changed his career for ever – while questioning the options chosen by Eça. It wasn't by any means a casual insight, though. At the age of 38, Machado had meticulously prepared himself *to gain an insight* into his own limits as a writer so he could consciously expand them, as he actually did. However, *gaining an insight* requires, say, a trigger, and the trigger might have been Eça's novel O primo Basílio.[13]

Let's consider, just for a moment, that this hypothesis is true. Under those circumstances, Machado wrote Brás Cubas – to a degree, at least – in response to O primo Basílio, or rather, against O primo Basílio. Eça's novel therefore *invented* – albeit unintentionally – the second and definitive Machado. On the other hand, Machado, with his review and the debate it provoked, established the reception of Eça in Brazil, which, as already mentioned, was more favorable overseas than in Portugal. In the months following Machado's review, O primo Basílio continued to be commented on, either in literary notes or in comic news cartoons. Eça's phenomenon went even further, indeed: the novel received two theatrical adaptations, the first in May and the second in July 1878.[14] Machado made remarks on

---

13 João Cezar de Castro Rocha discusses this topic at length in his Machado de Assis: Towards a Poetics of Emulation, trans. Flora Thompson-DeVeaux (East Lansing: Michigan State UP, 2015).
14 On the reception of O primo Basílio in the months following its arrival in Brazil, see Sílvia Maria Azevedo, "A recepção de O Primo Basílio na imprensa brasileira do século XIX: caricatura, humor e crítica literária," Patrimônio e Memória, vol. 8, no. 1 (Jan.–Jun. 2012), 27–42.

the latter in a *crônica* published in July of that year, when he reaffirmed his admiration for Eça and his animosity towards the school of Naturalism.¹⁵

This animosity expressed and reiterated by Machado contradicts one of his propositions stated in "O ideal do crítico." In this article, Machado advocates for tolerance and impartiality towards different styles, which isn't practiced at all in his review of Eça's novel. Also, after a short period when the young Machado voiced strong opinions in the press, his overall conduct, both privately (as far as we know it) and in public, was strictly guided by cordiality to avoid controversy at all costs. As a cordial man to the core, Machado was promptly able to agree with his interlocutor just to stifle debate (see Chapter Eight, letter P). But, curiously enough, he wasn't feeling cordial on April 16, 1878, when he accused Eça's style of degrading itself by making "photographic and slavish reproductions of minimal and ignoble things," and when he blatantly pointed out that Luísa, Eça's heroine, was less a moral character and more like a "puppet."¹⁶ This man abhorred controversy, yet what he generated with these and other provocative words was ... controversy.

Machado's review caused such an upheaval among Eça's readers that the critic felt compelled to write a second article on April 30 to clarify some of the points that had been contested by others. He possibly felt compelled to rest his case by writing a third and more extensive response: *Brás Cubas*. The undisputable fact is that, after 1878, Machado wrote criticism only sporadically.¹⁷ Alfredo Pujol, Machado's first biographer, assumes that this debate over the review of O *primo Basílio* hurt Machado's feelings, and, consequently, he reduced his activities as a critic.¹⁸

The question now is to what extent *Brás Cubas* can be read as a critical response to O *primo Basílio* and/or to Zola's Naturalism. We could approach this question with a passage by Zola in which the French writer famously argues that "The author isn't a moralist, he's instead an anatomist

---

15 See Machado de Assis, *Crônica* from July 7, 1878. *Obra completa*, vol. III, 388–89.
16 Machado de Assis, "[Eça de Queirós: O *primo Basílio*]," *Obra completa*, vol. III, 904–05.
17 One remarkable exception is the lengthy article "A nova geração" ("The New Generation") published in December 1879. This is an important commentary on and analysis of poetry and poets then current in Brazil. The article has a commendable English translation by Robert P. Newcomb: "The New Generation," *Journal of Lusophone Studies* 1.2 (Autumn 2016), 262–308.
18 Alfredo Pujol, *Machado de Assis*, 2nd edn. (Rio de Janeiro: José Olympio, 1934), 270–71.

who'd be delighted to report his findings in a human cadaver."[19] For Zola, the author plays the role of a scientist whose investigations aim to find the naked truth. As in science, the ultimate goal of art should be the discovery of truth, no matter how inconvenient and shocking it is. In this context, sexuality itself, along with its perversions, gained a prominent place in the modern novel. But "the author isn't a moralist," and the modern novel isn't about being moral or immoral; the modern novel, in Zola's view, is about being true or untrue in capturing and depicting the human and social reality.

Machado, for his turn, instead of dissecting a "human cadaver," creates an author, Brás Cubas, who *is* a cadaver – a cadaver who talks about the living and dissects the human condition. Instead of dissecting a corpse in quest of scientific truth, Machado revives in nineteenth-century Brazil an ancient tradition: that of Menippean satire, in the lineage of Lucian of Samosata's *Dialogue of the Dead*, full of tongue-in-cheek wit, where truth is as solid as a soap bubble. ("Truth lies on this side of the Pyrenees, error on the other," was one of Machado's favorite quotes by Pascal.[20]) The sinuous trajectory of a soap bubble in the air, by the way, parallels the digressive (i.e. non-methodic, non-linear) style of Machado's second-phase novels. Brás Cubas himself acknowledges this fickle style by referring to his memoir, in the prologue, as a "diffuse work" in which he "adopted the free form of a Sterne or a Xavier de Maistre."[21]

Diffuseness and freedom of form are two aspects that can be viewed in opposition to logic and determinism, two principles closely aligned with the scientific premises of Naturalism. The list of opposing elements between those that Machado attacks in reviewing O *primo Basílio* and those that he embraces in his later fiction could go on and on. I'll just single out a final aspect to reinforce the idea that the Machado who criticized Eça's novel shows anticipatory signs of the future writer who would revolutionize Brazilian literature.

In the penultimate paragraph of the second article, or the second part of the review, Machado says: "Well, the Realism of Mr. Zola and Mr. Eça de Queirós, despite everything, hasn't exhausted yet every aspect of

---

19 Émile Zola, *Du roman: Sur Stendhal, Flaubert et les Goncourt* (Bruxelles: Éditions Complexe), 135.
20 Blaise Pascal, *Pensées and Other Writings*, trans. Honor Levi (Oxford: Oxford UP, 2008), 23.
21 Machado de Assis, *The Posthumous Memoirs of Brás Cubas*, trans. Flora Thompson-DeVeaux (New York: Penguin, 2020), 3.

reality. There are intimate and minimal acts, secret vices, social secretions that cannot be overlooked in the exhibition of all things."[22] Machado touches here on a central matter that is detectable in his mature style: the dialect of showing/hiding, saying/silencing. In other words, the second Machado, in contrast with "Zola's Realism" (i.e. Naturalism), and in contrast with his own Romantic vein, will hide to show, will silence to speak. In the works produced during his second phase, Machado maximizes the minimum, or, better yet, the minimum *is* the maximum. In this act of upending things, there exists a sort of humanistic metaphysics, that is, an invitation to see the spectacle of the world in its immanent nature, but also to see it through, going further and beyond its limits, from the visible to the invisible, from the sound to the silence.

"The risk involving the Realist movement," says Machado, "lies in the supposition – assumed by some – that the thick line is the exact line."[23] By "thick line" ("*traço grosso*"), Machado means the immoral, the unpleasant, the crude painting of reality done and brought to the forefront of a literary work under license from Science, or from the author being – supposedly – "scientific." At last, the way Machado the critic tackles science in his review of *O primo Basílio* sheds light on the way Machado the fictionist deals with science and rationalism in some of his later masterpieces, such as "O alienista" ("The Alienist") and *Quincas Borba*, for instance.

A Brief Conclusion on Machado the Critic

Machado's critical conception of nationalism in literature opened up an avenue for him, and other writers after him, to create a national literature without falling into the trap of exoticism (see Chapter Eight, letter N). Being national, in this context, doesn't necessarily mean being local or regional. But the other side of the spectrum may also be a trap. The main tenets of modern Western culture – capitalism, rationalism, Christianism, liberalism – tend to standardize all Western societies, or rather, all Western experiences. In this regard, the greed of a capitalist in Rio de Janeiro wouldn't differ much from the greed of a capitalist in London. After all, both capitalists are products of the same economic system. Through this

---

22 Machado de Assis, "[Eça de Queirós: *O primo Basílio*]," *Obra completa*, vol. III, 913.
23 Ibid., 908.

perspective, Westernization opposes nationalization, particularly in the case of a colonized (i.e. Westernized) country such as Brazil.

For Machado, however, this is as true as it is fallacious: Alencar's Indigenous characters, for instance, are depicted as Christians; that is to say, they appear to be authentic, or national, but, deep down, they are not. Similarly, Machado sees it as possible to portray an urban character whose Europeanized appearance encompasses national traits. In this respect, Brás Cubas, a capitalist living in Rio de Janeiro, bears similarities to other capitalists, such as Lisboan Basílio, from Eça de Queirós's *O primo Basílio*, or the American expatriate Gilbert Osmond, from Henry James's *The Portrait of a Lady* (published the same years as *Brás Cubas*, 1880–81). These three characters are snobbish and self-centered and their personalities are, indeed, molded by the social-economic environment in which they live.

Yet, in order to avoid schematism or reductionism, Machado, more so than Eça or James, individualizes his protagonist with the aim of rendering the character unique, or rather, with the aim of overcoming typification. Machado seems to be perfectly aware that between the social-economic environment, as a determining factor, and individuals, as products of this environment, there are always interstices and gray areas. As a fictionist, Machado targets these interstices and gray areas where we, as readers, may find – albeit scattered and blurred – the national element.

Also, in this process of deepening the individualization of his characters, Machado comes to reject Naturalism and its mechanical logic of causality based on strictly scientific premises. The complexity of Machado's characters, particularly at the psychological level, continuously breaks this logic and defies science. For Machado, in sum, human existence is far more unpredictable than scientific determinism might assume. His interest as a fictionist rests upon humans' unpredictability rather than upon natural laws dictating humans' actions and reactions. By pondering concepts such as nationalism and Naturalism, especially towards the end of the 1870s, Machado the critic somehow prepares for the advent of Machado the revolutionary fictionist who appears in 1880. Ultimately, Machado the mature fictionist emerged once he learned how to convert critical ideas into fictional narrative.

Machado as a Journalist and *Cronista*

Throughout this book, I have been using the Portuguese word *crônica* instead of the English *chronicle*, and you may have been wondering why. It's time, then, to explain this choice of use. The Portuguese word *crônica* has basically two meanings. The first means an account of historical events provided in chronological order. This meaning corresponds to that of the English term *chronicle*. The second meaning refers to a literary genre which was cultivated in nineteenth-century Brazil and is still being practiced. Major names in Brazilian literature wrote *crônicas*. Among them are Lima Barreto, Clarice Lispector, Carlos Drummond de Andrade, Rubem Braga, Luis Fernando Verissimo, and Machado de Assis. It is argued – and to some degree it is true – that *crônica* is an authentic Brazilian genre – not born but developed and practiced only in Brazil. It's unquestionably a Brazilian tradition. And because there is no immediate or precise parallel in English, we should use the Portuguese word. But what is *crônica*, then?

Think of a literary tradition with over a century of history and hundreds, maybe thousands, of writers. As you may imagine, it's unfeasible to reduce *crônica* to a single definition. It's better to start, let's say, with a historical-structural idea.

We already learned that in 1808 the printing press arrived in Brazil, brought by the Portuguese royal family and their delegation. The arrival of the printing press soon gave birth to … the press, the Brazilian press. The first newspaper to be published in Brazil, *Gazeta do Rio de Janeiro*, was released on September 10, 1808. On its four pages, one could read local news, reports from the metropole, and classified advertisements. Just to put this event into historical perspective, the first colonial paper in America, *Publick Occurrences Both Forreign and Domestick*, was printed in Boston in September 1690. The publication was discontinued after its first edition, though. Then, almost fourteen years later, in April 1704, *The Boston News-Letter* started circulating in Massachusetts and became the first regularly published newspaper in the colonies.

In France, the history of journalism goes back to 1631, when the weekly magazine *La Gazette* began reporting on local and international news. The history of Brazilian *crônica* has its origins in France, specifically from the issue of *Journal des Débats* released on January 28, 1800. In this edition, the French periodical reserved a space at the bottom part of its pages and coined the term *feuilleton* to name it.[24] *Journal des Débats* was a political paper established in 1789 and was initially committed to transcribing the debates occurring during the National Assembly. Over the years, the paper became an influential periodical devoted to French politics. In January 1800, its editors decided to make an additional space

---

24 Link for the January 28, 1800 issue of *Journal des Débats*: https://gallica.bnf.fr/ark:/12148/bpt6k415710x/f1.item

for non-political news: the *feuilleton* space. The idea was to create a counterweight section for readers to take a rest from political matters; or, to create a "vent" in the paper for readers to "breathe some fresh air" after reading the upper sections with their serious and important news; or, still, to widen the scope of topics in order to attract new readers and, that way, increase the paper's circulation.

In this regard, the *feuilleton* section should entertain the readers by focusing on areas of ... entertainment: music, theater, gastronomy, travelling, literature, and so forth. In the 1830s and 1840s, the *roman-feuilleton*, or a novel published in installments (the precursor of radio and TV soap operas), dominated the *feuilleton* sections of the main periodical press, both in France and Brazil (in the case of Brazil, novels were mostly translations of French *feuilletons*). From the 1830s on, roughly speaking, the *feuilleton* bifurcated into two main forms: the literary, or *roman-feuilleton*, and the *feuilleton de variété*, a free form addressing a variety of current topics, which was primarily associated with the arts of entertainment. The *feuilleton de variété* was also referred to as *feuilleton-causerie*, or conversational *feuilleton*. In this type of writing, the tone – i.e. conversational – was the determining aspect of the text.

The Brazilian *crônica* derives directly from the *feuilleton-causerie*: its tone is predominantly conversational and its style primarily informal. However, as time went by, the Brazilian *crônica* took on its own shape and created its own identity similar to but also different from its French source. One important point to underline, before examining distinct aspects of the *crônica*, is its social function in nineteenth-century Brazilian society. A few paragraphs above, I mentioned a "historical-structural idea" regarding the genre *crônica*. Now, it's time to expand on this idea.

Oral Culture, Hummingbirds, and Fickleness

During Machado's lifetime, Brazil was a predominantly illiterate country. Brazilian culture, for its historical developments, was heavily oral based. In this respect, the conversational tone of *crônica* functioned – structurally considering – as a *bridge* between readers and journalism as well as readers and literature. To put it another way, *crônica*, through its stylistic balance between spoken and written word (i.e. the conversational tone or style), worked as an effective mediator between the traditional oral culture and the emerging literate and literary cultures. That's one of the reasons why, as a genre, *crônica* has had such traction in Brazil since its first appearance in the mid-nineteenth century up through the present day. Even nowadays, *cronistas* who contribute to the Brazilian press can still be viewed (and read) as mediators between the oral and written cultures in Brazil.

But what does oral culture mean in this context – since oral culture may have multiple implications? Oral culture, here, simply means the pleasure of companionship through the exercise of chatting away. It means, in this regard, relishing talking with friends about subjects picked at random, because talking in and of itself – as a way to feed and sustain friendly interaction – is important, whereas the content of the conversation isn't as relevant. So, does the content matter at all? Well, if we are looking for a pleasurable experience in talking for the sake of talking, it's recommended not to touch on controversial issues, such as politics, religion, or soccer. If one wishes to bring these matters into the conversation, it's advisable to do so with tact and openness.

Before Machado, the genre *crônica* incorporated political issues in a light, approachable fashion. The main *cronista* of that time, José de Alencar, wrote a series of *crônicas* that were suggestively entitled *Ao correr da pena* (*As the Pen Runs*). In these texts, which appeared in 1854 and 1855, Alencar tackles several topics, including politics. The way he tackles them somehow determined and defined the new genre of *crônica* as we now regard it. It's worth noting that, in a *crônica* dated September 24, 1854, Alencar compares the *cronista* to a hummingbird, who gracefully and weightlessly zigzags and hovers from flower to flower to drink their nectar. Likewise, the *cronista* approaches trivial events, go in zigzag fashion from one to another, and tries to extract sweetness from them.[25] Based on the movements of the *cronista*-hummingbird, Alencar identifies "fickleness" as one of the stylistic features that defines the genre.[26] Fickleness also characterizes Machado's digressive style as a *cronista* and mature fictionist, as we shall see. But before examining Machado's *crônicas* from a stylistic point of view, let's first focus on a turnabout that occurred on February 22, 1862. On that date, the trajectory of Machado as a *cronista* took a sharp turn. In the long run, this change would become decisive in helping the writer to find his own voice. Let's go to the facts.

---

25 José de Alencar, *Ao correr da pena* (São Paulo: Tipografia Alemã, 1874), 20. Machado repeats the comparison between the *cronista* and a hummingbird in an 1859 *crônica* entitled "O folhetinista," *Obra completa*, vol. III, 959 (*folhetinista* = *cronista*).
26 José de Alencar, *Ao correr da pena*, 20.

"Discontentment over Politics"

"I entered journalism [in 1860]," recollects Machado in a *crônica* of memoirs that he wrote thirty-eight years later, in 1898.[27] In this recollection, Machado recounts the context in which he was invited by Quintino Bocaiúva to work at the prestigious and influential *Diário do Rio de Janeiro*. (We referred to this event in Chapters Two and Three.) Before 1860, Machado had worked in the press as a proofreader. As a writer, he had contributed to short-lived periodicals. During this period, his most fruitful experience as a journalist occurred from September 1859 to January 1860, in working for the paper O Espelho. There, Machado was responsible for basically every step of the editing process as well as writing regularly for the periodical. It's possible to assert that Machado "entered journalism" *de facto* in 1859, when he started working at O Espelho. The following year, though, he entered the big press. He left behind his activities as a dilettante journalist, a gig with most likely little to no pay, to become a professional, full-time journalist paid on a salaried basis.

In *Diário do Rio de Janeiro*, Machado was initially appointed as a reporter in charge of covering the Senate sessions. The next year, though, he made another professional leap: he was offered a regular column in *Diário*. He had been a permanent columnist writing theater criticism for O Espelho. Now, for the first time, he was going to write *feuilletons de variété*, or *crônicas*, on an assortment of topics. Also, for the first time, he was going to have a broad audience. Thus, from October 1861 to May 1862, he penned twenty columns for the series "Comentários da semana" ("Weekly Commentaries").[28] In these columns, Machado the *cronista* mixed literary and theater reviews with general commentaries about recent events. These events could be anything from a regatta in Guanabara Bay, to the church bell with no clapper, to the prejudice in the press against fortune tellers, to political news.

As for the latter, Machado's commentaries weren't laid-back notes. On the contrary, Machado the *cronista* took politics seriously enough to level bitter criticism at politicians. From a political perspective, the

---

27 Machado de Assis, "O velho senado," *Obra completa*, ed. Afrânio Coutinho, vol. II (Rio de Janeiro: Nova Aguilar, 1997), 636.
28 Although the *crônicas* of "Comentários da semana" can be referred to as *feuilletons de variété*, they didn't occupy the bottom of the page in *Diário do Rio de Janeiro*. This space was usually occupied by a chapter of a *roman-feuilleton*, i.e. a serialized novel.

Machado we see in "Comentários da semana" is a young journalist committed to fighting for his ideas with courage and determination. He bashes legislators and state ministers with sharp irony and daring attacks – so much so that he appears to have been instructed by one of *Diário*'s directors to moderate his voice.[29] Probably in response to this and other pressures, Machado closed his *crônica* of February 22, 1862, with a downhearted remark on politics entitled, quite appropriately, "Discontentment over Politics."

In that closing note, Machado deplores the spectacle of "political miseries" that makes the "public spirit disappointed and nauseous"; Machado feels deeply sorry that the men responsible for that pitiful spectacle are the ones who lead the country. "It's tedious," says Machado "to see how characters are slandered, how opinions are distorted, how ideas are upended, all in favor of transitory and material interests, all in favor of the exclusion of every view that contradicts the prevailing opinion." And he finishes by evoking Don Quixote. Machado argues that the famous Spanish knight-errant, with "the sincerity of his ridiculousness," makes us laugh, at least; the despicable men in power can't even do that.[30]

Following this despondent note, Machado wrote two *crônicas* on March 24 and April 1, 1862, on the topic of the inauguration of the equestrian statue of D. Pedro I, which occurred on March 25. Both texts are fiercely critical of the conservative cabinet of the Marquis of Caxias, who was then in office. The *crônica* of April 1 was the penultimate of the series. In the last one, dated May 5, 1862 (note that the frequency of the *weekly* commentaries wasn't regular), the *cronista* goes on to campaign openly for the fall of Caxias cabinet, which eventually happened two weeks later, on May 24. On May 5, though, the Machado *cronista* who engaged in partisan politics leaves the public stage once and for all. The spirit of his note "Discontentment over Politics" guides his pen from then on. Machado's *crônicas* thereafter scrupulously avoided controversy. Avoiding controversy, however, didn't mean overlooking politics. It simply meant looking at politics from a different angle.

---

29 Jean-Michel Massa, *A Juventude de Machado de Assis*, trans. Marco Aurélio de Moura Matos (Rio de Janeiro: Civilização Brasileira, 1971), 308.
30 Machado de Assis, *Comentários da semana*, eds. Lúcia Granja & Jefferson Cano (Campinas: Unicamp, 2008), 178.

What is *Crônica*, Again?

As a genre, *crônica* shares close similarities with other literary genres. So much so that, in the first attempt to publish the complete works of Machado – the thirty-one volumes of Jackson's edition, 1937 – his February 22 *crônica* was moved, with no explanatory note, into the volume that comprises his literary criticism. A recent edition, fortunately, corrected this error.[31] Maybe *error* is too strong a word since the nature of *crônica* is so variable and absorbing that it's not all that easy – even nowadays – to demarcate its limits. Some *crônicas*, for instance, can be read as short stories and vice versa. To minimize confusion, it's useful to have a definition, one we can lean on whenever we need to differentiate *crônica* from other literary forms or genres.

Before jumping to a definition, though, one brief note. Over the forty years Machado dedicated to journalism, he penned, according to Afrânio Coutinho, 614 *crônicas*.[32] In Jackson's edition – which is not complete, by the way – the *cronista*'s production is spread over seven of the volumes, comprising more than 2,000 pages. To count the number of *crônicas* Machado wrote isn't a simple task because a great number of them, following a convention of that time, were signed under several different pseudonyms. Consequently, we have found over the years new *crônicas* that are presumably authored by Machado, and others whose authorship has since been contested. The sure fact is that, in terms of absolute numbers, the production of *crônicas* far surpasses other genres that Machado cultivated. This extensive production also demonstrates Machado's profound commitment to journalism. Different from poems, stories, or serialized novels, *crônica* is a product of journalism and also became an intrinsic part of it. In other words, if *crônica* is derived from newspaper (and it is), *cronistas* are also journalists. Thanks to the talent of Brazilian *cronistas*, like Machado, *crônica* also became literary, even though its origins and nature, as we have seen, are primarily journalistic.

As for the origins of the genre, Machado presents his own ironic, mythical version in a *crônica* dated November 1, 1877:

> I can't say for sure which year *crônica* was born; but it's quite probable that its birth was contemporary with the two first ladies who were

---

31 Ibid., 173–79.
32 Afrânio Coutinho, *Machado de Assis na literatura brasileira* (Rio de Janeiro: ABL, 1990), 295.

next-door neighbors. These neighbors, between lunch and the afternoon snack, sat by their doors to pick at the happenings of the day. They likely started by complaining about the hot weather. One said she couldn't eat at lunch; the other replied that her shirt was wetter than the herbs she had eaten. Going from herbs to the vegetable garden of the neighbor who lives in front of them, and then to his adventurous romantic affairs, and so forth, was the easiest and most natural thing to do. And herein lies the origins of *crônica*.[33]

And herein also lies the definition I promised to spell out. Machado defines *crônica* as a conversation between the *cronista* and the reader, as if they were two next-door neighbors talking about whatever topics come to mind. In this informal conversation, one topic sparks and brings in another, and this sparks and brings in another, and another, and another ... The style of *crônica* is defined, thus, as both conversational in tone and tessellated in content. As for the latter, it structurally resembles a mosaic, or, better yet, a patchwork quilt. Politics may feature in this conversation as long as the topic doesn't create conflict between the *cronista* and the reader. *Crônica* aims to create community, intends to strengthen the bonds between readers and the newspaper. For this to happen, the *cronista*, like a Turkish sultan, should "smoke quietly the pipe of his fatalism," writes Machado in 1878. "The *cronista*," he continues, "is not in charge of souls, he neither evangelizes, nor warns, nor straightens out the crooked people in the world; he is a mere spectator."[34]

Being a "mere spectator" doesn't exactly align with the image (*ethos*) of the social-political absentee that some critics describe Machado to be. At this point, it's useful to differentiate the man from the writer. Machado the man had an interest in politics just as much as any citizen who knows about their civil rights and duties, and who is aware that political decisions have an impact on their life. Machado the writer, though, had a different involvement with politics, one that was neither null nor pragmatic, neither absent nor interventionist. When tackling the topic of politics, Machado the writer prefers adopting a skeptical and ironic approach.

In order to illustrate this last argument, I've selected one *crônica* to unpack and discuss in the section below. As you may imagine, one sample is too little to show for such a huge task. But it can be helpful, anyway. I

---

33 Machado de Assis, *Obra completa*, vol. III, 370.
34 Machado de Assis, *Notas semanais*, eds. John Gledson & Lúcia Granja (Campinas: Unicamp, 2008), 223.

tried to stick to the idea that the *cronista* is someone who talks informally to his readers and doesn't intend to "evangelize" or "warn" them. The *cronista*'s primary aim is to forge a friendly alliance with readers.

A Paradigmatic *Crônica* by Machado

The corpus of Machado's *crônicas* contains, in 614 small segments, the author's whole plural and complex universe. So selecting just one, I should say, was a thorny task. After much hesitation, though, I came to choose the *crônica* dated November 12, 1893, published in *Gazeta de Notícias* under the series "A semana" ("The Week"). The aim of this reading, besides understanding as much as possible the text under analysis, is also to prepare ourselves for approaching Machado's fiction, which we'll be focusing on in the next chapters.

Before starting the analysis, though, we need to get a sense of the historical context surrounding the *crônica*. So here we go. From September 1893 to March 1894, Rio was the battleground in a civil war between the Brazilian navy and army. The conflict went down in history as the second *Revolta da Armada* (Naval Revolt). The first one had occurred in November 1891 and caused the resignation of the first president of the Republic of Brazil, Deodoro da Fonseca, who governed the country after the military overthrew the monarchy, through a *coup d'état*, and implemented the republican system. As in any war, the Naval Revolts were involved in a series of entangled events that gradually evolved into an armed conflict. I will try to simplify these events as much as I can in the following eight brief and consecutive points.

1. During the Second Reign (1841–89), the navy was the apple of Emperor D. Pedro II's eyes. The army occupied a secondary position in terms of prestige. After the Proclamation of the Republic on November 15, 1889, led by the army, the status of these bodies switched, with the navy being tacitly relegated to a position of less importance. This change of power created friction between the two military forces – the navy resented the loss of distinction.

2. The first president of the Republic of Brazil was Marshal Deodoro da Fonseca. The new government, which – let me repeat – came to power through a *coup*, declared itself provisional. Deodoro da Fonseca then called a constituent assembly to draft a new constitution, which was eventually promulgated in February 1891. Under the laws of the newly established Republic, the members of Congress elected Deodoro da Fon-

seca to be the first president of Brazil. Thus, still in February 1891, the provisional president became the president-elect, lawfully endowed with a four-year term to govern the nation, starting in February 1891.

3. The 1891 Constitution determined that the 1891 presidential election would exceptionally be indirect (i.e. through Congress). Subsequent presidents would be elected, instead, by popular vote – with the law restricting the vote to prevent women, illiterate men, members of the Catholic Church, members of the military, and men under 21 years old from voting. One section of the Constitution stated that, if the president were unable to exert his mandate without completing 50% of his term, new elections must be called.

4. In November 1891, during a grave political and economic crisis, President Deodoro da Fonseca closed Congress through a unilateral decision that clearly violated the recently established Constitution. The closure of Congress was a desperate act committed with the aim of saving his presidential mandate.

5. Admiral Custódio de Melo – then the most powerful man in the navy – moved a fleet to Guanabara Bay and threatened to bombard the capital if the president didn't abide by the Constitution. Feeling cornered, weakened, and pressured, Deodoro da Fonseca resigned after nine months of a disastrous administration – which had *de facto* been initiated after the *coup* in November 1889. The occupation of Guanabara Bay by the naval fleet in November 1891 was called the first Naval Revolt.

6. Don't get lost with dates and facts. Let's recap before we continue. *November 1889*: Republic is established through a military *coup*. Deodoro da Fonseca is the president. A constituent assembly is called. *February 1891*: new constitution is promulgated. Deodoro da Fonseca is indirectly elected and starts his four-year term. *November 1891*: Deodoro da Fonseca closes Congress. First Naval Revolt. Deodoro da Fonseca resigns nine months after being elected.

7. The vice president, Marshal Floriano Peixoto, then took the presidential office. As stated by the Constitution, he was obliged to call new elections, but he didn't. His refusal provoked another military crisis. On September 13, 1893, the crisis reached its peak when a fleet led by Admiral Custódio de Melo bombarded forts on the coast of Rio. That's how the second Naval Revolt began. For the next six months, the army and the navy exchanged fire. Some of the civilians fled from Rio to mountainous or rural areas in the state; those who stayed could see and hear shots fired by cannons on land and at sea.

8. The second Naval Revolt opposed two military leaders: Marshal Floriano Peixoto and Admiral Custódio de Melo. The former fought against the navy (and against the Constitution) to remain in office until the end of Deodoro's term. The latter demanded that the Constitution be enforced, and new elections called. Custódio de Melo had a political career besides his military one, and was a natural candidate to run for president and replace Floriano Peixoto in the next election. So, below the Constitution, below the feud between the army and the navy, there were two individuals who had personal interests in fighting one another.

Please note: the above summary doesn't encapsulate to the whole picture, as the events briefly described are much more complex than that. Yet, without knowing these basic facts, we wouldn't be able to grasp the ironies of the November 12, 1893, crônica.

In November 1893, the Naval Revolt had been going on for two months. The *cronista* begins his text by remarking on the recurrence of cannon shots, which he compares to the bangs of a "huge clock."[35] From this comparison, he moves to Henry Longfellow's poem "The Old Clock on the Stairs" and its chorus that imitates a pendulum movement: "Never – forever. / Forever – Never." In the first paragraph, the *cronista* goes from war to clocks, and from clocks to poetry, and from poetry to the following conclusion: "Poetry, my friends, is in everything, in war as well as in love."

This rhythm of skipping from one topic to another continues into the next paragraph. The *cronista* starts it by asking readers to forgive him for speaking an "illustrious triviality," that of love being a war. In love as well as in war, we find "strife and battles," "wounded and dead people," "heroes and ignored crowds." The arenas where both love and war take place attract curious watchers. From this point, the *cronista* hops to the ancient Greek text *Daphnis and Chloe*, and then to the Crimean War, and then to memory and childhood, and then to Napoleon III, and then to D. Pedro I, and then to a recent piece of news about the issue of personal vouchers in three Brazilian cities, and then to a sarcastic and elusive remark about the Encilhamento – a catastrophic economic plan created by Rui Barbosa which caused the crisis that ended up causing Deodoro's resignation – and then to a prophetic vision, replete with irony, of people issuing their own money ... On that day, says the *cronista*, "hunger will die from hunger," for everybody will finally be

---

35 Machado de Assis, [Crônica 81, 12 de novembro de 1893], *A semana: crônicas (1893–1893)*, ed. John Gledson (São Paulo: Hucitec, 1996), 328. All quotations are from this edition.

rich! Machado finishes the *crônica* by bringing back Longfellow's clock but takes a poetic license to slightly alter the poem's chorus; when everybody becomes rich by fabricating their personal currency, the clock will be loudly ticking: "Ever – forever. / Forever – ever."

This partial synopsis of the November 12, 1893, *crônica* underlines a structural aspect of the genre which is also a pivotal component of Machado's style: the digressive arrangement of a narrative, which seems disorganized, random, and as if it's lacking focus. However, that is the spirit of the conversational *crônica*: not having a focus, pushing the line of reasoning from one side to another constantly and playfully, painting a mosaic of topics apparently disproportional, and overlaying everything with the glaze of humor. Without irony and humor, the entire structure would fall apart. Digression and satire, therefore, must go hand in hand. This unpretentious way of approaching the facts imparts freedom to the *cronista*, who, like a modern *flâneur*, follows languidly and from afar the everyday occurrences as if they were the spectacle of history. The *cronista*, however, occasionally finds a treasure among the knick-knacks. That's how the game works.

In the case of this *crônica*, there is a passage halfway through the text which, despite its ordinary nature, or maybe because of it, calls the readers' attention. In this passage, the *cronista* gets out of the trolley at Gloria Beach to watch the bombings. He is standing there for about ten minutes when a man approaches him and notes in a placid voice that "the shots were necessary, particularly those fired by the Hotchkiss revolving cannons, and the explosions of gunpowder magazines, too." Without agreeing or disagreeing, the *cronista* assumes that the man is a mere rubbernecker. Nevertheless, a second man gets closer and says, once the first goes away: "He's a glazier; he doesn't wish that people die, he just wishes for broken glasses." And the second man continues and argues that he abhors wars because no one is safe; no one walking in the streets knows whether they will be able to go back home or not; stray bullets render existence more vulnerable than ever. These are the reasons why he has already made his last will and testament. "I enjoyed listening to this man," says the *cronista*. "He made a judicious and melancholic contrast to the first," he concludes. After the second man leaves, the *cronista* asks a third man: "Who was that gentleman?" "He's a notary," the third man replies.

The irony of this passage has several layers. In the middle of a civil war – with politics on shaky ground, with the president of Brazil fighting against the head of Brazilian navy, with the army artillery and the navy fleet bombarding each other, with these bombardments putting the lives of civilians in danger – the *cronista* decides to tell us a casual anecdote involving a glazier and a notary. Both apparently in contrast: the *explosive* glazier contrasting with the "melancholic" notary. This contrast, though, immediately dissolves when we, the readers, realize that both are equally looking out for number one, that both can only gaze at their own navels, that both are primarily concerned about their own personal interests. At first, the glazier and the notary seem to occupy opposing, or at least different, sides. But, deep down, they don't; they are the same, they mirror each other, like ... Marshal Floriano Peixoto, the president of Brazil, and Admiral Custódio de Melo, the head of the Brazilian navy. They, too, seem to occupy opposing sides. But, deep down, they don't, they are the same, they mirror each other. The lust for power equalizes both the marshal and the admiral. Or rather, the *love* of power – with love, in this case, being the primary cause of the war. Love and war: opposing or complementary forces?

Machado's *crônica* doesn't take the discussion to this level of abstraction (love vs. war), or beyond the level of the popular saying ("love is a war"), or to the level of high-ranking military politicians (marshal vs. admiral). Why? Because, essentially, *crônica* is a lowbrow genre. It lives on the ground floor of the literary genres building. It stays at the level of the common people, like glaziers and notaries. It communicates in everyday language. It looks at events from afar and from the periphery. It capriciously shifts from one topic to another. It has a sharp eye for detail while ignoring the grandiose landscape.

Machado's *crônica* apparently refrains from discussing the political issues of the day, particularly the ongoing outcomes of the second Naval Revolt. The *cronista* seems unwilling to put his finger on this topic directly. However, he does – not by taking a side in the conflict but simply by showing us how the engine works. The *crônica*, in this regard, provokes the reader to ask what kind of fuel keeps this engine working, and how dangerous and destructive this engine can be, with powerful men making war and ordinary people trying to garner personal advantage from it.

The writer could, obviously, raise his voice to condemn the war and its atrocities (Lima Barreto did it, in a way, in the last chapters of his *Triste fim de Policarpo Quaresma* [*The Sad End of Policarpo Quaresma*]). But *crônica* isn't a channel for civil activism, and the *cronista* doesn't intend to "straighten out the crooked people in the world," as Machado said in 1878. *Crônica* is a hybrid form of literature and journalism, permanence and contingency, fiction and history. The *cronista*'s primary goal is to draw unchangeable meanings from transient events.

Machado didn't shut his eyes to the social issues surrounding him, as his detractors like to argue. He wasn't an aesthete who cared little or nothing about the main political topics of his days. As a citizen, Machado held his own political views. He was highly critical of the republican regime in Brazil, for instance, and we can read his criticism in his *crônicas*. But, as a journalist, Machado was a *cronista* – not a political analyst or a pamphleteer – and, as such, his main aim was to create an interval between events and the news, to set up a rhetorical space for readers to take a break from the political debate inevitably pervaded by lies, hypocrisy, greed, jealousy, and resentment. The role of Machado as a *cronista* was not to recycle these low sentiments and send them back to his readers. As the comments above on his *crônica* suggest, the role of the *cronista*'s calling was to lend a new frame through which to observe ongoing events, so they could be viewed from a different angle and by a different light.

This new frame entails digression (i.e. the art of transitioning from one topic to another) and irony, as we have seen, along with the confluence of history and fiction. Person and persona may converge in a *crônica*, but this convergence isn't imperative. In other words, the "I" of Machado the *cronista* doesn't necessarily mirror that of Machado the citizen. The anecdotes about the glazier and the notary were most likely fictional, although the idea behind them corresponds to that embraced by the actual flesh-and-bone Machado. We, the readers, then, can read Machado's *crônicas* either from a fictional or from a historical standpoint, or even both combined. The genre *crônica* stems from these double and conflicting dimensions: on the one hand, it is deeply grounded in the current events that the *cronista* observes and comments on; on the other hand, these comments, at times, transcend the historical facts by transforming their particular, accidental nature into universal claims. The *cronista*, then, goes into the changing nature of history to eventually draw out the unchanging laws of human nature. The *crônica*, in this respect, balances between ephemeral and metaphysical meanings.

Final Remarks

Diving into the circumstances of a historical fact to bring back a universal idea – a metaphysical concept or a moral meaning – was neither new nor original during Machado's lifetime. In fact, it's as old as Homer and his epics. If *crônica* as a genre presents any novelty, it is through the angle from which a historical episode is captured. If it were possible to take a modern *cronista* back to the time of the Trojan War and its aftermath, for instance, they would probably focus on the talk of the Trojan women while washing clothes at the banks of Scamander River; or how one of these women accidentally met the blacksmith who designed Achilles' helmet and how they started a forbidden affair; or how the Olympian gods overlooked this affair while laughing and dancing and refusing to rule over the fate of humanity; or what thoughts crossed Argos's mind when the dog saw his master, Odysseus, back in Ithaca twenty years after he left; or how Argos died with simplicity, without revealing the identity of his master; or, finally, what simplicity in the act of dying means.

Machado, by the way, loved dogs. He and Carolina didn't have children, but they did have a pet dog, Graziela, named after an Alphonse de Lamartine heroine. When Graziela died – old, blind, and toothless – Machado wrote a curious poem about her entitled "Um óbito" ("A Death"), which was published in 1892, in *Almanaque das Fluminenses* (*Almanack of Women from Rio*), but was never collected in a book.[36] Machado didn't approach this topic in a *crônica*, for it was too personal (hence why it was addressed in a poem). And *crônica* is not about the *cronista*, it's about time, instead (from the Greek term *chronos*, meaning *time*), the time of the *cronista*.

Thus, for instance, on December 29, 1895, Machado comments in a *crônica* on the recent news about a certain Mr. Estruc, who was swimming at Flamengo Beach, suffered a sudden discomfort (most likely cramps), and would have drowned had he not been rescued by his brave dog. The *cronista* draws on this news to reflect on the profound sentiment of gratitude dogs feel for their owners.[37]

In terms of animals, however, those most often referred to in Machado's *crônicas* are not dogs but (likely) donkeys. And this is not by chance, as far as I'm concerned. Through one of his characters, in the *crônica* dated February 13, 1889, Machado says, "if we find friendship in a dog, pride in a horse, etc., solely in a donkey we see philosophy."[38]

And Machado makes donkeys express their philosophical thoughts in two anthological *crônicas*: that of October 16, 1892, and that of April 8, 1894. In the former, the *cronista* gets on an animal trolley, pulled by two donkeys, at night. The city is quiet, the streets are empty, and he starts

---

36 See Augusto Fragoso, "Achegas à bibliografia machadiana," *Revista do Livro*, no. 11 (Sept. 1958), 137–39.
37 See Machado de Assis, [Crônica de 29 de dezembro de 1895], *Obra completa*, vol. III, 693–94.
38 Machado de Assis, Crônica 35, *Bons dias!*, ed. John Gledson (Campinas: Unicamp, 2008), 237.

listening to the conversation between the two donkeys. The electric trolley has just begun operating in Rio, and the animals talk about their future. One expects to retire soon. After all, with the electric coming in to replace the animal trolley, donkeys won't be useful anymore. The other, however, doesn't share the same optimism. Donkeys won't be useful to work in trolleys, but they will still be able to pull carts. Modernity, thus, doesn't come to save the donkeys or change their fate. Modernity comes just to change the hands that whip their loins.

The second *crônica* shows an abandoned, dying donkey lying on a vacant lot. The *cronista* approaches the animal as other passers-by are standing around with a mix of indifference and superiority as they watch the spectacle of death: the death of *the other*. The *cronista*, then, acts to humanize the donkey by deciphering his last thoughts. The animal reviews his whole existence as he lies at the threshold of death. His soul-searching doesn't convey despair or regret, though, but rather stoical serenity and conformity. If philosophizing is to learn how to die, as Cicero states via Montaigne,[39] this is what Machado's donkey somehow does via the *cronista*, who translates the animal's thoughts and feelings into human language.

In both *crônicas*, donkeys are philosophers – ironic philosophers in the first example and a tragic philosopher in the second. Also, in both examples, *crônica* borders on fable due to the presence of the talking animals. Despite its lightness, *crônica* can be surprisingly philosophical; despite being deeply rooted in social reality, it can, at times, incorporate fantastic elements. *Crônica*, in short, has a free form, and, as such, it relates closely to the formal experiments Machado implemented in his fictional works. *Brás Cubas*, for instance, balances ironic and tragic philosophy while its narrator writes his memoirs from the afterlife.

The bottom line is that there exists a synergy between Machado the *cronista* and Machado the fictionist that, to a degree, makes one resemble and complement the other. The inherent realism of the *crônica* as a genre, for instance, surely had an impact on Machado's fiction in its trajectory from Romanticism to Realism. In other words, the practice of writing *crônica* in the 1860s and 1870s somewhat pushed Machado away from Romanticism and towards Realism. This realism, though, could not be that of Zola and Eça. It had to be distinct and personal. This personalism has some of its roots in the *crônica* genre, with its informality, hummingbird-digressive style, and attentiveness to small things. "I enjoy picking

---

[39] See Michel de Montaigne, *The Complete Essays of Montaigne*, trans. Donald M. Frame (Stanford: Stanford UP, 1958), 56.

the minimal and hidden things. Where no one sticks their nose, I stick mine, with a close and sharp curiosity that unveils what goes undercover."[40] These words are from Machado the *cronista*, but they could also be from the fictionist; or rather, they accurately describe his prose fiction.

In the next two chapters, while discussing some of Machado's major stories and novels, we'll expand more on this idea.

---

40 Machado de Assis, *Obra completa*, vol. III, 772.

Figure 1. Machado de Assis, c. 1864, by José Insley Pacheco, Academia Brasileira de Letras.

Figure 2. Machado de Assis, c. 1880, by Marc Ferrez.

Figure 3. Portrait of Machado de Assis, in O *Álbum*, Ano I, n° 2, January 1893.

Figure 4. Carolina Augusta Xavier de Novais, when she was 44. Picture by Pacheco & Filho. Arquivo Nacional (Brasil), Fundo Correio da Manhã.

Figure 5. The house where Machado lived in the neighborhood of Cosme Velho.

Chapter Five

Short Stories: The Dialectical Other

What Is Dialectics?

YOU MIGHT HAVE heard about Hegel's dialectics. You might have also heard about Marx's dialectical materialism, which was Marx's response, or reaction, to Hegel's proposition. Both Hegel and Marx were highly influential nineteenth-century thinkers; we can, thus, conclude that the nineteenth century and the dialectical method have a significant connection. This doesn't mean, however, that dialectics is a concept born in the nineteenth century: the history of the concept goes back to ancient Greece and Plato. Defining dialectics, therefore, is not all that easy. Without going into the specifics just yet, we can come up with a fair, relatively simple, and helpful definition.

Imagine that everything in this world has a double. Not a double like a doppelgänger, such as William Wilson in Poe's homonymous story, or Borges himself in "El otro" ("The Other"), but double in a sense that every unity contains within itself two conflicting forces. For instance, every human being (a unity) consists of a material body and a non-material, abstract soul; or, in Freud's theory, every mind (a unity) is comprised of consciousness and the unconscious. For a unity to exist, in brief, these opposing forces – body/soul; consciousness/the unconscious – must function in conjunction. If you separate them, the unity falls apart. What we call the dialectical method, then, can be roughly described as an analytical mode that reflects on and unveils the nature and the role of the element placed on the other side of the unity's spectrum – like soul in relation to body, the unconscious in relation to consciousness, or the non-Western aspects of Brazilian culture in relation to the Western ones.

In Chapter Three, I argued that "Brazilian culture is deeply rooted in a complex dialectics of conflicting forces between Western and non-Western (i.e. African and Indigenous) values." Therefore, what upholds Brazil as a unity is this permanent clash of vectors that pushes Brazilian culture in distinct and, at times, opposing directions; this clash can be summarized, parodically speaking, through the dilemma: "To be or not to be *Western?*" That is to say, under the appearance of "Westerness," there is a set of fundamentally non-European practices and ideas which shape Brazilian culture while also constantly defying Brazil's Western heritage. In this respect, or in this "Westerness dialectics,"[1] the non-Western values represent the *dialectical other* of Brazilian culture.

So, what is dialectics, again, in the context of this chapter? Simply put, it is the composite of two contrasting parts – one manifested and the other concealed – that makes the existence of a given unity fully fledged. What role does this concept play in Machado's stories? It is possible to identify a dialectical approach to human behavior and social reality in his tales. By and large, we will build our analysis on this approach. Let me start, then, by illustrating the interrelated concepts of *dialectical approach* and *dialectical other* through a fictional passage from a story by the nineteenth-century Russian author Anton Chekhov. The story is "The Lady with the Dog," and it was published in 1899. Let's dive in.

A Literary Example: Chekhov and Machado

In Chekhov's story, the protagonist, Dmitri Gurov, has a "double life." But he doesn't fully realize it until a moment, towards the end of the story, when he suddenly recognizes his duality. Gurov is a married man, who is having an affair with a married woman whom he casually encountered during a vacation in Yalta. In the last section of the narrative, he takes his daughter to school before heading to meet his lover at an obscure place in Moscow. His daughter asks him a question about nature. While answering her, Gurov starts thinking about his whole situation:

> As he [Gurov] was speaking, he kept reminding himself that he was going to a rendezvous and that not a living soul knew about it, or, probably, ever would. He led a double life – one in public, in the sight of all whom it concerned, full of conventional truth and conventional

---

[1] Mario Higa, *Modos de leitura: crítica & tradução* (Cotia: Ateliê, 2022), 164. The original phrasing is "Dialética da Ocidentalidade."

deception, exactly like the lives of his friends and acquaintances, and another which flowed in secret. And, owing to some strange, possibly quite accidental chain of circumstances, everything that was important, interesting, essential, everything about which he was sincere and never deceived himself, everything that composed the kernel of his life, went on in secret, while everything that was false in him, everything that composed the husk in which he hid himself and the truth which was in him – his work at the bank, discussions at the club, his "lower race," his attendance at anniversary celebrations with his wife – was on the surface. He began to judge others by himself, no longer believing what he saw, and always assuming that the real, the only interesting life of every individual goes on as under cover of night, secretly. Every individual existence revolves around mystery, and perhaps that is the chief reason that all cultivated individuals insisted so strongly on the respect due to personal secrets.[2]

In this passage, Gurov has a sudden and startling revelation: "the only interesting life of every individual goes on as under cover of night, secretly." He abruptly realizes that truth flows "in secret," while lies dwell "on the surface" of things. There is a private, rich, true life for Gurov that exists behind his social image, or "the husk in which he hid[es] himself." And for Chekhov, as well as Machado, one of the goals of fiction consists in dialectically dealing with this complex dichotomy so that the concealed truth can reveal itself. The act of coaxing truth to emerge from hiding, rise to the surface, and reveal itself through a "quite accidental chain of circumstances" is – to parody Chekhov's wording – "the kernel of *fiction's* life."

Machado, for his part, addresses the dialectics between the social "I" and the secret, or the other, "I" in one of his best-known stories: "O espelho" ("The Mirror"). In this tale, the main character, João Jacobina, narrates an episode of his life to illustrate his "new theory of the human soul" – "A Brief Outline of a New Theory of the Human Soul" is the story's subtitle. According to Jacobina and his theory, "every human creature contains two souls: one that looks inside out, and the other that looks from the outside in," the latter being the external soul which, when combined with the internal one, "complete[s] the man."[3] Jacobina is a middle-aged man

---

[2] Anton Chekhov, "The Lady with the Dog," trans. Ivy Litvinov, *Anton Chekhov's Short Stories*, ed. Ralph E. Matlaw (New York: W. W. Norton & Company, 1979), 233.

[3] All citations from Machado's "The Mirror" come from *The Collected Stories of Machado de Assis*, trans. Margaret Jull Costa & Robin Patterson (New York:

when he recounts the episode that occurred when he was 25 years old. At that younger age, as a poor man, he was made a second lieutenant in the National Guard, "the very lowest rank of commissioned officer." Despite being a lowly position, the event of Jacobina's promotion had a huge impact on his family: his mother – who then insisted on addressing him as "*her* lieutenant" – along with his cousins, aunts, uncles, "everyone was bursting with the purest, sincerest joy."

One of his aunts, Dona Marcolina, begs Jacobina to come and see her at her "remote and isolated farm" located "many leagues from town," and to bring his military uniform. At his aunt's request, Jacobina decides to go for a brief visit. Excited by her nephew's presence on her property, Dona Marcolina declares she won't let Jacobina return home "for at least a month." "And how she hugged me!" says Jacobina, who concludes: "She, too, called me *her* lieutenant." This turns out to be just a fraction of the reverential treatment he receives while in his aunt's house:

> She [Aunt Marcolina] pronounced me a handsome devil and, being a rather jolly sort herself, even confessed to envying the girl who would one day be my wife. She declared that there was not a man in the entire province who was my equal. And it was always lieutenant this, lieutenant that, every hour of the day or night. I asked her to call me Joãozinho as she used to, but she shook her head, exclaiming that, no, I was "Senhor Lieutenant" and that was that. One of her brothers-in-law, her late husband's brother, who lived in the house, also refused to address me in any other way. I was "Senhor Lieutenant" not in jest but perfectly seriously, and in front of the slaves as well, who naturally followed suit. I sat at the head of the table and was always served first.

To honor the presence of "Senhor Lieutenant" still further, Aunt Marcolina places the most dignified piece of furniture in the house in her nephew's room: a large mirror, which had been given to Aunt Marcolina by her godmother, "who had inherited it from her mother, who had bought it from one of the Portuguese noblewomen who came to Brazil in 1808 with the rest of King João VI's court." This show of attention, affection, and kindness brings about a transformation in the young Jacobina, who, in one key passage of the narrative, defines this change by stating that "The officer eliminated the man."

Jacobina describes this transformational process in terms of a fight, a combat, a battle, out of which his "original nature gave way to the other;

Liveright, 2018), 444–52. For the sake of readability, I'm not adding footnotes for each quoted section related to this source.

only a tiny part of [his] humanity remained." Up until that point, Jacobina's *external soul* had been "the sun, the air, the rolling countryside, and the eyes of young women." Then, it became the bowing, the flattery, the compliments, all the adulatory treatment that took place in the house; "everything," says Jacobina, "that spoke to me of my rank, and nothing about me, the man."

After three weeks, not even a tiny part of Jacobina's humanity remains: he is "all lieutenant and nothing else." At this point, the narrative takes a turn. Aunt Marcolina receives news that her daughter, who lives 5 leagues away, is ill, "perhaps dying." She leaves the farm with her brother-in-law and asks Jacobina to stay and take charge of the property, which he does. Left alone with a couple of enslaved individuals, Jacobina feels his external soul "contracting," "for now it was limited to a handful of half savages," he says, and comments that "the officer continued to hold sway within me, albeit less intensely alive and less fiercely conscious."

The narrative then takes another turn. The enslaved people plot an escape and run away during the night. "I found myself," says Jacobina, "completely alone, with no one else within the four walls of the house, staring out at the deserted yard and empty countryside beyond. Not a single human breath."

Jacobina thinks of going out to meet his aunt to tell her that the enslaved people have run away, but he soon gives up the idea. It would only heighten Aunt Marcolina's distress "without providing any remedy." After three days of complete solitude, Jacobina begins "to feel decidedly odd, like someone who has lost all sensation in his nerves and can no longer feel his muscle move." Minutes, hours, and days last an eternity. Jacobina tries to read, to write, to do gymnastic exercises, but nothing, absolutely nothing works. Without recognition, his external soul gradually fades away, slowly dying out. Jacobina states he would have definitely preferred literal death to being what he was: "a dead man walking, a sleepwalker, a mechanical toy." Sleeping and dreaming were the only relief he had: "in eliminating the need for an external soul, sleep gives free rein to the internal one," he explains. However, on waking, he realizes that his "internal soul had lost its exclusive power of action, and was once again dependent upon the other, the external soul, which stubbornly refused to return."

At this point, the story is about to reach its climax. "There's worse to come," warns Jacobina, who tells his story to an audience of four curious men. While alone, Jacobina hadn't even once looked in the mirror. Not for any specific reason, though. Perhaps, he was unconsciously fearful of finding two of him, "at the same time, in that solitary house." The ambiguous atmosphere of the story continues to thicken. "If that is the true explanation [i.e. that Jacobina was fearful of finding two of him by looking in the mirror]," says Jacobina, "then there is no better proof of man's contradictory nature, for, a week later, I got it into my head to look at the mirror with precisely the aim of seeing myself twice over." After a week of total loneliness, Jacobina stands in front of the mirror and recoils. The glass doesn't show him "as a sharp, complete image, but as something vague and hazy, diffuse, a shadow of a shadow."

It's worth noting that Jacobina, with this remark, doesn't lead the story into the realm of the supernatural, as could easily have happened. It remains a realistic tale. As such, the narrator – after losing his self-image – observes: "The laws of physics will not allow me to deny that the mirror did indeed reproduce my shape and features accurately, for it must have done, but that was not what my senses told me." This is to say, although the mirror reflects Jacobina's image, Jacobina himself cannot see his image reflected in it. At this point, he fears for his sanity and decides to leave. He starts getting dressed when "some inexplicable flash of inspiration" gives him an idea: to put on his lieutenant's uniform. "I did so," reveals Jacobina, "every last bit of it, and, as I stood in front of the mirror, I raised my eyes and ... I hardly need say it: the mirror now showed my whole figure, with not a feature or a line out of place." The lieutenant, says Jacobina, "had finally rediscovered his external soul."

Every day, for two to three hours, Jacobina now puts on his lieutenant's uniform and sits in front of the mirror, "reading, looking, and meditating." By sticking to this habit, he was able to endure the following days of solitude, "without the slightest problem."

The Dialectical Other as the "Other"

The above summary of Machado's "O espelho," albeit long, does not reflect all the complexities associated with the story's structure. But it's useful, anyway, for our purpose of illustrating Machado's dialectics. His approach to the topic is different from that of Chekhov. For the Russian author, as we saw in the passage above, every human is a dual being comprising an external appearance (i.e. the social "I," whose actions are controlled by social forces) and an internal essence (i.e. the true self, hidden inside or behind the social "I," waiting to emerge). Implicit in this theory is the idea that we should find our true selves behind the masks that society constantly forces on us – the Freudian notion of the unconscious somehow relates to this idea. We can then conclude that appearance versus essence, each in opposition to the another, constitute the basic dichotomic elements of Chekhov's dialectics.

In Machado's dialectics, as shown in "O espelho," the opposing elements of appearance versus essence also repeat themselves; their dynamics, however, are fundamentally *othered*, since, for Machado, appearance coincides with essence, or rather, appearance *is* essence. When, in the story, the "officer eliminated the man," appearance, or the *external soul*, became the essence of Jacobina's identity. Essence, therefore, functions as an empty mold to be filled up with the external soul which, for its turn, can vary depending upon the circumstances. "I know a lady," says Jacobina, "who changes her external soul five or six times a year." The nature of any essence lies in its immutability. So here is one conclusion according to a syllogistic logic: if, as Jacobina's story shows, appearance *is* essence, and appearance is also mutable, then *essence doesn't exist* since the nature of essence lies in its immutability. Or, to put it another way, in every human psyche, appearance and essence wrestle to take control over one another by fighting a life-and-death battle. In the case of Jacobina, appearance (or the *external soul*) won, and, consequently, suppressed essence.

But, in the story, there is a pivotal detail: the *weapon* used by appearance to defeat essence was ... the mirror. Two mirrors, more specifically. The sight of the Other (family members, friends, enslaved people) was the first mirror.[4] In the eyes of the Other, Jacobina's external soul consolidated itself and gained ground. When the Other vanished completely, the lieutenant's external soul became debilitated and almost lost its battle against the internal one. That's when the second mirror, the literal mirror, was called in. It doesn't reflect the man since the lieutenant had "eliminated" the man, but the lieutenant himself had also lost his image. At this point in the story, Jacobina lives in a sort of an existential limbo, a parenthetical time wherein he is neither the lieutenant nor the man, not appearance nor essence, not dead nor alive; he is, in his own words, "a dead man walking." Jacobina the lieutenant recovers his image and regains his strength only when he gets dressed in his military uniform and stands in front of the mirror. Although temporary, the reflection of the mirror replaces the eyes of the Other, which, in a larger sense, represents social recognition.

---

4   Alfredo Bosi, *Machado de Assis: O enigma do olhar* (São Paulo: Ática, 2003), 99.

Hegel's Dialectics

"O espelho" can be read as a modern fable, or a theory-tale, about human consciousness. Its modernity, though, has Shakespearean roots. Jacobina himself declares it in quoting *The Merchant of Venice* to explain the concept of external soul: "Shylock, for example. The external soul of that particular Jew was his ducats; to lose them was the same as dying. 'I shall never see my gold again,' he says to Tubal; *'thou stick'st a dagger in me.'*" Nonetheless, despite Shakespeare's presence, it's possible to read Machado's story also in parallel with Hegel's dialectics of the lord and the bondsman (a.k.a. the master–slave dialectics), which he developed in his 1807 *Phenomenology of Spirit*.

This dialectics occupies paragraphs 178 to 196 of *Phenomenology of Spirit*.[5] In this short section, Hegel creates an allegory to expatiate on the nature of self-consciousness. The allegory's underlying question could be summarized as follows: can we legitimize our existence and find true meaning in it without the endorsement of other human beings? Or rather, can human consciousness be fully aware of itself, or simply *be*, independent from other human consciousnesses? Hegel, then, imagines a context in which two self-consciousnesses "prove themselves and each other through a life-and-death struggle."[6] The allegory that expresses this struggle involves a lord, the one who achieves recognition, and a bondsman, the one who recognizes. The implications of this strife go beyond the scope of our analysis; the point to be underlined here is the issue of pure individuality as a self-resourceful existential entity (consider, for instance, Descartes' famous proposition "I think, therefore, I am"). For Hegel, and for Machado, "human existence is primordially a matter of mutual recognition, and it is only through mutual recognition that we are self-aware and strive for the social meanings in our lives."[7] In other words, "otherness cannot be abolished or destroyed, without destroying oneself."[8] In "O espelho," the complete absence of Otherness (i.e. social recognition) pushes Jacobina's existential life to the edge of self-destruction.

---

5 G. W. F. Hegel, *Phenomenology of Spirit*, trans. A. V. Miller (Oxford: Oxford UP, 1977), 111–19.
6 Ibid., 113–14.
7 Robert Solomon, *Continental Philosophy Since 1750: The Rise and Fall of Self* (Oxford: Oxford UP, 1988), 68.
8 David Duquette, "Hegel: Social and Political Thought," *Internet Encyclopedia of Philosophy*, https://iep.utm.edu/hegelsoc/#H4

Brazilian Metaphysics?

For Machado's detractors, "O espelho" constitutes one glaring example – among others – of how Brazil or Brazilian themes are out of sight in Machado's fiction. After all, the story is a philosophical tale about true self and self-identity with no connection to the local culture beyond the fact that the narrative takes place in some rural area in the state of Rio de Janeiro. In this respect, Machado prefers to be engaged in metaphysical issues over those of national history. It would be true if it weren't for one tiny detail: the history of the mirror, as briefly mentioned in the summary of the story above. Here it is again so we can take a closer look at it:

> It [the mirror] had been given to her [Aunt Marcolina] by her godmother, who had inherited it from her mother, who had bought it from one of the Portuguese noblewomen who came to Brazil in 1808 with the rest of King João VI's court. I don't know how much truth there was in this story, but that was the family tradition. Naturally, the mirror was very old, but you could still see the gilding, eaten away by time, a couple of carved dolphins in the top corners of the frame, a few bits of mother-of-pearl, and other such artistic flourishes. All rather old, but very good quality.

"If Machado's aim were only philosophical (i.e. concerned [with] the 'soul' and the question of personal identity)," notes John Gledson, "surely any mirror would do." And he asks: "Why mention the rotted frame and the tradition that it came from the Portuguese court?"[9]

We learned in Chapter One that the Portuguese royal family transferred the court to Rio de Janeiro in 1808. We commented, too, on what this transfer represented for Brazil, and the many, deep changes it brought. Indeed, it's possible to draw a parallel between the country in 1808 and Jacobina in Machado's story. Both have their status significantly increased; Brazil starts the process of becoming a modern nation, and Jacobina begins his career as an officer in the National Guard. Both also initiate a journey towards finding their own identities. In this regard, as Gledson notes, Jacobina and the mirror reflect each other: "Jacobina, too, is an empty space surrounded by a decorative frame – the uniform he puts on to protect himself from disappearing."[10] In terms of identity,

---

9 John Gledson, "Brazilian History in Machado de Assis's *Papéis Avulsos*," *Portuguese Studies*, vol. 11 (1995), 113.
10 Ibid., 113.

Brazil bears a resemblance to Jacobina. The country as well, in 1808, was "an empty space," or a blurry image of itself, "surrounded by a decorative frame": the legacy of the Portuguese culture that Brazil inherited, and that was seen as worn and obsolete.

The issue of recognition, or to be seen in the eyes of the Other, is pivotal to young Jacobina as well as young Brazil. Both are in search of validation from, respectively, other people and other nations. Such validation would corroborate their ascending social status and economic prosperity. If this parallelism between Jacobina and Brazil is correct, as Gledson proposes it to be, the story opens up two hermeneutical avenues for readers to explore: the philosophical and the social-historical; or even both, since they are not, in principle, mutually exclusive.

"O espelho" and Other Stories

At the time of writing, "O espelho" has five translations – or one translation and four retranslations – into English.[11] This number speaks for itself of the literary importance of Machado's story. What other nineteenth-century foreign author has five or more English versions of one of their stories? Certainly not many. What nineteenth-century *Latin American* author has five or more English versions of one of their stories? To the best of my knowledge, only Machado de Assis. And, speaking of numbers, let's take a brief look at a few more noteworthy stats.

From 1858 to 1906, Machado wrote about 200 stories. According to Cláudio Weber Abramo, who has researched this topic in depth, Machado wrote "at least 206 stories."[12] Luis Filipe Ribeiro opines that the final figure may actually be 218.[13] The authorship of a few of these tales has been questioned as several of them were published under pen names.[14] Unquestionably, of *about* 200, 76 were included in the seven volumes of

---

[11] "The Looking Glass," 1963, Helen Caldwell; "The Mirror," 1995, Wilson Loria; "The Mirror," 2008, John Gledson; "The Looking Glass," 2013, John Chasteen; and "The Mirror," 2018, Margaret Jull Costa & Robin Patterson.

[12] Cláudio Weber Abramo, "Distorções perpétuas." *Folha de São Paulo*, Oct. 1, 2000. Available at: www1.folha.uol.com.br/fsp/mais/fs0110200006.htm

[13] Luis Filipe Ribeiro, "Machado, um contista desconhecido," *Machado de Assis em linha*, no. 1 (2008), 10. Available at: http://machadodeassis.fflch.usp.br/sites/machadodeassis.fflch.usp.br/files/u73/numo1artigo02.pdf

[14] See Jean-Michel Massa, *A juventude de Machado de Assis*, trans. Marco Aurélio de Moura Matos (Rio de Janeiro: Civilização Brasileira, 1971), 552–65.

stories that Machado published during his lifetime. Here is a list of the volumes:

> *Contos fluminenses* (*Rio Tales*), 1870
> *Histórias da meia-noite* (*Midnight Tales*), 1873
> *Papéis avulsos* (*Miscellaneous Papers*), 1882
> *Histórias sem data* (*Undated Stories*), 1884
> *Várias histórias* (*Assorted Stories*), 1896
> *Páginas recolhidas* (*Collected Pages*), 1899
> *Relíquias de casa velha* (*Relics from an Old House*), 1906

"O espelho" appeared in the 1882 collection *Papéis avulsos* after being published that same year in the pages of the periodical *Gazeta de Notícias* (seventeen years, therefore, prior to Chekhov's "The Lady with the Dog"). For these stories, too, we can draw a line that separates the pre-1880 Machado from the post-1880 one. "O espelho" was written by the latter. Beyond its historical importance and centrality in Machado's oeuvre, the story typifies the philosophic-psychological idea of human duality – the "I" and its dialectical other – as developed in Machado's other narratives. In "O espelho," however, this duality reveals a third element: the eyes of the Other, or Hegelian otherness, described as an establishing factor of human existence and a shaping component of human personality. Also, the story incorporates, with Machadian subtlety, aspects of Brazilian history which – far from being merely decorative – enable the narrative to generate parallel, alternative meanings. Jacobina as a metaphor for the country, as Gledson proposes it, doesn't invalidate the philosophic-psychological approach but rather opens up another possibility of approach – or another *story*, if you will – to be explored.

That said, it's time to clarify the strategy adopted here in presenting Machado's stories. While planning this chapter, two basic options came to the fore: either offering a broad overview of Machado as a story-writer by making brief remarks on dozens of his most famous narratives, or examining a few of them in depth. It was like choosing between surfing and diving. And after weighing the pros and cons of each method, I decided to dive. Why? Machado is a complex author; by choosing to comment on a handful of his tales, I intend to provide a brief glimpse of this complexity. At the end of this chapter, I've provided you with a short list of Machado's top stories.

Dialectics, or the dialectical other, or even the dialectical method, has functioned in this chapter as a conceptual common ground, or a unifying concept, to examine across each of the stories presented. There isn't, as you may imagine, a single critical key capable of opening all 200 of Machado's stories. It's possible, though, to assert broadly that Machado's fiction is driven by an impulse to go beyond appearances; to reveal what is behind social reality; to investigate the hidden, deep meanings inside the attributed, superficial ones. It's not by accident, therefore, that Machado's works relate to Hegel's, and even more closely to Marx's, Nietzsche's, and Freud's. All of them were dialectical thinkers. All of them dealt with the immeasurable complexities of the human mind, not just to disclose concealed secrets, as in a game of hide-and-seek, but ultimately to force us to face up to the most frightening parts of ourselves, as in a "life-and-death struggle."

Dialectics and Feminism: "Missa do galo"

Now, it's time to keep the promise I made in Chapter One: to examine "Missa do galo" ("Midnight Mass"). In this story, as I said, nothing happens except a miracle. Or, to put it another way, a miracle happens where apparently nothing happens. But first: an important note about the context.

As mentioned, we don't know for certain how many stories Machado wrote, since a number of them were written under pseudonyms and were only later ascribed to him. According to Luis Filipe Ribeiro's calculation – also mentioned earlier – he wrote 218. Let's take that figure for our purposes. We know for sure that 8 of the 76 stories which appeared in book form were never published before. This means that 210 out of 218 stories were published in periodicals. Which periodicals? The most relevant, quantitatively speaking, were *Jornal das Famílias*, *Gazeta de Notícias*, and *A Estação*. In the first, Machado published 85 stories; in the second, 53; and in the third, 43.[15] These three periodicals, thereby, received 181 of Machado's stories, or more than 80% of his entire output in the genre.

Of these three periodicals, two – *Jornal das Famílias* and *A Estação* – were illustrated publications dedicated to a specific target audience: the family woman, be she young or mature. This means that the 128 narratives Machado wrote for these magazines – almost 60% of his stories – were addressed primarily (though not exclusively) to women. The creation and release of these 128 narratives was spread over thirty years – from 1868, when Machado's stories started appearing in *Jornal das Famílias*, to 1898, the year of his last contribution to *A Estação*. We can conclude from this

---

15 Luis Filipe Ribeiro, "Machado, um contista desconhecido," 12.

context that Machado grew largely as a fictionist by writing to a female audience. This somehow explains two hallmarks of his fiction: his extraordinary ability to create female characters (he needed to deeply understand his female audience to establish a fruitful communication with them), and his mark of feminism, as already discussed in Chapter Three.

"Missa do galo" is a story that contains a feminist infra-message and a memorable female character, Conceição. The story was published in 1894 in the periodical *A Semana* – which was not a gender-specific publication – and republished in 1899 in *Páginas recolhidas*. In terms of length, "Missa do galo" is about 20% shorter than "O espelho" – it's truly Machado's style at its best. In terms of plot, it could be outlined as simply a vague, ambiguous, and brief conversation between a 30-year-old woman, Conceição, and a 17-year-old male student, Nogueira, on the night of Christmas Eve. This conversation, however, generates *parallel plots* which are not directly expressed in the story. It's up to us, the readers, to gather the scattered clues and assemble these secret, latent plots.

The story's famous opening line sets the tone and the main structural elements of the narrative: "I've never quite understood a conversation I had with a lady many years ago, when I was seventeen and she was thirty."[16] The narrator, Nogueira, is trying to reconstruct an event from years past with the help of his memory. At the time of the event, he was a student from a town, Mangaratiba, that lies approximately 85 kilometers from Rio. He had gone to the court a few months before with the aim of studying for his "university entrance exams." While in Rio, Nogueira stayed in the house of the notary Meneses, who had been married to Nogueira's cousin. Meneses' second wife is Conceição. In the house, besides the couple, live Dona Inácia, Conceição's mother, and two enslaved women.

Once a week, the notary went to the theater and did not return home until the following morning. After some time, and some gaffes, Nogueira learned that *going to the theater* was a "euphemism in action." Meneses was, in fact, having an "affair with a lady who was separated from her husband." And Conceição was aware of it. At first, she was deeply wounded by the discovery; as time went by, though, she "resigned herself," grew "accustomed to the situation," and, in the end, "decided that there was nothing untoward" or even blameworthy "about it at all."

---

16 All citations from Machado's "Midnight Mass" come from *The Collected Stories of Machado de Assis*, trans. Margaret Jull Costa & Robin Patterson, 806–13. For the sake of readability, I'm not adding footnotes for each quoted section related to this source.

Nogueira provides the reader with a physical as well moral portrait of Conceição. Here it is. We'll comment on it below.

> Good, kind Conceição! People called her "a saint," and she did full justice to that title, given how easily she put up with her husband's neglect. Hers was a very moderate nature, with no extremes, no tearful tantrums, and no great outbursts of hilarity. In this respect, she would have been fine as a Muslim woman and would have been quite happy in a harem, as long as appearances were maintained. May God forgive me if I'm misjudging her, but everything about her was contained and passive. Even her face was average, neither pretty nor ugly. She was what people call "a nice person." She never spoke ill of anyone and was very forgiving. She wouldn't have known how to hate anyone, nor, perhaps, how to love them.

Nogueira's description of Conceição plays a crucial role in the narrative. The "no extremes," "neither-nor," "very moderate" depiction of her ends up depriving her of everything remarkable: she has neither personality nor beauty (or ugliness). Her "niceness," in the end, means nothingness. Her "averageness" means emptiness. As described, Conceição appears to be, fundamentally, a nonentity. Her humiliating existence blanks her out. Like Jacobina in his loneliness, Conceição is a "shadow of a shadow." However, in the case of Jacobina, the lack of Otherness transforms him into that shadow; in the case of Conceição, the Other, i.e. the oppressive patriarchal culture, as embodied in the character of Meneses, is the factor responsible for her transfiguration.

Once a week, Meneses humiliates Conceição by "going to the theater." It's worth noting, in this regard, that male adultery was then widely practiced and normalized in Brazil. The leniency of Brazilian legislation regarding male adultery fostered this situation (on the other side of the spectrum, the legal response to female adultery was much more severe).[17] Although widespread and normalized, that didn't mean male adultery had no effect on the wives, like Conceição, who had to deal morally with it. It surely did. And Machado's story tackles this delicate matter.

But, at the same time, wives were, for the most part, totally dependent on their husbands. They had to learn by themselves how to endure and cope with this situation with no help from Brazil's social and legal systems. For women in nineteenth-century Brazil, marriage was a *career*. First, they had to *get a job* by marrying a man; then, they had to maintain

---

17 Gustavo Silveira Siqueira, "Uma história do crime de adultério no Império do Brasil (1830–1889)," *História do Direito: RHD*, vol. I, no. 1 (2020), 122–31.

their position in the marriage. Sticking with this metaphor, Conceição *got a job* – a good one, where she could bring along her mother. Conceição, therefore, had to be grateful that Meneses accepted her and her mother, Dona Inácia, into his house. Otherwise, she would have had a huge problem on her hands. After all, her mother depends on her, and she, in turn, depends on Meneses, and he, in his turn, depends on someone else in his work more powerful than him. In this chain of dependencies, the more dependent a person is, the less powerful they are. And, in Meneses' house, everybody depends on him; everybody, thus, must subject themselves to him in order to survive. The subjection to the patriarch (i.e. Meneses) is a life-and-death issue for Conceição, as is the subjection to social recognition for Jacobina in "O espelho."

However, in "O espelho," this issue receives a primarily existential frame; whereas, in "Missa do galo," the frame is heavily social. Also, if the "officer eliminated the man" in the former story, the submissive wife didn't eliminate the woman in the latter, as we shall see. This is quite understandable if we think that being an officer, or lieutenant in the National Guard, was a socially desirable position for a young, poor man like Jacobina. When Jacobina the officer experiences overt flattery, he uses his power to overthrow Jacobina the man. As a poor woman, Conceição's condition is entirely different. Although marrying a man was critical for her and her mother's survival (the other option would be living on the streets, or in complete poverty), being a married woman entailed acting as an obedient wife – a role far from desirable for those who had to play it. On the night of Christmas Eve in "1861 or 1862," however, Conceição plays another, more pleasant, role. At least, in the eyes of Nogueira, the narrator of "Missa do galo."

On that night, "the notary went off to the theater," says Nogueira, who, at that point, should have been back in Mangaratiba for the holiday but decided to extend his stay in the court a few more days because he "wanted to see what midnight mass was like in the big city." Customarily, everybody in Meneses' house retires to bed at 10 p.m. and falls soundly asleep half an hour later. With Meneses out and the women of the house sleeping, Nogueira remains awake in the front room while he waits just before midnight, at which time he can leave without disturbing anyone and call on a neighbor to wake him up and take him to midnight mass. To fill the time, he reads. Nogueira has with him an edition of Dumas' *The Three Musketeers* and, "by the light of an oil lamp, while the rest of the house [is] sleeping," he "climb[s] onto D'Artagnan's scrawny horse and set[s] off on adventure."

When the clock strikes eleven, Nogueira hears footsteps which rouse him from his reading. "I looked up," he says, "and, soon afterward, saw Conceição appear in the doorway." The original sentence reads (italics mine): "levantei a cabeça; logo depois vi *assomar* à porta da sala o *vulto* de Conceição." In Portuguese, the verb *assomar* presents at least two meanings: "to appear" and "to ascend, to go up, to appear at the top of a high place." Its Latin root, *summus*, means "the highest point (of something)."[18] This second meaning often has a religious use, and it recalls Conceição as she was previously described as "a saint." The noun *vulto*, for its part, is also ambiguous and is thus employed in the sentence; it means, vaguely, "someone with a particular type of appearance," but it also means "someone who is important," like the word *figure* in English. So, when Conceição first appears in the narrative here, she is surrounded by an atmosphere of ambiguity. She is someone simply coming into sight, like an appearance, but she is also someone who is unexpectedly *becoming visible*, like an *apparition*. After emerging in the scene, Conceição asks Nogueira: "Still here?" This utterance is the first time we, as the readers, hear her voice: the voice of a voiceless woman.

From this line on, the narrative gains the structure of a drama. We watch the strange dialogue between a mature woman, Conceição, and a young student, Nogueira, in the dark living room of a small, cozy house in Rio, on Christmas Eve, about an hour before midnight. On this night, Meneses isn't the only one who "goes to the theater"; Conceição does, too. Each in their own way, of course. In the case of Conceição, she enters onto the "stage" of her living room and plays the role of a character who has been out (and ousted) for a good while: she plays the part of *herself*. "Still here?" With this utterance, the voiceless woman eventually recovers her voice.

After asking Nogueira that question, Conceição comes into the room. It's a magical entrance: her "white dressing gown, loosely tied at the waist," with the contours of her thin body seen through the fabric illuminated by the oil lamp, "lent her a romantic air, rather in keeping," says Nogueira, "with my adventurous story." Nogueira, who is then "completely intoxicated by [the story of] Dumas," will become vertiginously intoxicated by Conceição. Not the Conceição he met a few months ago and became accustomed to by living in the same house; but *another* Conceição, full of mysterious enchantment, like a romantic character, who reveals herself to Nogueira only that night.

---

18 *Dicionário Houaiss da língua portuguesa* (Rio de Janeiro: Objetiva, 2001), 324.

In consonance with the title, "Missa do galo" narrates a story of an epiphanic revelation: the apparition of a woman. Conceição's presence fills the room: she leads the conversation, moves around with grace, gets closer to Nogueira, brings the talking down to a whispering volume so her "Mama" won't wake. She is a woman. She dominates the scene with her will and beauty. Because now she *is*, or rather, *becomes* beautiful: "One memory does still remain fresh," says Nogueira, "at one point, she, who I had only thought of as 'nice-looking' before, looked really pretty, positively lovely." That's the epiphanic moment, the revelation, the miracle. After all, it is Christmas time. Magic is in the air.

Nevertheless, although Conceição has the name of a Catholic saint, and this is referred to in the narrative – "In my prayer niche," Conceição says to Nogueira, "I have a really beautiful statuette of Our Lady of the Conception ["Conceição," in Portuguese], my patron saint"; and "people" also "called [Conceição] 'a saint,'" – the miracle that Nogueira attests and of which he gives us an account is not divine in nature. Conceição is not a saint. She is, instead, a sexualized woman: a woman sexually repressed, full of sexual energy. Sexuality, thus, pervades the entire conversation of that night, and it reaches its climax in the following passage:

> She [Conceição] gradually leaned forward, resting her elbows on the marble table-top, her face cupped in her outspread hands. Her unbuttoned sleeves fell back to reveal her forearms, which were very pale and plumper than one might have expected. This was not exactly a novelty, although it wasn't a common sight, either; at that moment, however, it made a great impression on me. Her veins were so blue that, despite the dim light, I could count every one. Her presence was even better at keeping me awake than my book.

The miracle that happens that night of Christmas Eve – let me repeat – consists of the apparition of a woman; a woman of flesh and blood and "veins" and desire; a woman to the fullest extent of her womanness; a woman who progresses from exhibiting "a romantic air … in keeping with [Dumas'] adventure story" to being "better at keeping [Nogueira] awake than [Dumas'] book"; from "neither pretty nor ugly" to "really pretty, positively lovely." In brief, in an adverse soil poisoned with systemic patriarchalism and female oppression, Conceição manages to bloom beautifully. Even though it's only for an hour, she still does it. Miraculously, she does it. So much so that even the perception of time gets lost in this miraculous moment. At one point, someone bangs on the window outside and shouts: "Midnight mass! Midnight mass!" Nogueira, who was supposed to wake the neighbor up, asks: "Is it midnight already?"

Nogueira and the neighbor set off to church. During the mass, more than once, "the figure of Conceição interposed itself between me and the priest," says Nogueira. The next morning, over breakfast, he describes the mass and the people in the church, "but Conceição showed not a flicker of interest," Nogueira finishes. The humanly divine Conceição had vanished without trace. Forever? The story ends with Nogueira going back to Mangaratiba and returning to Rio in March. By that time, Meneses had died of a stroke, and Conceição had moved to another neighborhood in the city. "I neither visited her nor met her again," says Nogueira, who closes his account with the following remark: "I later heard that she had married her late husband's articled clerk." Was Conceição, while married, having an affair with her husband's clerk? It's possible, not provable, though. What lies beyond reasonable doubt is that Conceição made her way back into marriage and, consequently, into a familiar, toxic environment. Why? Because, in such a patriarchal society as nineteenth-century Brazil, there was virtually nothing available outside marriage for poor women like Conceição.

So, feminism – where in the text is it? When we think of feminism, particularly nowadays, one of the first words comes to mind is *empowerment*, or, more specifically, *female empowerment*. In his fiction, Machado often – and to a degree, foresightedly – empowers his female characters, like Helena in *Lição de botânica* (see Chapter Three), and Conceição in "Missa do galo." Both are empowered and powerful characters. Both – as well as a number of Machado's other heroines – give messages of female power to readers. Is it, then, a revolutionary form of feminism? It's not. It's a *literary* form of feminism, intended not – or not *primarily* – to provoke a revolution, but instead to bring about, along with social awareness, literary fruition. Machado's goal as a writer was to create clever, entertaining stories and captivating, convincing characters. What readers would do with them was none of his business. The question "Missa do galo" seems to pose to its readers is not what we, as a society, should do in order to improve the lives of unhappy wives like Conceição and so many others in the nineteenth to twenty-first centuries. The question Machado's story asks, according to Michael Wood, is: "What does it mean when nothing happens, and that same nothing lingers unforgettably in your life?"[19]

---

19 Michael Wood, "Foreword," *The Collected Stories of Machado de Assis*, xv.

The Satirist: "The Alieninst"

The post-1880 Machado is fundamentally an ironist, a satirist, a humorist. "O espelho" and "Missa do galo" don't display these facets fully, but other stories do. Such is the case of the novella "O alienista" ("The Alienist"), one of the most notable works by Machado. On a separate note – but linked to this topic – it's worth mentioning that among the authors who were canonically chosen to represent their culture or country – for instance, Shakespeare, Dante, Goethe, Borges, Kafka, Camões – only Cervantes and Machado are essentially satirists. Shakespeare wrote comedies, and Kafka had a rich vein of dark humor; nevertheless, they are not considered satirists at their core. In Cervantes and Machado, however, satire represents the backbone of their style. Through satire, their skeptic and corrosive wit was able to deconstruct and relativize certain established truths.

Madness, for instance, is deconstructed and relativized in both *Don Quixote* and "O alienista." Moreover, instances of intertextuality – with Cervantes's novel feeding Machado's novella – are clearly noticeable. Let's see an example. The action of "O alienista" is set in Itaguaí, a town which lies approximately 70 kilometers from Rio. The alienist, or psychiatrist, Dr. Simão Bacamarte, had dedicated his life to the study and practice of medicine. For his devoted commitment to science, he was deemed the "greatest physician in Brazil, Portugal, and the two Spains."[20] When he decided to immerse himself in research of "cerebral pathology" and "requested permission from the council to build a hospital that would provide treatment and lodgings for all the lunatics of Itaguaí and the surrounding towns and villages," Father Lopes recommended that Dona Evarista, the alienist's wife, take her husband with her on a trip to court, arguing that "all this studying can't be good for him [Simão Bacamarte]; it gives him all sorts of strange ideas."

The equivalence between *too much study* (or *reading*) and *insanity* – or the former eventually causing the latter – became paradigmatic through Cervantes's story of Don Quixote. In "O alienista," however, Machado plays with this equivalence. By dint of his excessive studying, Simão

---

[20] All citations from Machado's "The Alienist" come from *The Collected Stories of Machado de Assis*, trans. Margaret Jull Costa & Robin Patterson, 316–62. For the sake of readability, I'm not adding footnotes for each quoted section related to this source.

Bacamarte attains, indeed, a perfect equilibrium of mental, moral, and emotional faculties. His discernment and moderation are simply flawless.

As the narrative evolves, Simão Bacamarte determines that nearly every adult in Itaguaí ought to be taken as an inpatient to Casa Verde – the madhouse he founded – to be studied and treated. Invested with the power of Science – which means the power of Truth – Bacamarte sends to the asylum, first, those who act like lunatics. Later, those who show any behavioral deviation, such as little manias. When eventually four-fifths of Itaguaí's population resides in Casa Verde, Bacamarte decides to discharge all the patients and bring into the asylum, instead, those who behave in total conformity with reason and moral patterns. In the end, Bacamarte discovers that no one is completely sane after all; no one is endowed with absolute mental health; and, therefore, everyone has a weakness, a flaw, a deviation, morally and intellectually. In short, everyone – to a degree – is crazy. Everyone … but him. Bacamarte can't find any imperfection in himself; he asks around and everyone promptly reassures him of his utter sanity. Simão Bacamarte is, no doubt, perfectly sane. Upon acknowledging and pondering on this fact, Bacamarte locks himself in Casa Verde as its sole patient: he is the only *abnormal* person in Itaguaí!

Rationalism and Thomas Mann's *The Magic Mountain*

There is a passage in Thomas Mann's *The Magic Mountain* that speaks directly to Machado's notion of *relativism of absolute values*, like absolute health, as presented in "O alienista." In this passage, Hans Castorp, a young engineer, goes to a sanatorium in the Swiss Alps to pay his tubercular cousin a visit. There, he is introduced to Dr. Krokowski, who asks whether Castorp is a patient. Castorp replies that he isn't and politely chats about general topics, such as his recent university exams and the time he plans to spend in the sanatorium while visiting his cousin. Read the following brief passage, and I'll comment on it afterwards:

> In answering, he [Hans Castorp] said something about three weeks, mentioned his exams, and added that, thank God, he was perfectly healthy.
> "You don't say!" Dr. Krokowski replied, thrusting his head forward at a derisive slant and smiling more broadly. "In that case you are a phenomenon of greatest medical interest. You see, I've never met a perfectly healthy person before."[21]

---

21 Thomas Mann, *The Magic Mountain*, trans. John E. Woods (New York: Everyman's Library, 2005), 19.

Castorp sees himself as a healthy person, and, to a degree, he can be. What he, or anyone, cannot be – and this is why Dr. Krokowski reacts ironically by calling him "a phenomenon of greatest medical interest" – is *perfectly* healthy. Castorp perceives his own physical and mental condition in binary terms: he is either *sick* or *healthy*; if he is not sick, then he is healthy. Dr. Krokowski, for his part, has a more nuanced perception of this matter. No living human being is perfectly healthy or completely sick. Or, as he says to Castorp later in the novel: "I was articulating my doubts that the words 'human being' and 'perfect health' could ever be made to rhyme."[22] Departing from Dr. Krokowski's sentence, one could say that this is a linguistic issue: the problem lies in the way one uses language, like the word *perfect*, for instance. But it's also right to say that language and perception are intimately connected.

Under the premises of nineteenth-century rationalism, for example, people were classified as either sane or insane: there weren't nuances between these two classifications. Reason and madness were two poles apart; like "human being" and "perfect health" in Dr. Krokowski's proposition, they didn't rhyme. If one given person was considered sane, this would make them free from any stigma associated with mental health issues. Insanity, then, would be characterized as the Other. Upon determining who the Other is, science comes to occupy the center of society and starts ruling over it, as Simão Bacamarte does in "O alienista." And the issue of the health–sickness dichotomy dangerously becomes an issue of power–powerlessness. In other words, the risk that the establishment of binary categories, such as health and sickness, poses to humanity is that the powerful tends to – and, at some point, inevitably will – control the powerless. If science promises progress, it also implies power. According to this logic, power constitutes the dialectical other, or the Other, of science. And, to a great extent, "O alienista" is a story about power, not about science; or rather, it's about power as the dark side of science.

The act of relativizing absolute values – such as reason and madness – corresponds to the act of relativizing power. In 1924, when Thomas Mann published *The Magic Mountain*, this daring act was, say, more predictable in terms of availability and expectation than it had been in 1881–82, when Machado published "O alienista," first in *A Estação* and later in *Papéis avulsos*. To a great degree, the twentieth century defined itself as the age of relativism, that is, the age of questioning and undermining sources of truth, such as rationalism, science, and metaphysics, as well as truth itself as a product of these sources. The problem, pragmatically

---

22 Ibid., 227.

speaking, doesn't lie in the process of logically conceiving a universal truth: the problem is how this truth (or the Truth) is going to be *used* by the instances that create it, and which, by creating it, inevitably become instances of power.

Simão Bacamarte, for example, by virtue of scientific knowledge, rules Itaguaí as an autocrat. The more scientific knowledge he acquires, the more autocratic power he achieves. Despotism, thus, just changed hands from monarchs endowed with hereditary rights, as in the *Ancien Régime*, to scientists who rightfully fought against superstitions and old traditions with the weapons of reason. For Machado, though, reason paradoxically became the *superstition* of modern times. And, as such, who would be able to fight against it? What was as powerful as modern science and reason? Fiction, maybe; or rather, *modern* fiction. In that case, the seriousness of the claim – that of reason being a new form of superstition – could not be fictionally confronted in serious terms. It had to be in parodic and satirical ones. That's when Cervantes was called in. It was time to dismantle modern beliefs, and Cervantes's style, where gravity and lightness intertwine to confound readers, might contribute towards accomplishing this task. Simão Bacamarte, in this respect, embodies the new Quixote – the one who became *perfectly sane* by cause of excessive study.

Machado insists on not hiding the Cervantean source, though. In Chapter Three, for example, Dona Evarista leaves Itaguaí to spend some time at court. She takes a few guests with her, among them the apothecary's wife. Simão Bacamarte stays and so does Crispim Soares, the apothecary. Both go to say farewell to the group at a place in town. When the travelers depart, Simão Bacamarte and Crispim Soares return to their houses, each carried by their own mount:

> And so the entourage left. As the apothecary and the doctor returned home, Crispim Soares kept his gaze fixed firmly between the ears of his mule, while Simão Bacamarte's eyes were fixed on the horizon ahead, leaving his horse to deal with how to get home. What a striking image of the genius and the common man! One stares at the present, filled with tears and regrets, while the other scrutinizes the future with its promise of new dawns.

What a striking image of a modern Quixote and a modern Sancho Panza!

Structure and Beyond

The narrative structure of "O alienista" also resembles that of *Don Quixote*. As in Cervantes's novel, the narrator of Machado's novella states that his account rewrites the chronicles of past historians. This artifice creates the illusion that the narrative recounts a historical event. In the case of Machado's story, "O alienista" recounts the establishment of the first madhouse in Brazil by the first physician in the colony who dedicated himself to study of the human mind. The establishment of the Casa Verde by Simão Bacamarte occurred in Itaguaí at some point between 1789 and 1808.

One character describes Casa Verde as a "Bastille of the human reason," when a group of dissatisfied common people carry out a revolution, resulting in civilian casualties, against the alienist in Itaguaí. The narrative parodies, on a much smaller scale, the events of the 1789 French Revolution. This particular historical reference reinforces the argument that, in Machado's view, scientists were among the new enlightened tyrants of modern (i.e. post-French Revolution) Western society. Despotism, I repeat, just changed hands.

However, different from France in 1789, Brazil or, metonymically, "Itaguaí," says the narrator, "like all other towns, villages, and hamlets throughout the colony, had no printing press." This note demarcates another time frame in the narrative. As we learned in Chapter One, the arrival of printing presses in Brazil occurred in 1808 along with the Portuguese royal family. By fictionally recreating the foundation of the first mental hospital in Brazil within the time frame that goes from 1789 up to 1808, Machado points out a dialectical aspect of Brazilian society that is, indeed, recurrent in his fiction. I'm referring to the coexistence of two opposite and complementary countries: the *modern* and the *archaic* Brazil. The former is represented by Simão Bacamarte and Casa Verde and the latter by a pre-printing press society. In other words, it's ironic that in a town where news circulated "either by nailing a handwritten notice to the doors of the town hall and the parish church, or by means of the town crier, who would roam the streets of the town with a rattle in his hand," there is avant-garde medicine with a distinguished doctor and a pioneering hospital doing cutting-edge research on the innovative topic of mental health. These pieces simply don't fit together.

What is the historical reality, then? Historically speaking, the Royal Charter that created the first school of medicine in Brazil was signed by the Prince Regent, D. João, on November 5, 1808.[23] Thirty-three years later, that is, in 1841, on the very day of his July 18th coronation, the then 15-year-old Emperor Pedro II issued the decree establishing the first lunatic asylum of Brazil. Following European models, the asylum operated in a separate building, only dedicated to inpatients with psychological disorders. This isolation increased the stigma attached to people in need of mental care. It also encouraged doctors to conduct coercive experimental treatments where inpatients were subject to all sorts of punitive psychiatric therapy, which included ice-water baths, straitjackets, barbiturates, electroshock, and psychosurgery. The death toll in psychiatric hospitals used to be exceedingly high. In one institution alone, Hospital Colônia de Barbacena, it is estimated that 60,000 inpatients died from medical malpractice and torture from 1903 to 1980.[24]

At the time of writing, there are no longer lunatic asylums in Brazil. But the history of psychiatry and mental hospitals in this and other countries – particularly during the nineteenth and twentieth centuries – continues to haunt and fright us more than any horror movie. And that's for a single, basic reason: it happened in real life, to real people. Curiously enough, one author of horror stories, when developing the theme of the lunatic asylum in one of his narratives, decided to approach it in a satirical fashion. I'm referring to Edgar Allan Poe and his 1845 tale "The System of Doctor Tarr and Professor Fether." Machado most likely read it before writing "O alienista." It's possible, indeed, to identify intersections between the two stories – the satirical approach to the topic of madness and the madhouse being just one of them.[25] At one point in Poe's story, Monsieur Mallard, a madman feigning to be the superintendent of a madhouse called Maison de Santé, says to the unnamed, naïve narrator: "When a madman appears *thoroughly* sane, it is high time to put him in a straitjacket."[26] Had Machado chosen this sentence to serve as the epigraph to "O alienista," it would have been a quite suitable choice.

---

23 www.medicina.ufrj.br/pt/conteudos/paginas/historia/principal
24 See Daniela Arbex, *Holocausto brasileiro* (São Paulo: Geração Editorial, 2013).
25 See Ivan Teixeira, *O altar & o trono* (Cotia: Ateliê, 2010), 319–25.
26 Edgar Allan Poe, "The System of Doctor Tarr and Professor Fether," *Poetry and Tales* (New York: Library of America, 1984), 713.

In Conclusion

We commented in Chapter Four on how Machado reacted to reading Eça de Queirós's O primo Basílio. In reviewing this novel, Machado harshly criticized the scientific premises of Émile Zola's Naturalism, which Eça – according to Machado – had followed closely. This reaction, or the awareness that stemmed from it, seems to have provided the basis for the second Machado to emerge, as critics have claimed. Machado, no doubt, was highly critical of any school of thought aligned with scientific determinism. However, Zola's Naturalism and Auguste Comte's Positivism – to name the two most influential schools – enjoyed an outstanding reputation among Machado's fellow countrymen. Machado wasn't aligned with them on this topic, and, from Brás Cubas on, his fiction can be read as a critique of the absolutism of reason that dominated nineteenth-century culture.

In replacing religion as the dominant discourse of the nineteenth century, science promised to foster progress and justice, to lead civilization to its highest level of modernity. In making such a bold promise, science presented itself as the only righteous way for humanity to achieve what it had been looking for over the course of millennia: the Truth. Not the superstitious truth that had been offered by religion, but, instead, the ultimate truth: the logical, undeniable truth of reason. "Let's see," Simão Bacamarte says to himself in the last segment of "O alienista," "let's see if I can finally reach the ultimate truth." As a scientist, Bacamarte's utmost goal could not be any other truth than that of reason, or rather, the Truth.

As a disciple of Pascal, Machado didn't believe in absolute truth. On this topic, he would prefer offering one of his favorite Pascalian quotes (as already cited in Chapter Four): "Truth lies on this side of the Pyrenees, error on the other." Besides being a satirist, the post-1880 Machado was also a skeptic. To a great degree, both satire and skepticism define the final Machado. And, as a skeptic, he doesn't just doubt whether absolute truth exists, but, most importantly, he wonders what would happen if it existed and what would occur if a few people *owned* it. Would truth be used for the improvement of humanity? Or, would it be utilized instead as a tool to wield power for personal interests? If you believe in altruism and altruistic values and that humanity is remediable, you'll probably reply *yes* to the first question. Machado and his fiction said *yes* to the second. For Machado – and this is the pivotal point to be underlined – reason, knowledge, and experience are virtuous *per se*; that is to say, the problem does not lie in them: the problem, instead, is what we *do* with them.

Reason, knowledge, and experience can be used to promote justice, but they can also validate arbitrariness and violence. They form a dangerous double-edged sword. For centuries, Portuguese and Brazilian elites justified slavery with *reasonable* arguments. The patriarchal order that oppressed women was protected by law during Machado's lifetime. Scientific experiments conducted in mental asylums during the nineteenth century ultimately led the scientific community to back eugenics and eugenic policies in the twentieth century. Eugenics, as we unfortunately know, shaped and gave rise to the Nazi movement and what followed.

In Book II of Plato's *Republic*, Glaucon describes the ring of Gyges, whose magic powers granted its wearer the ability to become invisible at will.[27] By Glaucon's account, under the safeguard of invisibility – which allows the invisible person to act freely with no consequences – "the just man would differ in no way from the unjust, but both would follow the same course."[28] In the nineteenth century – always according to Machado's view – reason became a sort of ring of Gyges. Under the protection of reason, or on its behalf, people received tacit permission to do virtually whatever they wanted. The line separating justice and injustice, then, became very fine indeed.

"O alienista" can be read as a satire of this tragedy. The story seems to question not reason itself, but its harmful consequences. Machado doesn't appear interested in what reason *is*, but rather, in what reason is able to *do*. In practical terms, there was (and there still is) a blatant contradiction between what reason promises and what it actually delivers. In many ways, Machado's fiction points to and denounces this contradiction. His stories and novels, for that matter, seem to occupy the space between the agency and practice of human reason.

Ten Stories for You to Enter Machado's World (If You Haven't Already)

Let's do the math. Machado wrote 200-something stories. Ten stories out of this grand total corresponds to approximately 5%. That's very few. Nevertheless, I believe that with some judicious selection it is possible to put together a relevant group of ten stories. But first, we need to define

---

27 Plato, *The Republic*, 2nd edn., trans. Desmond Lee (New York: Penguin), 43–44.
28 Ibid., 44.

the criteria. My goal in making this list was not *exactly* to choose the top ten stories by Machado. My goal, instead, was to create a list of representativeness. In other words, I aimed to select a corpus of ten stories – aside from the ones we've already discussed: "O espelho," "Missa do galo," and "O alienista" – that will give you, the reader, a fair sense of Machado's style and his *Weltanschauung* (i.e. worldview) as a fictionist.

All of the ten selected tales listed below have English translations. If you want to find all of them in one volume, an excellent option is *The Collected Stories of Machado de Assis*, translated by Margaret Jull Costa and Robin Patterson. Note: the English titles indicated after the original titles come from this edition; and the dates refer to the first separate edition of each story followed by the date of their publication in book form.

1. "O enfermeiro" ("The Gentleman's Companion") (1884, 1895)

It's not by chance that "O enfermeiro" was – as we learned in Chapter One – the first piece by Machado to be translated into French in 1909, just one year after his passing. It's not by accident either that the story introduced Machado to the English-speaking world in 1921 – with the title "The Attendant's Confession," "O enfermeiro" is the opening story in the first volume to present Machado in English: *Brazilian Tales*, translated by Isaac Goldberg and published in Boston. "O enfermeiro" is, in fact, Machado's *tour de force*; it's Machado at the fullest expression of his abilities as a storyteller. The plot revolves around the narrator, Procópio Valongo, who, on the brink of death, writes to confess a crime he committed – two crimes, indeed. Through his crimes, he became a rich man. He then asks for mercy. His confession, however, is one whereby regret intertwines with cynicism and self-justification. For a cynical bourgeois like Procópio Valongo, remorse is just the antechamber that leads to self-deception.

2. "Pílades e Orestes" ("Pylades and Orestes") (1903, 1906)

"Pílades e Orestes" is one of the most complex and fascinating stories by Machado. As do other tales – such as "O anel de Polícrates" ("Polycrates' Ring"), "Uma visita de Alcibíades" ("A Visit from Alcibiades"), "Viver!" ("Life!") – "Pílades e Orestes" attests to Machado's passion for ancient Greek culture. Following Greek sources – Aeschylus' *The Libation-Bearer*, Euripides' *Electra*, and Sophocles' *Electra* (although only the latter is mentioned in the text) – the story transports Pylades and Orestes to nineteenth-century Rio de Janeiro as the characters Quintanilha and Gonçalves, who form a love triangle with Camila. In "Pílades e Orestes,"

Machado approaches the topic of male homoeroticism, which also appears in another of his stories, "As academias de Sião" ("The Academies of Siam").

3. "O diplomático" ("Mr. Diplomat") (1884, 1895)

Machado's obsession with *Othello* led him to rewrite Shakespeare's hero and his misfortunes several times over. In "O diplomático," Rangel is about to propose to Joaninha during a night party. His lack of confidence, though, makes him repeatedly delay his plan. Meanwhile, a new guest, Queirós, arrives; his radiant personality and charisma gradually conquer and seduce everyone in the party, except Rangel. In the end, Rangel neither marries nor kills Joaninha, thus not quite repeating the history of Othello and Desdemona. Instead, Rangel … Well, you'll have to read it for yourself to find out.

4. "D. Benedita: Um retrato" ("Dona Benedita: A Portrait") (1882, 1882)

"The most difficult thing in the world, apart from governing a country, must surely be that of guessing Dona Benedita's exact age."[29] With this ironic opening line, the narrator initiates the portrait of Dona Benedita, for whom the most difficult thing in the world is to govern her own desires, or lack thereof. In "D. Benedita," Machado dives deep into a woman's psychological universe – as he does in other stories, such as "O segredo de Augusta" ("Augusta's Secret"), "Confissões de uma viúva moça" ("Confessions of a Young Widow"), "Uma senhora" ("A Lady"), and "D. Paula" ("Dona Paula"), for instance.

5. "A sereníssima república (Conferência do cônego Vargas)" ("The Most Serene Republic [Canon Vargas's Lecture]") (1882, 1882)

In this allegorical story written in the form of a scientific lecture, Canon Vargas announces to his audience that, after long years of research, he has managed to decodify the language of spiders. Capable of listening and talking to them, he decides to carry out a social experiment with his 490 spiders: helping them implement a political system in their society. Canon Vargas, then, chooses an old political model to implement: the Venetian Republic. In his speech, he focuses on the electoral system, and the impasses, drawbacks, and contradictions that arise as it is practiced

---

[29] Machado de Assis, "Dona Benedita: A Portrait," *The Collected Stories of Machado de Assis*, 390.

among the arachnids. With humor, "A sereníssima república" unveils and gives a glimpse into Machado's skeptical view on politics. The story also reveals an important facet of the author's style: the approach to fantastical realism. Brás Cubas, who narrates his memoirs after death, is always referred to when it comes to Machado's fantastical realism. In the circle of stories, however, those of a fantastic nature include "Uma visita de Alcibíades" ("A Visit from Alcibiades"), "Entre Santos" ("Among Saints"), and "O imortal" ("The Immortal").

6. "Pai contra mãe" ("Father Against Mother") (1906; not published separately)

"Taking Assis's story ["Pai contra mãe"] to its logical paroxysm," asserts Fernando Rocha, "the most severe result of our refusal to face the consequences of the slavocratic disaster is a microcommunity of Afro-descendants who control, punish, and annihilate each other for the benefit of white elites."[30] "Pai contra mãe" is one of the four Machado stories that approach the topic of slavery. The other three are: "Virginius," "Mariana" (1871 – there is another story entitled "Mariana" which was published in 1895), and "O caso da vara" ("The Cane"). Besides being the most somber story of this group – and possibly the most somber story Machado ever wrote – "Pai contra mãe" displays another particularity: its plot focuses on Afro-Brazilian characters only. The narrator doesn't reveal the racial background of the three central characters – Clara, Cândido Neves, and Mônica – but pieces of evidence in the narrative suggest that they form a group of non-white people, as Fernando Rocha demonstrates in his study.

7. "Noite de almirante" ("Admiral's Night") (1884, 1884)

"Noite de almirante" is a beautiful love story with no happy ending – at least not for Deolindo, who loves Genoveva but has to embark on an offshore training trip. Before leaving, however, the couple decide to take an oath of fidelity. Deolindo departs and then comes ashore ten months later. He rushes down the streets towards Genoveva's house to finally see her again. She's not there, though. Something has happened during those ten months of Deolindo's absence ...

---

30 Fernando Rocha, "'Father versus Mother': Slavery and Its Apparatuses," *Emerging Dialogues on Machado de Assis*, eds. Lamonte Aidoo & Daniel Silva (New York: Palgrave Macmillan, 2016), 91–103.

8. "Um homem célebre" ("Fame") (1888, 1895)

Machado was passionate about music, which frequently appears in his fiction. "Um homem célebre" narrates a story of a composer, Pestana, who is famous for his polkas but dreams about composing concert music. Psychologically ripped apart by the eternal conflict between his classical ambition and his popular vocation, Pestana, says the narrator, is a person "at peace with his fellow men and at war with himself."[31] Other stories where music plays an important part in the narrative are "O machete" (the *machete* was the Portuguese ancestor of the ukulele), "Cantiga de esponsais" ("Nuptial Song"), and "Trio em lá menor" ("Trio in A Minor").

9. "Uns braços" ("Her Arms") (1885, 1895)

"Uns braços" is a coming-of-age story about 15-year-old Inácio, who temporarily lives in the house of his father's friends, the couple Borges and Severina. During his stay, the teenager falls in love with Severina, who perceives that she's loved. It's a story full of lyricism, delicacy, and sensuality.

10. "A causa secreta" ("The Secret Cause") (1885, 1895)

Fortunato derives pleasure from watching others (humans or animals) undergoing pain. He is a sadist who befriends Dr. Garcia and establishes a private hospital with him where he, Fortunato, works as the chief nurse. Against his will, Dr. Garcia falls in love with Fortunato's wife, Maria Luísa. In "A causa secreta," the narrative blends cruelty, love, and analysis. The latter comes to characterize the main intellectual feature of Dr. Garcia. "The young man [Garcia]," says the narrator, "had a nascent ability to decipher men and deconstruct characters; he loved analysis and possessed the gift, which he prized above all others, of being able to penetrate numerous emotional and spiritual layers until he grasped the inner secret of a human organism."[32] Dr. Garcia's "ability to decipher men and deconstruct characters" perfectly coincides with that of his creator, Machado de Assis.

---

[31] Machado de Assis, "Fame," *The Collected Stories of Machado de Assis*, 666.
[32] Machado de Assis, "The Secret Cause," *The Collected Stories of Machado de Assis*, 679.

Chapter Six

Novels: Lights! Camera! Digression!

The Importance of Schopenhauer

WHEN *BRÁS CUBAS* was released, first in installments (1880), and then in book form (1881), the reaction from its readers was either coldness or perplexity. In 1883, Araripe Júnior alluded to Machado's novel as "the most whimsical book of those published in the Portuguese language."[1] *Brás Cubas* was then viewed as the odd one out, the offbeat fiction, the outlandish novel. Novel? "Is *The Posthumous Memoirs of Brás Cubas* a novel?" wonders Capistrano de Abreu.[2] This question was, indeed, quite pertinent. After all, at the time, there was no parallel to *Brás Cubas* in the Portuguese language to help define it in terms of literary form or genre – the only exception, or the closest model, was perhaps the 1846 novel *Viagens na minha terra* (*Travels in My Homeland*) by the Portuguese writer Almeida Garrett.[3] Therefore, the puzzlement that *Brás Cubas* caused in its first readers is quite understandable.

---

[1] Araripe Júnior, *Lucros e perdas* (Rio de Janeiro: Livraria Contemporânea de Faro, 1883), 61–62. See also Hélio de Seixas Guimarães, *Machado de Assis, o escritor que nos lê* (São Paulo: Unesp, 2017), particularly the chapter "Um escritor de exceção."

[2] Machado de Assis, "Prologue to the Fourth Edition," *The Posthumous Memoirs of Brás Cubas*, trans. Flora Thomson-DeVeaux (New York: Penguin, 2020), xliii. As a matter of fact, this prologue was written to the third edition of the novel.

[3] The critic Macedo Soares pointed out Garrett's *Viagens na minha terra* as an ancestor of *Brás Cubas*. Machado mentions this fact in the prologue to the

But, what was considered so odd about *Brás Cubas*? Basically, everything. However, we need to put this *everything* into context. So, let's recap. We've already examined – albeit rather schematically – the cultural conditions of colonial Brazil. We've discussed the changes brought by the Portuguese royal family when Prince Regent D. João transferred the court from Portugal to Brazil in 1808. We've also mentioned the "French Mission" of 1816, when a group of French artists, who were invited and sponsored by D. João, moved to Brazil with the aim of modernizing the country by spreading French ideas and culture. As a matter of fact, the French Mission's contribution to Brazilian culture was invaluable.

One general effect of this contribution lay in the fact that Brazil became openly Francophile, culturally speaking, during the nineteenth century. French became the second language of every educated Brazilian. French was the first foreign language Machado learned and the one in which he was most proficient.[4] Machado, too, was Francophile. But, different from most of his peers, he widened his scope by reading and studying authors from other cultures, particularly Britain and America: Shakespeare, above all, but also Poe, Swift, and Sterne, as we've discussed in previous chapters. Regardless of languages and cultures, Machado was a friend of the classics: ancient Greeks, Dante, Camões, Cervantes, Goethe … This made him one of the few Brazilian intellectuals of his generation whose cultural background wasn't founded almost exclusively upon French culture.[5]

The literary lineage of *Brás Cubas*, in this respect, has deeply English roots, as Machado himself – speaking through Brás Cubas – acknowledges in the novel's prologue. There, Brás Cubas cites Sterne and *Tristram Shandy*'s "free form" as one of his major sources of influence.[6] In mentioning "free form," he implicitly alludes to the eighteenth-century British digressive novel tradition, whereof Sterne's *Tristram Shandy* constitutes a paradigmatic model. It's true that Brás Cubas also alludes to Xavier de Maistre in the same prologue; but de Maistre's *Voyage autour de ma chambre* (*Voyage Around My Room*) takes *Tristram Shandy* as its model as well, structurally speaking.

---

third edition of *Brás Cubas*.

4 See Jean-Michel Massa, *Machado de Assis tradutor*, trans. Oséias Silas Ferraz (Belo Horizonte: Crisálida, 2008).
5 See Otto Maria Carpeaux, "Contos de Machado de Assis," *Teresa: revista de literatura brasileira*, no. 20 (2020), 34.
6 Machado de Assis, *The Posthumous Memoirs of Brás Cubas*, 3.

The eighteenth-century British digressive novel basically combines two interrelated compositional aspects: first, the inner life of the main characters prevails over their outer life; and second, as a consequence, the narrative action is reduced to a minimum. The minimal action along with the correspondent maximization of the characters' inner lives defines, generally considering, Sterne's *Tristram Shandy*. These features in *Brás Cubas*, though, baffled Machado's audience, who were accustomed to reading novels of action, or episodic narrative, in which action constituted one of the nuclear structural components. Following Sterne and de Maistre, Machado replaces action with digression, which breaks action into smaller, loosely interconnected pieces, thus defeating the general readers' expectations.

The question is why did Machado decide to follow Sterne's model and replace action with digression, even knowing that, in doing so, he would confound and confront his readers' horizon of expectation? Before bringing Schopenhauer into this discussion, let's briefly recap another point: Machado's biography could be defined, as we did in Chapter Two, as perfectly unadventurous; the main *event* – or one of them – being the mystery surrounding the composition of *Brás Cubas*, given its unpredictability and what it represents in Machado's career as well as in Brazilian literature. Over the years, critics have tried to understand what could have enabled this turning point. As we discussed in Chapter Four, *Brás Cubas* might have been written in response to and against Eça de Queirós's *O primo Basílio*. In addition to this hypothesis, or rather, connected to it, critics also mention – as we did in Chapter Two – Machado and Carolina's stay in Nova Friburgo from December 1878 to March 1879. During this period – the first in which Machado took a break from his multiple, exhausting jobs – something might have occurred that helped him redefine the course of his fiction.

In this string of hypotheses, I want to suggest another one, not to challenge the prior claims but possibly to complement them. At some point, before conceiving *Brás Cubas*, maybe while resting with Carolina in Nova Friburgo, Machado read Schopenhauer's ideas on the novel as a genre and might have been inspired by them. We know for certain that he was an avid reader of Schopenhauer. We also know for sure that Schopenhauer's ideas shaped Machado's fiction in many ways. Machado's allegorical story "Viver!" ("Life!"), for instance, which originally appeared in 1886, is deeply Schopenhauerian. Also profoundly Schopenhauerian is the celebrated Chapter VII of *Brás Cubas*, "The Delirium." The close link between "The Delirium" and Schopenhauer indicates that Machado was somehow in contact with the German philosopher's works by the time he conceived of and wrote *Brás Cubas*.

It's plausible, though, to imagine that Machado read Schopenhauer's notes about the novel as a genre around this time. In one of these notes, the philosopher argues: "A *novel* will be the higher and nobler the more *inner* and less *outer* life it depicts."[7] Connected to this argument, Schopenhauer came to list "four novels [that] are the crown of the genre." For him, the jewel in the crown is – you guessed it – *Tristram Shandy*. One remarkable feature that Schopenhauer finds in Sterne's novel is … its lack of action: "*Tristram Shandy*," he says, "to be sure, has as good as no action whatever." Following Sterne's work, Schopenhauer lists Rousseau's *La nouvelle Héloïse* and Goethe's *Wilhelm Meister*. "How very little action there is in [them]!" exclaims the philosopher. The list is completed by Cervantes's *Don Quixote*, which presents "relatively little [action], and what there is is very trivial, amounting to no more than a series of jokes," he says. Schopenhauer closes his comments on novels and novelists with the following statement: "The task of the novelist is not to narrate great events but to make small ones interesting."[8]

This closing remark could encapsulate Machado's conception of fiction. It might perfectly serve as the epigraph for all his second-phase fiction. In the specific case of *Brás Cubas*, the novel focuses more on the inner and less on the outer life of the protagonist, whose actions, therefore, are shortened to the minimum and where even the smallest events are made interesting. It's the confluence of Schopenhauer's views on the novel and Machado's achievements in *Brás Cubas* that makes us assume the direct influence of the former on the latter.

When *Brás Cubas* came out, Machado's achievements bewildered readers, because the horizon of their expectation could hardly accommodate such *eccentric* compositional features. Among other factors, this mismatch can be explained through the discrepancy of cultural backgrounds between Machado and his contemporary readers. This is to say, whereas the latter had strong French foundations, based on schools of thought such as Naturalism and positivism – besides French Romanticism – Machado went beyond and forged his fiction on the basis of alternative models, such as Schopenhauer and Sterne, as well as Shakespeare and Cervantes. Obviously, French authors were not out of Machado's literary

---

7   Arthur Schopenhauer, *Essays and Aphorisms*, trans. R. J. Hollingdale (New York: Penguin, 2004), 165.
8   Ibid., 165.

melting pot, but, even when it comes to Francophone writers, Machado had a particular taste for *rebellious* or *inconvenient* ones, such as Pascal, Voltaire, and Rousseau.

But, Before *Brás Cubas*...

Before *Brás Cubas*, Machado wrote four novels:

1. *Ressurreição* (*Resurrection*), 1872
2. *A mão e a luva* (*The Hand and the Glove*), 1874
3. *Helena*, 1876
4. *Iaiá Garcia*, 1878

This group of novels, written by the young Machado, is generally deemed a sort of preparation before the leap into his glorious, mature period. In this section, I will draw on some ideas from this first group of novels. To make my remarks more organized, I've separated them out into the following eighteen points:

1. *Two Phases*: Machado wrote a prologue for the second edition of *Ressurreição*, which was released in 1905. In it, the novel is referred to as belonging to the "first phase of [Machado's] literary life."[9] Therefore, the indisputable concept of the existence of two "Machados" was first put forward by, yes, Machado himself. Critics, then, have naturally divided his oeuvre into pre- and post-*Brás Cubas* works. The first group is generally aligned with ideas of Romanticism, whereas the second is associated with premises of Realism.

2. *Romanticism*: What is Romantic about Machado's first novels? There are several aspects. Conformism, or idealization of the upper class, can be viewed as just one of the Romantic aspects. Overall, the moral standards that guide and define the behavior of the main characters in Machado's first novels mirror those that permeated and shaped the civil society that he inhabited. The patriarchal system, for instance, is somehow validated and naturalized in these novels. But, note: *overall* doesn't mean *always*. There are layers of social criticism that exist, albeit subtly, in these works (see point 11 below). Yet, the level of conformism, or idealization, far surpasses that of criticism.

---

9 Machado de Assis, *Resurrection*, trans. Karen Sherwood Sotelino (Pittsburgh: Latin America Literary Review Press, 2013), 23.

3. *Point of View*: The first novels by Machado each present a third-person narrator who acts as an intermediary of – and a sort of an accomplice to – the upper-class main characters. This mediation generally operates with Romantic lenses that make the surface of things shiny and mostly conventional. The shift of point of view that comes in *Brás Cubas* – from third to first person – changes everything. In *Brás Cubas*, the upper class speaks for itself through its protagonist. By giving a voice to a representative of the Brazilian elite, Machado succeeds in skillfully exposing contradictions in the way the ruling class thinks and behaves. These contradictions are hardly pointed out in Machado's first novels.

4. *Intertextuality*: In the prologue to the first edition of *Ressurreição*, Machado asserts: "My idea when I wrote this book was to put into practice Shakespeare's thought: 'Our doubts are traitors, / And make us lose the good we oft might win, / By fearing to attempt.'"[10] With this note, Machado did not remove but, at least, relativized the Romantic dimension of the novel. Romantics placed great value on the idea of subjectivity as the main source of artistic creation. Machado, for his turn, insists on making it clear, from the outset, that his novel, or its main idea, was conceived and outsourced from other literary works, namely, Shakespeare's *Measure for Measure*, from where the quotation in the prologue came.

5. *First Novel*: *Ressurreição* narrates the story of Félix, a young doctor who doesn't work and lives off of savings. He's a cynical character who deeply distrusts love. His dead heart comes to be *resurrected* by Lívia, a young and beautiful widow. This resurrection, though, lasts just a little while. Soon, even in desiring to love, Félix's heart succumbs again to dark feelings of jealousy and fear of being deceived by others. Ultimately, Félix is deceived by himself; and thus, the topic of self-deception starts its long trajectory in Machado's fiction. "We find in him [Félix] the refusal to yield that typifies the Sophoclean hero," rightfully argues Helen Caldwell, whose primary field of expertise was classical literature.[11] "Prototypical of Machado's greatest characters, Felix is his own worst enemy," claims Earl Fitz.[12] Despite Félix's tragic nature, he doesn't end up going to a monastery and locking himself up in a cell. His personality proves to be as tragic as it is fickle. "If the painful impression of the events you readers have followed left him [Félix] deeply worn, it soon faded," says

---

10 Ibid., p. 26.
11 Helen Caldwell, *Machado de Assis: The Brazilian Master and His Novels* (Berkeley: U of California P, 1970), 41.
12 Earl Fitz, *Machado de Assis* (Boston: Twayne, 1989), 47.

the narrator. "His [Félix's] love was extinguished like a lamp out of oil. It was the young woman's company that had nurtured the flames. When she disappeared, the exhausted flame expired."[13]

6. *Ressurreição Versus Dom Casmurro*: In developing themes such as jealousy and distrust, *Ressurreição* (1872) anticipates *Dom Casmurro* (1899), and, likewise, Félix can be viewed as a prototype of Bento Santiago, *Dom Casmurro*'s protagonist. However, there is a noteworthy difference between them. Depicted by and described through a third-person narrator, Félix becomes aware of his own moral weaknesses; whereas Bento Santiago, as a narrator of his own story, has to hide his vulnerabilities in order to convince the reader of his case. As the narrative goes on, Bento Santiago's account becomes unreliable. It is as though he tries to deceive the reader without realizing that he is, in fact, deceiving himself. From this perspective, Bento Santiago, too, can be viewed as "his own worst enemy."

7. *Analysis of Characters*: In the year following the publication of *Ressurreição*, Machado wrote his well-known and well-regarded article "Instinto de nacionalidade," which we discussed in Chapter Four. While reflecting on the state of the Brazilian novel, Machado asserts:

> Instances in which passions and characters are analyzed, and that would satisfy critics, are much less common, though there are some of unquestionable value. This is, in truth, one of the most difficult and also one of the greatest aspects of the novel. Naturally it requires of the writer rare powers of observation that even in more developed literatures are uncommon and are not possessed by the majority.[14]

Machado, here, identifies a vulnerable point in the state of the Brazilian novel – it's "much less common" to find novels where "passions and characters are analyzed." We can deduce then that Machado wrote fiction that contributed towards changing this state of things, or making this state of things less evident. In his first novels, he endeavored to create plots that were conducive to the analysis of the characters since, to him, this was the superior form of the novel.

8. *Episodic Novel*: Machado never wrote novels of action. On the contrary, as digression expands in the novels of his second phase, narrative action tends to become more and more rarefied, as we've already

---

13 Machado de Assis, *Resurrection*, 160.
14 Machado de Assis, "Reflections on Brazilian Literature at the Present Moment – The National Instinct," trans. Robert P. Newcomb, *Journal of World Literature* 3 (2018), 410.

discussed. In his first novels, though, the analysis of the characters and action are somewhat balanced out. *Helena*, in this respect, stands out as the most Romantic of Machado's novel with its twists and turns and the *pathos* of the protagonist.

9. *Divisions and Subdivisions*: As already stated, Machado himself divided his works into two phases. It's possible, though, to divide the novels of his first phase into two sub-groups. In this new division, *Ressurreição* would stand in a sub-group solo due to its self-destructive hero. The other three novels could be grouped together as they present a plot pattern that repeats itself, with variations. In *A mão e a luva*, *Helena*, and *Iaiá Garcia*, we follow three remarkable Romantic heroines: Guiomar, Helena, and Iaiá Garcia. Each of them is endowed with a strong personality, comes from lower-middle class origins, and ends up successfully ascending in the social structure by earning the trust of powerful landowners and winning the hearts of young male characters, all of them elegant, educated, and wealthy.

10. *The Author in Disguise (Part One)*: The critic Lúcia Miguel-Pereira claimed that Guiomar, Helena, and Iaiá Garcia are all, to a degree, Machado in disguise. If I may quote myself from Chapter Three: "Like Guiomar, Helena, and Lina (Iaiá) Garcia, Machado was also a member of the lower-middle class struggling to thrive in a social milieu to which, hierarchically considering, he didn't belong. Machado, then, would have created these ambitious heroines, in Miguel-Pereira's view, in order psychologically to justify and ethically to legitimize his own ambition to himself" (Chapter Three).

11. *Subordination Versus Non-Passivity*: In a slaveholding, patriarchal society such as nineteenth-century Brazil, the master's moral shaped the social rules; the unquestionable and inviolable master's will defined the interaction between masters and their dependents (i.e. women, workers, *agregados*, and enslaved individuals). These interactions were determined by the notion of subordination: dependents were subordinate to their masters. This subordination was tacitly justified by the fact that dependents *owed* their masters the *favor* of being rescued from living in miserable conditions at the edge of society: "To possess her [Iaiá Garcia] was to do her a favor," thinks Procópio Dias, a 50-year-old capitalist, in the novel *Iaiá Garcia*. Note the correlation between *possessing* and *favoring*.[15] For dependents, therefore, subordination was not exactly an option: it was,

---

15 Machado de Assis, *Iaiá Garcia*, trans. Albert I. Bagby, Jr. (Lexington: UP of Kentucky, 1977), 97.

instead, an act of survival: "The truth is," says Helena to Estácio, "only the wings of your favor protect me."[16] In another passage of the novel, Estácio "coldly" asks Helena: "'Have we ever denied you any pleasure you wished?' Helena trembled, and also turned serious. 'No,' she murmured, 'my *debt* has no limits'" (emphasis added). But, if Helena – and also Guiomar and Iaiá Garcia – shows subordination to those whom she is in "debt" to and who "protect" her, she is also astute enough to act to her own benefit with clever slyness. Machado's heroines, in this respect, are unable to change history, but they are perfectly able to, at least, change *their* own histories, when successfully finding love and social ascent. To do so, they are subordinate but not passive; or rather, they are deceitfully subordinate. And this balance between subordination and non-passivity, as embodied by Machado's heroines, challenges, to a degree – or, better yet, to the degree possible – the social structure and hierarchy.[17]

12. *Psychology*: The analysis of characters and the "power of observation" cited by Machado in "Instinto de nacionalidade" imply some sort of knowledge – intuitive or non-systematic – of human psychology. Nietzsche's "power of observation," for example, made him a pre-Freudian psychologist. In this respect, Machado could be paired with Nietzsche since in his novels and stories, from both phases, he strives to reveal the characters' concealed feelings and intentions that lay on the fringes of their awareness. See, on this subject, the speech of Father Melchior to Estácio in the novel *Helena*. Estácio thinks that Helena is his sister (she isn't, but he hasn't learned this yet). He struggles with the fact that he is in love with her, but he can't consciously admit this feeling – a feeling which Father Melchior, who knows Estácio quite well, distinctly perceives:

> "Your heart," says Father Melchior to Estácio, "is a great unconscious offender [*um grande inconsciente*, reads the original]; it is restless, it mutters, it rebels, it goes astray in the guise of an ill-expressed, ill-understood instinct. Evil pursues you, tempts you, envelops you in its hidden golden snares; you do not feel it nor see it; you will shrink from yourself in horror when you come face to face with it. God who reads you knows in his perfection that there is a thick veil between your heart and your

---

16 Machado de Assis, *Helena*, trans. Helen Caldwell (Berkeley: U of California P, 1984), 73.
17 See Sidney Chaloub, *Machado de Assis, historiador* (São Paulo: Companhia das Letras, 2003), particularly the first chapter entitled "Paternalismo e escravidão em *Helena*."

conscience, separating them and preventing them from joining in a partnership of crime."

"Crime, Reverend Father?"

Melchior leaned over and looked hard at him, his eyes a cold polished mirror meant to reproduce the impression of what he was going to say. "Estacio," he said slowly and distinctly, "you are in love with your sister."[18]

Father Melchior skillfully understands and explains the internal mechanism whereby Estácio's own mind and emotions hide from himself the truth about his incestuous feelings towards Helena. "God who reads you," says Father Melchior, who, as an intermediary of God, also *reads* Estácio. Both God and Father Melchior, by looking through the "veil" that separates Estácio's "heart" from his "conscience," act as effective psychologists.

13. *The Will to Power*: "Ambition is no defect," says Guiomar. "On the contrary, it is a virtue," replies Luis Alves. This exchange is from the last paragraphs of *A mão e a luva*. It occurs one month after Guiomar and Luis Alves get married. Guiomar recognizes in Luis Alves "a strong man," and she praises "all the power of his will." Luis Alves, for his turn, says he relies on Guiomar to achieve his goals, as she "will be a new source of strength to [him]."[19] Machado's first novels give relevance to the idea of *will to power* in a sense that bears a resemblance to Nietzsche's famous concept, that is to say, as desire for both self-overcoming and sociopolitical domination (we'll expand on this idea in the next chapter). Nonetheless, it's worth noting that Machado's heroines, socially considering, cannot overcome their subaltern condition by themselves: they depend on the *favor* of a well-positioned man to help them accomplish their goal. Their unflinching determination, however, is an asset. "Will and ambition," asserts the narrator of *A mão e a luva* about Guiomar, "when they truly dominate, can struggle with other feelings, but they are sure to win, because they are the weapons of the strong, and victory belongs to the strong."[20] In *Quincas Borba*, a novel from Machado's second phase, these ideas on power reappear, but in a satirical and ironic form. Victory still "belongs to the strong," but the story, conversely, focuses on the trajectory of a character, Rubião, who is defeated by "the strong."

---

18 Machado de Assis, *Helena*, 155.
19 Machado de Assis, *The Hand and the Glove*, trans. Albert I. Bagby, Jr. (Lexington: UP of Kentucky, 1970), 116.
20 Ibid., 102.

14. *The Morality of Ambition*: Female social climbers are commonly depicted as anti-heroines, or villainesses, within the context of the nineteenth-century novel. Becky Sharp from Thackeray's *Vanity Fair* (1848) and Sofia Palha from Machado's *Quincas Borba* are two models of determined, cunning, manipulative, and cynical women whose cold opportunism furthers their driving ambitions. That's not the case with Guiomar, Helena, or Iaiá Garcia, though. Machado's first heroines are as morally good as they are ambitious. Through them, Machado tries to legitimize ambition, or rather, the *good ambition*. Ultimately, moral virtue in and of itself doesn't count; for virtue to be recognized, it needs the endorsement of someone from the upper class. Machado's heroines are virtuous women seeking recognition. And, for Machado, there is nothing morally or ethically reprehensible about that.

15. *The Author in Disguise (Part Two)*: Luis Garcia, Iaiá Garcia's father, is described as a "skeptical, austere, and [an] honorable man."[21] He is deemed the first *alter ego* representation of Machado (the other is Counselor Aires). The description below depicts Luis Garcia's daily routine and temperament, which in many ways (if not all) resemble those of Machado:

> Luis Garcia's life was like his personality, taciturn and withdrawn ... He would rise with the sun, take the watering pot and give the flowers and plants a drink; then he would withdraw to do some work before breakfast, which was at eight o'clock. After his breakfast he would take a leisurely walk to the administrative branch where he worked, and if he had a little time he paged through the daily newspapers rapidly. He worked silently, with a cold serenity of method. At closing time he returned home immediately, rarely stopping on the way.[22]

16. *The Morality of Money*: Unlike Luis Garcia, the main characters in Machado's novels – particularly the male characters – don't work. They are capitalists, landowners, plantation owners, heirs, and/or nobles, who live entirely off of investments. Although the plots don't establish money in and of itself as a sole theme, although it seems a distant shadow or a background to the narrative, money is in fact an all-pervasive force that presides and rules over characters' choices, behaviors, and even feelings. In this respect, psychology and capitalism – or, the psychology *of* capitalism – go hand in hand in Machado's fiction. However, in his first

---

21 Machado de Assis, *Iaiá Garcia*, 10.
22 Ibid., 2.

novels, Machado doesn't use this connection to criticize those who have the power. That is to say, being rich doesn't necessarily mean being bad (just as being ambitious doesn't lead perforce to villainy in the case of Machado's heroines). This conservative moral alignment between Machado and the upper classes takes a sharp turn in the author's second phase. In terms of style, metaphors associated with the lexicon of economics are abundantly used by both the first- and the second-phase Machados. Brás Cubas famously commenting that "Marcela loved me for fifteen months and eleven thousand milréis [the then-Brazilian currency]"[23] is just one of these metaphors – in this case, one full of irony.

17. *Love Triangles*: The plot of *Iaiá Garcia* advances via love triangles: Luis Garcia/Estela/Jorge; Procópio Dias/Iaiá Garcia/Jorge; and then Iaiá Garcia/Jorge/Estela. In Chapter Five of this book, we also mentioned love triangles in Machado's short stories. In terms of novels, *Dom Casmurro* is structured around a love triangle (Bentinho/Capitu/Escobar). *Esaú e Jacó* is, too (Paulo/Flora/Pedro), and so are *Brás Cubas* (Brás Cubas/Virgília/Lobo Neves), and *Quincas Borba* (Rubião/Sofia/Cristiano). Structurally speaking, love triangles play a vital role in both Machado's first and second phases.

18. *The Closing Statement*: "Something escapes the shipwreck of illusions," reads the final sentence in *Iaiá Garcia*, the last novel of Machado's first phase.[24] In the context of this novel, the closing statement emerges as a well-turned phrase, whose meaning relates to a specific event in the narrative. However, when reading this phrase in the context of Machado's oeuvre, it takes on a distinct meaning. Machado finishes the first phase of his career by saying that "something escapes the shipwreck of illusions"; but, two years later, when *Brás Cubas* comes to light, *nothing is going to escape the shipwreck of illusions*.

---

23 Machado de Assis, *The Posthumous Memoirs of Brás Cubas*, 50. In the novel's endnotes, the translator Flora Thomson-DeVeaux calculates that eleven thousand milréis "would amount to at least a few hundred thousand dollars today" (306).
24 I use Flora Thomson-DeVeaux's translation, which is in João Cezar de Castro Rocha, *Towards a Poetics of Emulation*, trans. Flora Thomson-DeVeaux (East Lansing: Michigan State UP, 2015), 12. The same sentence appears in Albert I. Bagby, Jr.'s translation as "Something, at least, is salvaged from the shipwreck of illusions" (*Iaiá Garcia*, 166).

Looking at Machado's Two Phases in Parallel

Let's take a comparative look at two passages from two novels by Machado: one from his first and one from his second phase. Let's see how he handles similar topics in these two distinct moments of his career. The excerpt below was extracted from the Chapter III of *Iaiá Garcia*. Here's some context:

The sixteen-year-old Estela is the daughter of a widowed clerk, Mr. Antunes. For years, Mr. Antunes had worked for an appellate judge, now deceased. The judge's widow, Valéria, became fond of Estela years ago, when she and her parents, Ms. and Mr. Antunes, were invited to dine at the judge's house. Valéria's son, Jorge, comes back home after graduating from the Law School in São Paulo, where he stayed for four years. Jorge and Estela will eventually fall in love, but a man from the upper class, like Jorge, can't marry the daughter of a clerk, no matter how virtuous and beautiful she is (and Estela is indeed morally virtuous and beautiful). In the excerpt to follow, Estela draws the attention of Jorge who, then, starts to look at her in a different way. Pay close attention to the sections marked in italics as they will be referred in the comparative analysis. (Note: Italics are not in the original; they are added for emphasis.)

Free of adornments, her [Estela's] dress emphasized her graceful, lofty, and lissome form. Nor was she accustomed to dressing any other way, except for some trinket or piece of lace which the widow gave her from time to time. *Of her own volition she refused every kind of embellishment, accepting neither ruffles nor earrings nor rings.* At first glance one would have called her a feminine Diogenes whose threadbare cape left visible *the vanity of a beauty that wished to assert itself just as it was, without any other artifice*. But, given the girl's character, one might guess two motives – a *natural inclination toward simplicity*, and, even more, *the consideration that her father's means did not allow for expensive furbishings and that therefore it was not wise for her to become attached to luxury.*

"Why don't you put on the *earrings* Mother gave you last week?" Jorge asked Estela one day when there were guests for dinner.

"The most beloved gifts are put aside," she answered, looking at the widow.

Valéria pressed the edge of the girl's chin between her thumb and forefinger: "How poetic!" she exclaimed, smiling. "You don't need *earrings* to be pretty, but go put them on; they suit you well."

It was the first and last time that Estela put them on. Her intention was too obvious not to be noticed, and Jorge did not forget either the girl's answer or the constraint with which she *obeyed*. ...

Jorge began to find the house a more pleasant place to be than the street.[25]

Now, an excerpt from Chapter XXXII of *Brás Cubas*. But first, some context – in this case, a more complex introduction is needed. In 1814, Brás Cubas is a spoiled nine-year-old boy. His parents host a dinner on their estate for a number of select guests and powerful figures of Rio to celebrate Napoleon's first fall.[26] After dinner, one of the guests, Dr. Vilaça, begins improvising sayings, in verse, about random topics that the other guests throw at him. The improvisations go on and on and delay dessert indefinitely; at least for Brás Cubas, who then starts to complain and is thus quickly dragged away from the dinner table by his aunt. The boy silently blames Dr. Vilaça for his removal. A while later, when the guests are talking in the house's backyard, Brás Cubas watched Dr. Vilaça wherever he goes. The boy wants to get back at Dr. Vilaça for the loss of his dessert. Dr. Vilaça, "forty-seven years old, married and with children," finds himself chatting to D. Eusébia, "the sister of a Sergeant-Major Domingues, a robust spinster, who, though not pretty, was hardly homely." At one point, Brás Cubas sees that Dr. Vilaça and D. Eusébia "ducked into a small thicket." It is dusk. He follows them in, eavesdrops on the dialogue between the two, whereby he listens to the advances of Dr. Vilaça, the refusal of D. Eusébia, and eventually "the light smack of a kiss, the most timorous of kisses." Upon hearing this, Brás Cubas starts running across the ground, still full of guests, and yelling "Dr. Vilaça kissed D. Eusébia!"[27]

Years then pass. Brás Cubas experiences his first passion for Marcela (who loves him "for fifteen months and eleven thousand milréis"), goes to Europe, graduates from Coimbra University, travels through other countries in Europe, and makes his way back home to Rio only when he is informed that his mother is dying. After her passing, Brás Cubas decides to spend some time at the family's property in Tijuca, a rural neighborhood on the outskirts of the city. A week later, when he is about to leave Tijuca to go back to his father's house, he learns that D. Eusébia just moved to a neighboring house. Somewhat against his will, but pushed by the fact that

---

25 Machado de Assis, *Iaiá Garcia*, 25–26.
26 In Machado's day, lunch (*almoço*) was usually served in mid-morning (8:00 to 10:00 a.m.), and dinner (*jantar*) in early afternoon (noon to 2:00 p.m.).
27 Machado de Assis, *The Posthumous Memoirs of Brás Cubas*, 38–39.

she offered companionship to his mother in her last days, Brás Cubas pays D. Eusébia a visit. And here, the episode begins.

At D. Eusébia's house, Brás Cubas meets the 16-year-old Eugênia, the illegitimate daughter of Dr. Vilaça. Brás Cubas silently recalls the 1814 episode involving D. Eusébia and Dr. Vilaça and calls Eugênia in his mind "the flower of the thicket" – an expression full of ironic meanness. While talking to Eugênia for the first time, Brás Cubas confesses – to himself and to the readers – that he "felt an itch to be a father,"[28] which is another malicious wording. Despite this "itch," Brás Cubas leaves D. Eusébia's house with no intention to return. The following day, he is all ready to go back home when D. Eusébia appears and invites him to dine at her house that day. He refuses the invitation, but she insists, and he then concedes, agreeing to go. When he gets there, Eugênia comes forward to greet him, and this is how Brás Cubas describes her (again, italics are mine for emphasis):

> Eugênia *disadorned* herself that day on my account. I believe it was on my account, but she might have gone about that way quite often. Not even the *gold earrings* she had worn the day before hung from her ears now, two finely shaped ears on the head of a nymph. *A simple white muslin dress; no brooch at the neck*, but a mother-of-pearl button, with another button at the wrist to fasten the cuffs, *and not a bracelet in sight*.
>
> That was the body; as for the spirit, it was hardly different. Clear ideas, simple manners, a certain natural grace, the air of a lady, and perhaps something else.[29]

Eugênia "disadorned herself" the same way that Estela appears "free of adornments." Eugênia has removed her "gold earrings" and there is "not a bracelet in sight"; Estela, for her part, "refused every kind of embellishment, accepting neither ruffles nor earrings nor rings." The "natural inclination toward simplicity" and the "natural grace" of Eugênia and Estela stand out in both passages. This naturalness, in both cases, is not disinterested; that is to say, it has a specific target: Jorge, for Estela; and Brás Cubas, for Eugênia. Think of the topic of female social dependency; again, both Estela and Eugênia depend on being accepted and favored by a powerful man – Jorge, Brás Cubas, or any other – whom they should marry in order to leave behind their adverse, marginalized social conditions.

---

28 Ibid., 81.
29 Ibid., 85.

By refusing to wear "expensive furbishings," Estela and Eugênia are clearly making a tacit but courageous statement: they wish to assert themselves just as they are. To put it another way, Estela and Eugênia don't want to show an artificial image of themselves: their beauty and dignity should appear with no filters, natural and authentic. For the ultimate truth is that, in the natural world, people should be viewed for who they *are* and not for what they *have*. That's the reason why Estela and Eugênia put aside every "adornment": they hope to be viewed – and maybe respected and loved – for who they truly *are*.[30]

This moral statement draws the attention of Jorge, who ends up falling in love with Estela; in the case of Brás Cubas, however, this statement awakes in him feelings of indifference and disdain for Eugênia. Brás Cubas would prefer a statement about *his* virtues and about *him* being as an asset to her. A submissive attitude towards him would articulate this. And here is the point where Estela and Eugênia diverge. Estela proves to be meekly obedient when she is asked by Valéria to wear the earrings. "Jorge did not forget … the constraint with which [Estela] obeyed [his mother, Valéria]." As for Eugênia, she apparently refuses to act with the docility *expected* from her. The day Brás Cubas met Eugênia, she later passes by him. Let Brás Cubas speak for himself: "That afternoon I [Brás Cubas] saw D. Eusébia's daughter riding by on horseback, with a slave following after her; she flicked her whip by way of greeting. I'll confess that I flattered myself with the notion that after a few paces she would look back; but she did not."[31]

Eugênia should have flattered Brás Cubas by gazing back at him, "but she did not." This was a mistake on her part since her goal was to win him over. If people should be evaluated for who they are, Eugênia should have showed herself to be more compliant towards Brás Cubas. That's how Brás Cubas's mind operates – that's how the patriarchal system, of which Brás Cubas is a product, operates. By affirming herself and her dignity as a young woman in the way she dresses and behaves, by doing this not exactly with boldness but with some sort of natural confidence, Eugênia is

---

30 Flora, the heroine from *Esaú e Jacó*, is also socially described through the image of earrings: "A creature [Flora] without a penny to her name, modestly dressed, no earrings, he [Nóbrega] had never seen earrings in her ears, not even two little pearls." *Esau and Jacob*, trans. Elizabeth Lowe (New York: Oxford UP), 222.
31 Machado de Assis, *The Posthumous Memoirs of Brás Cubas*, 82.

not only rejected by Brás Cubas, who still mocks and humiliates her, but also finishes her days in extreme poverty, dwelling in a tenement house.[32]

Besides being an illegitimate daughter, living on the outskirts of the city with her single mother, Eugênia carries another social stigma: she was born lame. This fact might lead readers to think that her disability condemns her and defines her sad destiny. To a degree, this conclusion is correct. But it's also right to say that, if Brás Cubas decided on a whim to marry Eugênia, who is also an educated and beautiful young woman, he could remove all her stigmas at once. Why doesn't he decide to do so? Using the logic of the patriarchal system, since it is the dominant logic of the novel, Eugênia's pride weighs more against her than her chronic disability.[33] Eugênia's disability, in fact, can be viewed as a deceptive factor that diverts readers' attention away from the focal point: patriarchalism in a slaveholding society and its nefarious effects.

Back to the 1814 Episode

"Patriarchalism in a slaveholding society and its nefarious effects" – what does this mean? Let's go back to the 1814 episode, when Brás Cubas secretly caught D. Eusébia and Dr. Vilaça in the act of kissing each other and then loudly spread the news. As stated already, the banquet was offered to members of Rio high society to celebrate Napoleon's first fall. Napoleon represented, at that point, despotism, or the betrayal of modern, liberal ideals. He was a traitor, a tyrant, an enemy of liberalism, progress, the future. Moreover, he humiliated the Portuguese royal family by forcing the court and their members to flee to Brazil. Thus, for political and historical reasons, the name of Napoleon, in Brazil, and in most parts of the Western world, was inevitably associated with obscurantism and obsolescence. Therefore, it would make sense to celebrate the news of his first fall by throwing a sumptuous dinner party. And that is exactly what Brás Cubas's parents did.

After the meal and before dessert, as we already know, Dr. Vilaça stands up and endlessly improvises occasional verses about circumstantial topics, some of them, obviously, against Napoleon. Brás Cubas walks among the

---

32 Ibid., 289.
33 See Roberto Schwarz, *A Master on the Periphery of Capitalism*, trans. John Gledson (Durham, NC: Duke UP, 2001), 56–68.

guests in between the poems. While walking around and waiting for dessert, the boy overhears random conversations. This is one of them:

> A fellow next to me [Brás Cubas] was telling another the latest about the new blacks that were coming in, according to letters he'd received from Luanda, one letter in which his nephew reported he'd already acquired around forty, and another letter in which ... He was carrying them right there in his pocket, but couldn't read them out just yet.[34]

Why can't this "fellow" read the letters out "just yet?" The implicit answer (not presented in the novel) is as simple as it is evident: it would not be appropriate to read letters about human trafficking at a liberal party where partygoers are cheering for modernity, progress, and civilization! In this environment, the "fellow" and his interlocutor act as if they are supporters of liberalism. After the party, in another, more convenient place, they can go back with ease to the topic of making profit from the slave trade.[35]

That's one of the lenses that readers can use to read *Brás Cubas*. The novel is about a narrator-protagonist – *Brás* Cubas – and a country – *Brazil* (*Brasil*, in Portuguese) – both of which want to sell an image of themselves as modern, progressive, and civilized, but whose social practices, deeply associated with slavery and patriarchalism, simply do not match the values they postulate and advocate. Brás Cubas cultivates a veneer of modern acceptability. Beneath the surface, though, astute readers are able to perceive that, beyond his self-perception, there is a narrator who is writing a book against himself without even realizing it. In terms of dialectics, Brás Cubas walks on the tightrope that separates *modernity* (as premise) and *backwardness* (as practice). Brás Cubas's self-confidence can only be compared with his self-deception. In this regard, Brás Cubas is a quixotic character (see Chapter Eight, letter Q). His seriousness should not be taken seriously; nevertheless, Brás Cubas does take his own seriousness seriously. The effect, rhetorically speaking, reveals itself through a playful utterance replete with fierce contradictions, irony, and humor. Brás Cubas mixes *hubris* (arrogance, impetus) with insurmountable moral flaws. His will is as strong as his lack of a fixed purpose and determination. He wishes to reach the summit of a mountain. Which mountain? Any mountain: "Perhaps a naturalist, a man of letters, an archaeologist, a banker, a politician, or even a bishop – even that would do – as long as it mean[s] rank, preeminence, a

---

34 Machado de Assis, *The Posthumous Memoirs of Brás Cubas*, 37.
35 See Roberto Schwarz, *A Master on the Periphery of Capitalism*, 73–75.

great reputation, a superior position."[36] In the end, he gets nothing. And, in the beginning, this fate emerges somewhat encrypted in the uncanny delirium that Brás Cubas experiences before dying.

In this delirious world, while riding a hippopotamus towards the origins of the ages, he encounters "the figure of a woman" who introduces herself to him: "Call me Nature or Pandora; I am your mother and your enemy."[37] They engage in a strange conversation whereby Pandora eventually declares – when Brás Cubas is about to finally step on the territory of death – "For you, great hedonist, there await all the sensual pleasures of nothingness."[38] In Pandora's speech, "the sensual pleasures of nothingness" corresponds to what Brás Cubas will find once he enters the realm of the dead. But, the concept can also be viewed in retrospect: Brás Cubas lives his entire life as a "great hedonist" who relishes "all the sensual pleasures of nothingness."

In this respect, it's worth noting the stark contrast between Machado's first-phase heroines and Brás Cubas. The former set a clear goal and act strategically, with straight determination, to achieve it; the latter steers the course of his life to where his huge, round, and hollow ambitions are circumstantially pointed out. The course of Brás Cubas's life and his attitudes are not the only aspects that take various and unfixed directions; his style, too, mirrors these volatile movements: "and this book and my style are like drunkards; they veer right and left, stop and go, grumble, bellow, cackle, threaten the skies, slip, and fall."[39]

Digression

Lúcia Miguel-Pereira famously argues that Machado's stories have at least one advantage over his novels, that of the concentrated plot that prevents the narrative from going astray, from "veer[ing] right and left,

---

36 Machado de Assis, *The Posthumous Memoirs of Brás Cubas*, 60.
37 Ibid., 21.
38 Ibid., 22. The sentence in Margaret Jull Costa & Robin Patterson's translation is: "O great libertine, what awaits you is the voluptuousness of the void." (*The Posthumous Memoirs of Brás Cubas* [New York: Liveright, 2020], 23) In Gregory Rabassa's version: "You great lascivious man, the voluptuosity of nothingness awaits you." (*The Posthumous Memoirs of Brás Cubas* [New York: Oxford UP, 1997], 18)
39 Machado de Assis, *The Posthumous Memoirs of Brás Cubas*, trans. Flora Thomson-DeVeaux, 153.

stop[ing] and go[ing]." "In [Machado's] novels," states Lúcia Miguel-Pereira, "even in the best ones, the deferrals, the narrator's interpolations lend a wavering and zigzagging aspect to the narrative, which has, at times, wide appeal, but that, in some cases, it turns out to be a bit annoying. This doesn't happen in the stories, though, where the narrative is forced to shrink, and the plot gains cohesion and strength."[40] For this reason, Lúcia Miguel-Pereira rates Machado the tale-writer over Machado the novelist.

Lúcia Miguel-Pereira's claim, albeit reasonable, is also debatable. What is not debatable about this issue, though, is the fact that digression, as a rhetorical device, does, indeed, leave readers unsettled. Why is digression unsettling? Because, when we open a fiction book, our logical mind expects a logical narrative. Digression, for its turn, breaks with some of these expectations. Our logical mind is also primarily teleological (*telos*, from the Greek "end," "goal"): it therefore anticipates a final purpose. In simple terms, the reason for reading a fiction narrative is to reach its conclusion, so that readers can rest and reflect on their experience. However, what digression does, in terms of reading effects, is delay the end of a plot by adding ancillary stories or parallel plots (not to be confused with *subplots*), thoughts, and comments that deviate from the main narrative. Also, as appendages to the central story proliferate, the structure of the narrative becomes non-linear, which also contradicts, and somewhat defies, the reader's logical mind.

How can digression, then, compensate for its unsettling effects? Simply enough: what seems to be gratuitous, off-target, and even disposable should turn out to be, in the end, indispensable. Take, for instance, the passage involving Brás Cubas and Eugênia once more. Midway through the episode, there is a famous digression: "The Black Butterfly" (Chapter XXXI). If we removed this digression, the episode as a whole would fall apart or, at least, become uneven. This digressive moment, in which Brás Cubas kills a black butterfly, sets the parameters through which we, as readers, come to understand the episode itself on a deeper level as well as the *logic* behind Brás Cubas's mindset and behavior. What apparently breaks the logic of the narrative – by inserting an episode within the episode – actually establishes its foundation.

The same could be said about Chapter VII in *Brás Cubas*, "The Delirium," in relation to the novel as a whole. "The Delirium" not only sheds light on the protagonist and his memoirs, but also sets the ground over

---

40 Lúcia Miguel-Pereira, *Machado de Assis (Estudo crítico e biográfico)* (São Paulo: Companhia Editora Nacional, 1936), 255–56.

which the plot plays out. Obviously, this claim requires a lot more discussion for it to be fully clarified and argued. We'll take another direction, instead – a more abstract direction.

There is the logic of the average reader who wants to move straight through the plot to its conclusion, and then there is the digression as an obstacle or deferring device that breaks the linearity of the narrative. So you may ask: what is the logic of a device that functions as a logic breaker? The logic of a logic breaker is … to break the logic, you could answer. Right! But that's too simplistic. There should be something else, like – dialectically speaking – a logic behind the logic.

Think of what we previously discussed in Chapter Two about the philosophical school of Idealism. According to Idealistic premises, objects independent of the mind don't exist, or rather, don't have *functional* existence. Let's go back quickly to this concept. Idealists claim that objects are ideas. Somewhat aligned with them, empiricists postulate that knowledge comes from our sensory experience. That is to say, we come to know what time is, for instance, by experiencing it in our bodies and minds. Thus, time as an objective reality is something like pure abstraction. The 60 seconds that I experience while watching a soccer game are not the same 60 seconds that I experience when I, say, take a test, or do something painful, or boring. In other words, time is relative, and 60 seconds does not last the same amount of time for me and for you in different circumstances. The time on the clock is a measurable reference (60 seconds) that we ourselves measure with a distinct "clock" (i.e. our experience), which provides different results (i.e. a *longer* or *shorter* 60 seconds).

These ideas were floating around during the eighteenth century, as the digressive novel took shape from the pen of writers such as Jonathan Swift, Denis Diderot, Xavier de Maistre, Henry Fielding, and, obviously, Lawrence Sterne. These authors – all references for Machado – took the road opened by *Don Quixote* and were not interested in reason and logic, or in using them as tools to understand and explain the world. The nineteenth-century authors aligned with scientific doctrines, such as Naturalism and positivism, were in charge of that. Sterne and his peers were, instead, more concerned with establishing the novel as a genre while, at the same time, expanding its rhetorical and discursive possibilities. This expansion entailed defying reason and logic, or rather, testing their limits. In this context, digression developed as a literary device. Its "free form" and non-linearity challenged the stable notion of temporality – for time is what digression is ultimately about.

And here lies a tricky point: defying reason and logic by twisting the linearity of time does not imply questioning the value of reason and logic. On the contrary, what digression does, in a sense, is exhibit *the other side* of reason, which, curiously enough, turns out to be the bright side rather than the dark. How so? Let me illustrate this argument with a practical example.

Digression as the Bright Side of Reason: A Practical Example

The phenomenon described in the lines below has happened to me a number of times; and it might have happened to you as well.

All of us, at some point, have had to solve a difficult problem. Students, for example, are constantly required to solve puzzling problems, like, say, math problems. Now, imagine, just for a second, the following situation: You are a high-schooler trying to solve an entangled math problem, but no matter how hard you try – and you have been trying for some time – you can't solve it; you keep getting stuck. The assignment is due tomorrow, and you have to get it done by today (the sooner, the better). You are tired, exhausted. Something is missing, though, for you to solve the problem. Something is missing, and you can't figure out what it is! After hours poring over the problem with no satisfactory results, you decide to take a little rest. You go to the kitchen for some snacks. Your mind soars away from the numbers and formulas. You think about the news, the weekend; you think of a friend whom you haven't seen lately; you hear the crunchy sound of the snacks in your mouth as you chew; you smell the scent of your dog who just passed by you, and … Aha! Suddenly, and unexpectedly, you find what was missing for you to solve the math problem. The answer seems to have magically popped into your head!

This phenomenon is commonly referred to as the *Aha! moment*, and everyone can experience it or has experienced it. But, what conclusions can we draw from the *Aha! moment*, and, most of all, how can we relate it to literary digression and Machado? First, the *Aha! moment* occurs for most of us when we are not concentrating on the problem we want to solve, that is, when our rational thinking is resting. In other words, when we think that we are not thinking, that's the time when we are, indeed, thinking the most. To put it another way, we can consciously exercise our rational thinking, but even when we are not consciously exercising it, our mind is doing so. And that is the first point to be underlined: based on the process whereby the *Aha! moment* generally ensues, it's possible to claim that our mind works better, or most effectively, when its non-rational (infra-rational or super-rational) side is on and in charge; or, when the energy of our rational thinking runs out, the non-rational side of our mind comes in to finish the job that the exhausted, logical mind has left behind.

The key point here is that well before Freud, there was the claim that *reason has its own limits* and, most importantly, that *beyond reason*, in deep compartments of the human mind, *there exist vigorous forms of thinking*. The *Aha!* moment reiterates this general concept. What about Machado in this context?

As we have been trying to demonstrate, from *Brás Cubas* on, Machado's fiction challenges the notion of rationality. Aligned with a literary tradition that goes back to Sterne and Cervantes, Machado endeavored to overcome reason by making creative use of metafiction and digression. In the case of the latter, here is the second point to be underlined: when the plot takes a turn from its central line and apparently *gets lost*, that's the moment when reasoning works to the fullest and the *Aha!* moment is potentially about to dawn. In Machado's novels, to put it another way, when the narrator's train of thought loses track and linearity, that's the moment when the narrative somehow, as a form of compensation, gains strength and density.

In this respect, "The Delirium" functions as the heart of *Brás Cubas* much as the philosophy of Humanitism – which first appears in *Brás Cubas* – is placed at the heart of *Quincas Borba*, and much as the allegory "life is an opera" pulses through all the narrative veins of *Dom Casmurro*. Without these digressive interpolations – and many, many others – the whole structure that upholds these novels would simply collapse. Also, as previously discussed, these structures would collapse because their plots – following Schopenhauer's advice, perhaps – are provided with only a vague line of action.

Machado's Second Phase

The five novels Machado wrote during the second phase of his career are:

1. *Memórias póstumas de Brás Cubas* (1880, serialized version; 1881, book form)
2. *Quincas Borba* (1886–91, serialized version; 1891, book form)
3. *Dom Casmurro* (1899; published in France, the novel arrived and started being commercialized in Brazil only in March of 1900. No serialized version. In 1896, Machado had published just a handful of chapters.)

4. *Esaú e Jacó* (1904; no serialized version)
5. *Memorial de Aires* (1908; no serialized version)

From this group, critics have elected the first three as Machado's Realistic trilogy. With them, the author reached the peak of his career as a novelist. From this trilogy, *Dom Casmurro* stands out as the most read and beloved work by Machado. Along with Guimarães Rosa's *Grande sertão: veredas*, *Dom Casmurro* is the greatest novel of Brazilian literature and, according to Helen Caldwell, "perhaps the finest of all American novels of either continent."[41] Ultimately, from the pages of *Dom Casmurro*, one character and one enigma emerge. The character is Capitolina, better known as Capitu, Machado's most commented-on character and one of the most complex in his gallery. The enigma that has puzzled readers for over a century is whether or not Capitu committed adultery as alleged by her husband, Bento Santiago, better known as Bentinho.

The Enigma Remains Alive (Another Personal Note)

In Chapter One's opening paragraph, I stated that, back in the mid-1980s, I was a high-schooler crazy about soccer, music, and books. In this respect, little has changed: although I'm no longer a high-schooler, I'm still crazy about soccer, music, and books. This somehow explains why, on June 26, 2021, at some point in the afternoon, I took a break from writing this book and went to the web to watch some news about soccer. It just so happened that I came across a curious headline about a soccer player who reviews books on his social media. I didn't know this! His name is Gustavo Scarpa. He plays midfield on the Palmeiras team, and his reviews had gone viral. In the video I watched, a reporter asks Scarpa questions about books and authors: Kafka, Dostoevsky, George Orwell, Machado de Assis … At the end of the interview, the reporter announces that she's forced to ask Scarpa *that* long-time controversial question. Scarpa smiles and says, "I think I know which one is this." The reporter, then, goes on: "In your opinion, did Capitu betray Bentinho or not?"[42]

---

[41] Helen Caldwell, *The Brazilian Othello of Machado de Assis* (Berkeley: U of California P, 1960), 1.

[42] https://g1.globo.com/educacao/noticia/2021/06/26/resenha-com-scarpa-jogador-do-palmeiras-viraliza-ao-comentar-classicos-da-literatura-e-dostoievski-e-seu-camisa-10-veja-video.ghtml

Machado Laughs

Every time I hear the question of whether or not Capitu betrayed Bentinho, I imagine the spirit of Machado laughing. It's well known that Machado enjoyed tricking his readers, and this controversy over the possible adultery is perhaps the major trick he played on his readers. Why a trick?

Critics and scholars commonly agree that the alleged adultery of Capitu functions as a pretext for the novel to raise other more important issues. In this respect, what seems to be central to the novel (i.e. the adultery) plays actually a secondary role, and what comes to be considered secondary should actually be placed at the center of the discussion. Earl Fitz, for instance, argues that *Dom Casmurro* "is only tangentially about adultery." Popular imagination, though, continues to picture the novel as about a possible case of adultery. Readers to date, like Gustavo Scarpa, remain intrigued by the question as to whether Capitu did or did not betray Bentinho. This doubt, however, although ever present, took a sharp turn in the year 1960.

"Nearly three generations, of critics at least, have found Capitu guilty. / Let us reopen the case." These are Helen Caldwell's words taken from her classic *The Brazilian Othello of Machado de Assis*, which was published in 1960.[43] With this study, Caldwell changed the way *Dom Casmurro* had been read. For sixty years, Machado's readers perceived Capitu as a sly traitor and a social climber, a woman who got close to Bentinho out of self-interest, cajoled him into marrying her, and later betrayed his trust by having an affair with his best friend, Escobar. From 1900, when the novel became available to readers, to 1960, Brazil was a society so deeply embedded in the culture of patriarchalism and slavery that, as a result, no one (or almost no one) questioned the "master discourse": the version of the story narrated by Bentinho, a white, well-positioned, and well-regarded man who wrote his memoirs with the intent of accusing his wife of adultery. No one said, "Wait a second! Why should I buy the narrator's version of the story, when the other side, Capitu, cannot speak for herself and in her defense? Why should I trust the word of a man who is prey to jealousy?" Jealousy? Yes; and here is where Helen Caldwell comes in and gives her invaluable contribution.

It was just said that for six decades *Dom Casmurro* was read through patriarchal and slaveholding lenses – that's the reason why the "master discourse" (i.e. Bentinho's first-person account) was never disputed.

---

43 Helen Caldwell, *The Brazilian Othello of Machado de Assis*, 72.

Bentinho was right, and Capitu was wrong. Simple. But, there is another lens to be used for examination: the Francophone lens.

We've already talked about how Francophile Brazilian culture was during Machado's lifetime. This Francophilia maintained its supremacy until the mid-twentieth century, when Brazil, and Latin America as a whole, gradually became Anglophile, or rather, more Anglophile than Francophile, culturally speaking.

What does this have to do with *Dom Casmurro* and its reception? In one of the novel's most famous chapters, Bentinho compares himself with Chevalier des Grieux, the hero of Abbé Prévost's *Manon Lescaut*, a novel published in 1731.[44] This comparison led readers to engage with Machado's novel through *Manon Lescaut* as the main point of reference. In actuality, readers find more allusions to *Othello* than to *Manon Lescaut* in *Dom Casmurro*; nevertheless, in the end, Prévost's novel prevailed over Shakespeare's play in becoming the backdrop to Machado's novel. In this respect, readers took it for granted that the young Bentinho was a version of des Grieux, and Capitu was a mirror of Manon Lescaut. What does this mean in practical, hermeneutical terms?

This means that Bentinho was perceived as a pure-hearted, trustworthy, kindly, and innocent man, like des Grieux, whereas Capitu was seen as an insinuating woman and a perfidious libertine, like Manon Lescaut. Jealousy, in this context, didn't play a part. After all, des Grieux isn't a jealous character as, for instance, Othello is.

Jealousy started playing a part – a central part, by the way – in the analysis of *Dom Casmurro* when Caldwell's book appeared.[45] One remarkable achievement of this study was to show, with a plethora of examples, how *Othello*, not *Manon Lescaut*, had served as the primary literary source for Machado in writing *Dom Casmurro*. This shift in paradigm, whereby Bentinho is paired with the tormented Othello, and Capitu with the innocent Desdemona, provoked a huge change in the way readers approached Machado's novel. Since 1960, Bentinho has been seen as an ambiguous character, one who projects his ambiguity onto Capitu; a tragic personality who blames Capitu for his own failures; and a bitter voice

---

44 Machado de Assis, *Dom Casmurro*, trans. John Gledson (New York: Oxford UP, 1997), 65. The chapter referred to is the one numbered XXXIII and entitled "Combing."

45 One remarkable exception is Roger Bastide who in "Machado de Assis, paisagista," published in 1940, alluded to Bentinho's jealousy (*Teresa: Revista de literatura brasileira*, 6/7 (2006), 426). See Chapter Eight, letter B.

who sees the world around him through the sick lens of jealousy. If we accept Bentinho's jealousy – which he strives to hide and, for sixty years, successfully did – his account becomes naturally unreliable. Bentinho is, in this respect, the paradigmatic model in Brazilian literature of an unreliable narrator.

Nevertheless, for sixty years, Capitu was placed under the spotlight as the unfaithful wife of the well-intentioned, respected, and *reliable* Bentinho. With a feminist and literary approach, Caldwell turned this interpretation upside down. Like Desdemona, Capitu was not just guiltless but also a victim in the hands of a troubled, sickly jealous man. After Caldwell, Capitu was ushered off the stage, and Bentinho was put under the spotlight. We, as readers, need to know him first in order to understand his accusations later – not the other way around.[46] Is Bentinho writing his memoirs, in which he accuses Capitu, as an act of self-defense, as he suggests, or as an act of self-deception (which is most likely the case)?

It's worth noting, however, that *Dom Casmurro* is a novel that can be read as a piece of accusation with no definitive proof. To make his case, Bentinho furnishes readers with his perceptions and presuppositions: first, the way Capitu looked at his best friend Escobar during his funeral (Escobar dies accidentally from drowning); second, the physical resemblance – in the eyes of Bentinho – between Ezequiel, Bentinho's son, and Escobar. These two scraps of evidence are presented in the novel along with the portrayal of Capitu as a girl of lower-class origins, endowed with a sly and clever spirit, who skillfully manages to win Bentinho's heart and marry him. Equipped with these arguments, Bentinho brings his case against Capitu.

In the end, we, as readers, leave *Dom Casmurro* without knowing *for sure* whether Capitu committed adultery or not. Textually speaking, it's not possible to know the answer. Nevertheless, readers tend to pick a side, either in favor of or against Capitu.

And I imagine the spirit of Machado laughing. Why? Because we don't need to pick a side in this conflict. Or rather, *Dom Casmurro* is not about whether Capitu cheated on Bentinho or not, in the first place. This is secondary element, or a *pretext*, in the *context* of the narrative. What is the novel about, then? In the most basic terms, Machado's novel is about the transformation of Bentinho into Dom Casmurro.

As the old Bento Santiago explains in the first chapter of his memoirs, he was nicknamed Dom Casmurro by a casual acquaintance after

---

46 See Hélio de Seixas Guimarães, *Machado de Assis, o escritor que nos lê*, 159–67.

nodding off in front of him while he was reciting a poem of his own during a short train ride. What does this nickname mean? "Don't look it up in dictionaries," Bento Santiago says. "In this case, *Casmurro* doesn't have the meaning they give, but the one the common people give it, of a quiet person who keeps himself to himself. The *Dom* was ironic, to accuse me of aristocratic pretensions."[47] So what did happen to the boy who was born into a wealthy family, who had access to education and everything he needed, who was loved and (over)protected by his widowed mother, who fell in love with his neighbor and eventually married her? What happened to him for that boy to become a disillusioned man full of bitterness, living out his life with the burden of a heavy, sour heart, and trying to hide himself under the shadows of his tortured mind? Trying to answer these questions is what *Dom Casmurro* is primarily about.

The 1999 Trial

In 1953, Helen Caldwell became the first English translator of *Dom Casmurro*. In 1960, she became the first scholar to publish a book – in any language – dedicated to analysis of one specific work by Machado de Assis. In 1987, after other translations of and critical works on Machado, Helen Caldwell died at the age of 82. She couldn't, therefore, see the celebrations that marked the centenary of *Dom Casmurro* in 1999.

The newspaper *Folha de S. Paulo*, for instance, promoted a legal and literary trial, open to the public, whereby lawyers, writers, and critics adjudicated on a court case. The defendant: Capitu. The complainant: Bentinho. The charge: adultery. The participants were divided into defense attorney, prosecutor, witness for defense, witness for prosecution, and a judge. After about three hours of arguments, counterarguments, and witness testimonies, the judge finally came to a decision and decreed that Capitu was … acquitted![48]

For sixty years, Capitu was found mostly guilty. A hundred years after the release of the novel, she was then declared acquitted in a symbolic trial. Helen Caldwell certainly wielded a great deal of influence over Capitu's acquittal. After all, it was she who changed this game. Well, did she really change it? In part, yes; but not fully. And this is the point: if adultery constituted a crime – and in Machado's day it did, when committed by a woman – libel did also – and it still does, indeed. In other words,

---

47 Machado de Assis, *Dom Casmurro*, 4.
48 *Folha de S. Paulo*, June 25, 1999, Caderno Ilustrada, 6–7.

if Capitu is innocent, Bentinho is guilty; if Capitu *is not* an adulterer, Bentinho *is* a libeler. Now that Capitu is acquitted of adultery, when will Bentinho be held responsible for *his* crime? If there is a new trial in 2049, when *Dom Casmurro* will celebrate its 150 years, where Bentinho is the defendant charged with paranoid fabrication and defamation, only then will Helen Caldwell at last fully rest her case. Up until then, though ...

Three (Curious) Notes and Three Bottom Lines:

Note 1: In the *Folha de S. Paulo* event, the judge who presided over the trial against Capitu was José Paulo Sepúlveda Pertence, who, at the time, held the position of federal judge in the Brazilian Supreme Court. To *Folha*, he said he decided to acquit the defendant for scarcity of proof. This was, however, a technical decision; in terms of personal convictions, he was convinced that Capitu committed an adulterous act. "If I had to vote secretly, as a juror," Sepúlveda Pertence declared, "I don't know if I could forgo my intimate moral conviction that the adultery did occur."[49] The burning question here is: if there is not enough proof against Capitu, why did Sepúlveda Pertence have an "intimate moral conviction" that she is guilty?

• *Note 2*: In answering the reporter's inquiry, the Palmeiras midfield player Gustavo Scarpa also said he believes that Capitu is guilty. Even though the accuser does not provide any irrefutable proof against her.

Bottom Line 1: Based on the statements above, made in two different moments – 1999 and 2021 – by two different people – an experienced judge and a young soccer player – we can fairly conclude that, *even acquitted, Capitu continues to be seen as guilty*.

Note 3: In the *Folha* trial, both sides – prosecutors and defendants – made remarks about Bentinho's latent homosexuality. It's possible, indeed, without reaching any definitive conclusion, to feel some homoerotic dimension and homosocial bond between Bentinho and his friend Escobar. Critics, particularly in recent years, have approached this topic. In the *Folha* trial, this argument was brought up *against* Bentinho in order to *defend* Capitu. Her adulterous act – if it did actually occur – should be seen not just as "defensible" but also "desirable," since Bentinho exhibited signs of homosexual propensity.[50]

---

49 Ibid., 6.
50 Ibid., 6.

Bottom Line 2: Maybe Capitu's case should be redirected to and analyzed by psychotherapists. Lawyers, historians, sociologists, and, above all, literary critics have – with a few exceptions – only messed things up.

Bottom Line 3: Brás Cubas says: "for this book's greatest flaw is you, reader."[51] Had Bentinho said this, it would make sense as well. In fact, more sense.

Point of View, *Alter Ego*, and Reliability

As characters, Bentinho and Brás Cubas have a lot of in common. Both write their memoirs. Both embody and exhibit the standard mindset of a representative from the Brazilian ruling class; the exhibition of this mindset can be used against them, but they seem not to realize that. Ultimately, Machado, as an author, appears to use both Bentinho and Brás Cubas to expose and denounce the contradictions and inconsistencies that defined Brazilian elites and, consequently, the country they ruled.

In the case of Brás Cubas, this contradiction consists in the erection of a façade of modernity – European progress – behind which lie retrogressive colonial practices, justified by cynical and hypocritical morals. In the case of Bentinho, it emerges from the process of self-deception and its use as a shield and weapon: as a shield to protect Bentinho from himself and from the moral assessment of the others, and as a weapon to accuse Capitu and use her as a scapegoat for Bentinho's own failures.

Brás Cubas and Bentinho are both first-person narrators. One basic way to look at Machado's second-phase novels is through their narrative points of view. *Brás Cubas*, *Dom Casmurro*, and *Memorial de Aires* are all first-person narratives, while a third-person voice constructs the narratives of *Quincas Borba* and *Esaú e Jacó*. In the first group of narratives, Brás Cubas and Bentinho are deemed unreliable narrators. In practical and specific terms, this means that the author tacitly invites astute readers to form an alliance with him against the narrators. In other words, the figure of the author, implicit in the text, requests that readers deconstruct the discourse and unveil the contradictions of the narrators. *Memorial de Aires*'s narrator, Counselor Aires, on the other hand, is considered to be an *alter ego* of Machado. As such, Aires constitutes, at least in theory, a more reliable voice, one that readers can feel is closer to the author's, especially when compared to the cynical Brás Cubas and the delusional Bentinho.

---

51 Machado de Assis, *The Posthumous Memoirs of Brás Cubas*, 153.

Counselor Aires appears in Machado's two final novels: *Esaú e Jacó* and *Memorial do Aires*. In the latter, he is the pseudo-author/narrator and protagonist; in the former, he is the pseudo-author/narrator who writes about himself (and others) through the third-person point of view. This image, mirroring Aires as a third-person narrator and Aires as a character, is consistent with the novel that centers around the twins Pedro and Paulo, whose origins, rivalry, and destiny are comparable to those of the biblical twins Esau and Jacob. This *hall of mirrors* ultimately establishes the narrative as a sort of labyrinth whereby readers are always prone to getting lost because their perception is constantly deceived. The plot apparently evolves from the love both Pedro and Paulo devote to Flora, who, for her part, seems to love them back as if they were one person. Flora dies an untimely death, while still undecided between Pedro and Paulo.

However, by examining the *trompe l'oeil* structure and technique, through which the narrator of *Esaú e Jacó* narrates himself as another, Stephen Hart builds a compelling hermeneutical hypothesis for a reading of the novel. Hart argues that the events presented by this narrator may function as a cover-up for an unrevealed plot that can be uncovered only by the astute reader (as happens, by the way, in *Brás Cubas* and *Dom Casmurro*). By supporting his arguments with plenty of textual evidence, Hart suggests that the love story involving Pedro, Flora, and Paulo may serve as a veil to hide an affair between Aires and Flora. Hart proposes three possibilities in this respect: "Aires' unconfessed love for Flora, Flora's unconfessed love for Aires," and a "third possibility" whereby "Aires and Flora are lovers."[52]

Hart's proposal of reading *Esaú e Jacó* as a *roman à clé* – which is just one out of four levels of meanings that he identifies and comments on in Machado's novel – should not be taken in terms of right or wrong, true or false. The opposition that better describes his hermeneutic efforts bifurcates into categories such as coherent versus incoherent, or plausible versus implausible. Ultimately, Hart's interpretation responds to a legitimate structural question that the novel tacitly asks its readers, one that shouldn't be overlooked: "Why does Aires write about himself in third person?"[53] Departing from this question, it's more than coherent and plausible to read *Esaú e Jacó* with one eye on the text and another

---

52 Stephen M. Hart, "Four Stomachs and a Brain: An Interpretation of *Esaú e Jacó*," *The Author as Plagiarist – The Case of Machado de Assis, Portuguese Literary & Cultural Studies*, 13/14 (Fall 2005/Spring 2005), 327; 329.

53 Ibid., 325.

on the blind spots of the novel. That's exactly what Hart does. One can agree or disagree with the results of his analysis, but the method employed is indisputably suitable for the work examined.

In terms of critical outcome, what Hart's reading ultimately does is make the formula "*alter ego* = (more) reliability" inconsistent. Counselor Aires is largely recognized by critics and critical readers alike as Machado's *alter ego*. In principle, the proximity of Counselor Aires to his creator makes the character's voice (again, in theory, as I said) more reliable. After all, Counselor Aires speaks for Machado – to a degree, at least. Nevertheless, according to Hart's hermeneutical approach, the effect in *Esaú e Jacó* is the exact opposite: Counselor Aires conceals more than he reveals. And it's up to us, the astute readers, to dig around in the narrative soil in search of what is covered up.

Skepticism

In *Memorial de Aires*, Machado's last novel, Counselor Aires returns as a first-person narrator, a traditional first-person narrator, though. The novel is written in the form of a diary in which Aires records and comments on the events that occurred between January 1888 and September 1889. The entry of May 13, 1888, the day when slavery was officially abolished, reads: "Finally, law. I have never been, nor did my position permit me to be, a propagandist for abolition, but I confess I had a feeling of great pleasure when I learned of the senate's final vote and the princess regent's approval."[54] The passage illustrates the singular position occupied by Counselor Aires through which he ideologically fluctuates between engagement and indifference regarding the major events going on around him. Like Machado, Counselor Aires places himself in a skeptical gap that opposes commitment and detachment. In other words, Aires is neither committed to nor detached from the world; he skeptically oscillates between these two opposite poles.

Skepticism, in this context, refers to a type of active doubt that grants the other, with whom one disagrees, the same consideration as one grants oneself. To put it another way, in a world where reason presides over ideological debates, every part in a dispute might, in principle, be right: one person or the other, one side or the other. This skeptical doubt can lead

---

54 Machado de Assis, *Counselor Ayres' Memorial*, trans. Helen Caldwell (Berkeley: U of California P, 1972), 44.

– and, in fact, led the post-modern twentieth century – to the abyss of relativism. Not in the case of Machado, though, who counterbalances the skeptical reason (relativism) with the destructive effects of social power (absolutism), be it derived from scientism (see Simão Bacamarte) or capitalism (see Brás Cubas and Bentinho). In other words, if skeptical reason renders truth *relative*, the consequences of rationalism, as manifested through its all-pervasive will to power, are *absolute* as they permeate, to a degree at least, every human action.

Counselor Aires is a retired diplomat, a former civil servant who is financially stable but not rich. Rubião, the protagonist of *Quincas Borba*, is not rich, either. He is a former elementary-school teacher who lives in Barbacena and, as a caregiver, takes care of Quincas Borba, a mad philosopher who had appeared in *Brás Cubas* and who came up with a philosophical system called Humanitism. When Quincas Borba dies, Rubião learns that he was named the philosopher's sole heir. The testator imposed, however, a condition for Rubião to receive the inheritance: he should look after Quincas Borba's dog, also named Quincas Borba, and treat him with food and affection – as if the dog were a human being – until his passing. Rubião agrees with the terms of the will and becomes a millionaire overnight. He then moves with the dog from Barbacena to the court. There, his (mis)adventures as a naïve nouveau riche begin.

Quincas Borba is the most raw and touching novel Machado wrote. It's a story about madness and greed, about humans turning other humans into objects, about sadness and indifference to the other. Its characters are planets that orbit around the sun of money and personal interest. Rubião, the quixotic protagonist, doesn't align with them. And because of this, he is deemed the pitiful, the ludicrous, the laughable one, and is mercilessly destroyed by the frivolous society. Ultimately, *Quincas Borba* dramatizes the concept of social Darwinism whereby the fittest – from the "survival of the fittest" – are also the slyest, most unscrupulous, rapacious, and wicked characters.

Critics, *Quincas Borba*, and *Mea Culpa*

From Machado's acclaimed trilogy, *Quincas Borba* has been the most underrated novel. In the English language, for example, we find three books entirely dedicated to analysis and interpretation of *Dom Casmurro*, one to *Brás Cubas*, and none to *Quincas Borba* (see Appendix Two). With regard to translations into English, we find (so far) five of *Brás Cubas*, three of *Dom Casmurro*, and two of *Quincas Borba* – one of them weirdly (to me, at least) entitled *Philosopher or Dog?* (see Appendix One). In terms of articles and essays, the picture is no different: *Dom Casmurro* and *Brás Cubas* have drawn significantly more attention than *Quincas Borba*. As for academic production in Brazil, the critical bibliography on *Dom Casmurro* and *Brás Cubas* far surpasses that of *Quincas Borba*. How to explain this imbalance?

Earl Fitz gives us a hint: "What was once considered the least experimental of Machado's three best known novels … is now, and rightly, judged to be one of his most accomplished efforts."[55] Fitz's hint, though, should be put into perspective. When he says "now," it's 2019. It will take time for the recognition of *Quincas Borba* as one of Machado's "most accomplished efforts" to translate into a more extensive critical debate about the novel. Finally, *Quincas Borba* has been "judged" as an "accomplished effort" by whom? Fitz's modesty doesn't allow him to convey that his is one of the few voices who are "now" working hard to shed new light on Rubião's story. More are needed.

To a considerable degree, *Quincas Borba* "was once considered the least experimental of Machado's three best known novels" – and, for the general reader, it continues to be seen as such – due to its change in the point of view from first person (as in *Brás Cubas*) to third person (like in Machado's first novels). This shift has been interpreted by many as a step back.[56] Paul Dixon, however, convincingly rebuts this argument in an article published in 2016.[57] Dixon even challenges the notion of third-person narration by reminding us that the narrator's perspective in *Quincas Borba*, at times, oscillates between first and third person – a rhetorical maneuver that is also present, albeit to a lesser extent, in Machado's first novels.[58]

Dixon's most notable argument, though, resides in the claim that *Quincas Borba* can be read in opposition *and* as a complement to *Brás*

---

55 Earl E. Fitz, *Machado de Assis and Narrative Theory: Language, Imitation, Art, and Verisimilitude in the Last Six Novels* (Lewisburg, PA: Bucknell UP, 2019).
56 Harold Bloom, in this respect, argues: "Still, a choice between *Brás Cubas* and *Don Casmurro* is between greatness, whereas the very interesting *Quincas Borba* I find uneven, partly because it is narrated in the third person, which is not Machado's mode." *Genius* (New York: Warner Books, 2002), 677.
57 Paul Dixon, "Quincas Borba: um passo atrás?" *Brasil/Brazil*, vol. 29, no. 53 (2016), 1–20.
58 I recall, more specifically, one of the final chapters of *Ressurreição* in which the narrator says: "Reader, let us understand each other. I am the one telling this story, and can assure you the letter was indeed from Luís Batista." Machado de Assis, *Resurrection*, 153.

Cubas. In Dixon's view, *Brás Cubas* is a novel that focuses on the story of the winners, whereas *Quincas Borba*, conversely, concentrates on the trajectory of the losers.[59] Rubião, indeed, loses everything, but his most significant loss is perhaps that of idealism, which causes Machado's hero to be comparable – like Simão Bacamarte and Brás Cubas – to Don Quixote.[60] Ultimately, Dixon's critical contention evolved into a book, released in 2020, entirely dedicated to *Quincas Borba*.[61] Both Dixon's article and his book were originally written in Portuguese.

In short, despite recent efforts to the contrary in both Brazil and the Anglo-American world, *Quincas Borba* continues to be the "ugly duckling" of Machado's major trilogy. The story of Rubião still deserves more critical attention. In this brief introduction to Machado de Assis, readers find more comments on *Brás Cubas* and *Dom Casmurro* than on *Quincas Borba*. This somehow helps perpetuate the imbalance between the first two and the latter. *Mea culpa*, I confess. Yet, by focusing more on *Brás Cubas* and *Dom Casmurro* and less on *Quincas Borba*, this introduction also reflects the actual state of Machado studies.

On a personal note, I remember the lasting impact of my first reading of *Quincas Borba* during my teenage years; it was far more profound than those caused by *Brás Cubas* and *Dom Casmurro*, which I couldn't understand when I first read them. I clearly recall the last scenes of Rubião, the biggest loser, walking the streets of Barbacena along with his faithful dog, Quincas Borba. I still see them confused and dripping wet due to a sudden heavy rainstorm. While wandering without any direction, Rubião repeatedly utters the Humanitism motto: "To the victor, the potatoes!" He is, then, deprived of money, friends – except for the dog – and reason. I'm still convinced that this is the most poignant and pathetic scene – in a sense that it makes us feel sadness and sympathy – ever written by a Brazilian author.

---

59 Paul Dixon, "Quincas Borba: um passo atrás?" 1.
60 Earl E. Fitz, "Machado de Assis' Reception and the Transformation of the Modern European Novel," *The Author as Plagiarist – The Case of Machado de Assis, Portuguese Literary & Cultural Studies*, 13/14 (Fall 2005/Spring 2005), 53–55.
61 Paul Dixon, *Por linhas tortas: Análise de* Quincas Borba *de Machado de Assis* (São Paulo: Nankin, 2020).

Chapter Seven

The World Keeps Changing to Remain the Same

Ecclesiastes

THE BIBLE IS one of the central literary sources for Machado. Despite not being a religious man, he was an avid reader of the Bible. One book, in particular, permeates his fiction with a vigorous presence: Ecclesiastes. Two of its most prominent messages can be summed up in the following quotes: "Vanity of vanities, said the Preacher, vanity of vanities; all is vanity" (1:2); and "The thing that has been, it is that which shall be; and that which is done is that which shall be done: and there is no new thing under the sun" (1:9).

Also an avid reader of the Bible, Shakespeare wrote his Sonnet 59 based on the abovementioned second premise:

If there be nothing new, but that which is
Hath been before, how are our brains beguiled,
Which, laboring for invention, bear amiss
The second burden of a former child!"[1]

The metalinguistic question that this quatrain raises can be viewed as not only Shakespearean but also Machadian: why write if everything has already been written? The answer for both – and for Rousseau, too – is

---

1   William Shakespeare, *All the Sonnets of Shakespeare*, eds. Paul Edmonson & Stanley Wells (Cambridge: Cambridge UP, 2020), 185.

perfectibility.[2] Ultimately, we, as humans, imitate imitations to make our own better ("Whether we are mended," says Shakespeare), although sometimes our attempts happen to be worse than ("or whe'er better they"), or even equivalent to ("Or whether revolution be the same"), that which preceded them.[3] Perfectibility, therefore, is linked to the notion of emulation, a concept that either directly or indirectly guides the literary creation of Shakespeare and Machado alike (see Chapter Eight, letter E).

"There is no new thing under the sun" inherently means, for its part, repetition. The world repeats itself, and history isn't a line whose events dialectically advance towards an ultimate goal, as Hegel and Marx held to be true. History, instead, is a circle. In this context, changes – if I may call a piece of contemporary popular culture into the discussion – are like rainbows: they "are visions but only illusions."[4] This doesn't mean that changes are useless or unnecessary. On the contrary, changes spin the wheel of history, make history come alive, and create a desired illusion of progress, while humanity – mostly without realizing it – continues to run around in circles, following the actual movement of history.

This explains, at least in part, the skepticism of Counselor Aires regarding the abolition of slavery, as commented on in Chapter Six: "I have never been … a propagandist for abolition, but I confess I had a feeling of great pleasure when I learned of the senate's final vote and the princess regent's approval."[5] On the one hand, Aires communicates his feeling of pleasure; on the other hand, this sentiment comes associated with an attitude of withdrawal. Why pleasure? For the conviction that this historical change was absolutely necessary. Why withdrawal? For the belief that this change was as necessary as precarious: humanity can stamp out one form of slavery, but other forms, inevitably, will remain or be reborn, always.

---

2   Jean-Jacques Rousseau, "Discourse on the Origin and Foundations of Inequality Among Men," *The Basic Political Writings*, 2nd edn., trans. Donald A. Cress (Indianapolis: Hackett, 2011), 45–92. On page 53, we read: "there is another very specific quality that distinguishes them [men from animals] and about which there can be no argument: the faculty of self-perfection." Rousseau tackles the topic of perfectibility in terms of self-perfectibility, that is, the human capacity to improve oneself over the course of a lifetime. It's different, therefore, from how Shakespeare and Machado dealt with the concept.
3   William Shakespeare, *All the Sonnets of Shakespeare*, 185.
4   "The Rainbow Connection," song by Paul Williams & Kenneth Ascher.
5   Machado de Assis, *Counselor Ayres' Memorial*, trans. Helen Caldwell (Berkeley: U of California P, 1972), 44.

Acts such as senators and the princess regent giving freedom to enslaved people are often, for Machado, misinterpreted as a manifestation of altruism, when they are indeed an expression of power. (Dialectics, or appearance versus essence, again plays a role here.) For Machado, the pro-slavery plantation owners were concerned about the decrease in their profits (as a result of the abolition of slavery), whereas the proponents of abolition viewed the pursuit of enslaved peoples' freedom as an opportunity to increase their own sense of power. The groups are not the same, for sure. They act differently and represent differing degrees and types of egoism; however, they share at least one point in common: the enslaved individuals were not their primary focus; those individuals were, in fact, a means for these powerful men to fulfill their own personal interests, either material or moral. The event that immediately follows Aires' remark supports this argument.

The episode begins with a statement that encapsulates a philosophy: "There is no public joy that is worth a good private one."[6] After the law abolishing slavery was signed, on May 13, 1888, public celebrations occurred throughout Rio. Counselor Aires heads to the house of some friends, where there is a celebration as well. He mistakenly thinks that they are celebrating the public act – but no. His friends Aguiar and D. Carmo are thrilled about another piece of news: the return of Tristão to Rio, after several years living in Europe. The couple, who have no children, grew very fond of Tristão when he was a little boy. The little boy grew up and took a trip to Portugal with his parents. They were supposed to come back six months later but decided to stay. Years passed by and Tristão, now a doctor, is coming back. "This is how," writes Aires in his diary, "in the midst of the general satisfaction, there can appear a private satisfaction to overshadow it."[7]

"Vanity of vanities; all is vanity." Private satisfaction, for Machado, prevails over ones that would benefit the collective. That's how human nature works. While history is condemned to repeat itself, we, as humans, are doomed to act egoistically according to our own interests and desires, even when we do something that *appears* to have the aim of benefitting the other(s). The episode involving Prudêncio in *Brás Cubas* illustrates, albeit ironically, this argument.

---

6 Ibid., 45.
7 Ibid., 45.

Prudêncio: History Repeats Itself

In his memoirs, Brás Cubas recounts his childhood and recalls instances in which he "played" with an enslaved boy named Prudêncio. Let Brás Cubas take up the story:

> Prudêncio, one of our slave boys, was the horse I rode around on; with his hands on the ground and a length of string between his teeth by way of a bit, I would climb astride his back with a little switch in hand, whipping him, riding up and down and around, and he would obey, moaning at times, but obeying without a word, or at most an "Ow, little master!" to which I would retort, "Shut your mouth, beast!"[8]

Brás Cubas then grows up, falls in love with Marcela, goes to Europe, graduates from Coimbra, spends some time in Italy, and travels back to Rio only because his mother becomes alarmingly ill. She then dies. Brás Cubas is supposed to marry Virgília. He doesn't. Then, his father dies. Brás Cubas meets with his sister to discuss the partition of the family property, and that's when he discovers that Prudêncio had been freed by his father two years earlier. Brás Cubas complains about his father's decision, but, at this point, what's done is done.

Virgília marries Lobo Neves. A while later, Brás Cubas and Virgília become lovers.

Years pass before Brás Cubas, while walking on the streets of Rio, bumps into the freed Prudêncio, who now owns – this was legally allowed – his own enslaved person. Right before this encounter, Brás Cubas was thinking of Virgília. Let him, again, take up the narrative:

> My reflections [of Virgília] were interrupted by a throng; a negro was whipping another in the square. The other did not dare flee; he simply moaned the words: "No, forgive me, master; master, forgive me!" But the first paid no mind, and at each plea he responded with a new lash of the whip.
>
> "Here, you devil!" he said. "Here's your forgiveness, you drunk!"
>
> "Master!" moaned the other.
>
> "Shut your mouth, beast!" retorted the whipper.
>
> I stopped and looked … Gracious heavens! Who was the one with the whip? None other than my slave boy Prudêncio, whom my father had freed some years earlier.[9]

---

8 Machado de Assis, *The Posthumous Memoirs of Brás Cubas*, trans. Flora Thomson-DeVeaux (New York: Penguin, 2020), 31.

9 Ibid., 148.

History repeats itself. In this case, identically. In the past, Prudêncio received the "benefit" of being whipped by Brás Cubas, his master. When Prudêncio, then, has a chance to become a master himself, he pays another the same "benefit." Again, "There is no new thing under the sun." Moreover, "all is vanity"; in this particular case, the vanity of being a master and acting as such.

Identical Twins: "Both Who?"

In *Esaú e Jacó*, monarchy and republic are symbolically embodied in two identical twins: Pedro and Paulo. The twins are rivals in politics as well as in love: both fight for the attention of the young Flora. The story is commonly interpreted as an allegory of the nation (Flora) undergoing a dispute between two opposing political forces, conservatives (Pedro) and liberals (Paulo), who, despite their angry rivalry, are exactly the same. The lust for power, as a converging point, unifies them and also magnifies their striking resemblance. They diverge in terms of the methods used to achieve their goal, but not in terms of the goal itself, which is to seize as many forms of sociopolitical power as possible.

Along with Counselor Aires, the mysterious Flora is endowed with a moral integrity that separates her from the rest of the characters in the novel, all of whom are sunk in frivolity and greed. In her lucidity and sharpness, she tends to view Pedro and Paulo as one person. Flora, thus, can't decide between the two, who assiduously court her. In the end, she "prefers" dying rather than being forced to choose between them. Why choose one when they *absolutely* don't differ? The twins' unity and sameness are ultimately highlighted by Flora's last, and apparently puzzling, words.

In one of the most poignant scenes ever written in the Portuguese language – the death of Flora – Flora is in bed, running a fever, awaiting death, when Natividade, the twins' mother, silently enters her room:

> "Who is it?" asked Flora, seeing her [Natividade] come into the room.
> "It is my sons, who both want to come in."
> "Both who?"
> That word made them believe that delirium had commenced, if it wasn't already ending, because in fact, Flora said nothing more. Natividade stuck to the delirium theory. Aires, when they repeated the dialogue to him, denied it was.[10]

---

10 Machado de Assis, *Esau and Jacob*, trans. Elizabeth Lowe (New York: Oxford UP, 2000), 228.

As a third-person narrator, character, and the one who has the most profound connection to Flora, Counselor Aires' perception should not be seen as deceitful: Flora, indeed, wasn't delirious when she asked, "both who?" (*ambos quais?* in the original). This wording ultimately illustrates Flora's deepest view of Pedro and Paulo – or, symbolically speaking, monarchy and republic, or conservatism and revolution, or any political agents in opposition – as one and the same, since one indefinitely alternates with the other, making the wheel of history spin and continuously repeat itself.

It's worth noting that this perspective is in line with a quote by Xenophon that appears in Chapter LXI of the novel. After the military coup on November 15, 1889, that overthrew the monarchical regime and established the republican system in Brazil, news and rumors about casualties were traveling through the city of Rio, then the nation's capital. Counselor Aires searches for reliable information. Upon hearing that the ministers and the emperor are safe and sound, he decides to have lunch:

> He [Aires] lunched calmy, reading Xenophon: "I considered one day how many republics have been toppled by citizens who desire another kind of government, and how many monarchies and oligarchies are destroyed by the uprising of the people, and of those who climb to power, some are toppled quickly and others, if they last, are admired for being able and happy."[11]

The wheel of history spins and continuously alternates between republicans and monarchists in power, observes Xenophon. His remark coincidently reflects the actual scenario in Brazil. However, there is a gap in time between the writer and the reader that is worth pointing out: Xenophon wrote his commentary at the turn of the fourth century BCE, whereas Counselor Aires read it at the turning of the twentieth century CE; that is to say, twenty-three centuries separate Xenophon and Aires!

---

11 Ibid., 137. Helen Caldwell notes that the quote of Xenophon in *Esaú e Jacó* has other implications. "Ayres resembled that Greek in certain other respects," says Caldwell and mentions a few of them. The main resemblance, in my opinion, lies in the fact that both Xenophon and Aires wrote their memoirs from a third-person perspective. By quoting Xenophon, Machado seems obliquely to state that the narrative structure whereby Aires, as a third-person narrator, narrates a story of a character named Aires, was inspired by the Greek. See Helen Caldwell, *Machado de Assis: The Brazilian Master and His Novels* (Berkeley: U of California P, 1970), 155–56.

A Moral Philosophy: Custódio's Dilemma

The awareness of the fact that "there is no new thing under the sun" and that "all is vanity," or the recognition that history inevitably repeats itself and that personal interests always prevail over collective values, led the mature Machado to the dark territory of pessimism and to areas of intersection, such as skepticism and Nihilism. However, in order not to succumb to pessimism, Machado found an antidote in humor. The result is a style that blends "the pen of mirth and the ink of melancholy," as Brás Cubas puts it in the Prologue of his posthumous memoirs (see Chapter Eight, letter Q).[12]

In the case of *Esaú e Jacó*, a satirical, three-chapter-long digression functions as a sort of counterweight to the tragedy involving Pedro, Paulo, and Flora, as well as a moral philosophy that somehow endeavors to respond to the ceaseless cycle of history, which, in its eternal repetition, gradually deprives life of meaning.[13] Here's a summary of this digressive incident:

A few days before the proclamation of the republic, a shopkeeper named Custódio from a nearby pastry shop came to talk to Counselor Aires. His story was, indeed, curious. After being convinced by his clientele, Custódio finally decided to repaint the old sign of his shop. The painter, however, told Custódio after examining the sign that it needed to be replaced. The wood was too old, splintered, and riddled with termites. Custódio insisted on repainting the old sign, but the painter refused to do it: "he was an artist and would not do work that was going to be ruined from the start." Counselor Aires agrees with the painter's view, saying: "New paint on old wood is worth nothing."[14]

Custódio, however, wanted to keep the old sign. In principle, he wanted it "more out of economy than out of affection" – Custódio is too miserly to pay for a new sign. But, now that he *has* to replace it, he finds that affection is worth a lot. "Now that he [Custódio] was going to exchange the sign," says the narrator, "he felt he had lost a part of his body." With a certain sarcasm, Counselor Aires thinks of "writing a Philosophy of Signs."[15]

---

12 Machado de Assis, *The Posthumous Memoirs of Brás Cubas*, 3.
13 I extensively discussed the semantic effects of repetition in my work *Matéria lítica: Drummond, Cabral, Neruda e Paz* (Cotia: Ateliê, 2016), 55–84.
14 Machado de Assis, *Esau and Jacob*, 109.
15 Ibid., 110.

Days pass and November 15 comes. After lunch, Counselor Aires' reading of Xenophon is disrupted by someone at the door of his house who wishes to talk to him. It is the desperate Custódio. Aires allows him to come in. "What's going on, Mr. Custódio?" asks Aires. The day before, November 14, Custódio had gone to see the sign; it was half done. The word *Confeitaria* (Pastry Shop) had been painted, as well as the letter *d* (for the Portuguese *do*, which, in English, translates to *of the*). "The letter 'o' and the word *Império* [Empire] were only outlined in chalk." Custódio "liked the paint and the color," but "urged haste." It was Thursday and "he wanted the sign inaugurated on Sunday."[16]

When Custódio wakes up on Friday the 15, the empire has fallen! "At first, in his shock, he [Custódio] forgot the sign," says the narrator. "When he remembered it, he saw it would be necessary to put the painting on hold. He dashed off a note, and sent a clerk over to the painter. He only said: 'Stop at the "d."'" But it's too late. Pressured by Custódio, the painter had woken up earlier that morning and finished the painting: *Confeitaria do Império* (Pastry Shop of the Empire). Custódio, then, tells the painter he will have to redo the second half of the sign. The painter, for his turn, replies by saying that Custódio will have to pay him what he initially owed first. After arguing over the payment, they eventually reach a deal. The first part, *Confeitaria*, will be kept, and Custódio has to choose which words will come after.

"Come to my aid, Excellency," says Custódio to Aires "Help me out of this predicament." If Custódio keeps the name *Império*, supporters of the republic could come at night and break the shop's windows. "You can call it 'Confeitaria da República' [Pastry Shop of the Republic]," says Aires at first. Custódio then argues that, in one or two months, there could be a counter-revolution: "I'd be back where I am now, and I would lose money again." Aires agrees, and so he proposes *Confeitaria do Governo* (Pastry Shop of the Government): "It will serve equally well for one regime as for the other." Custódio ponders the suggestion and finds a reason against it, too: "no government lacks an opposition. And the oppositions, when they come down the street, could give me a hard time ... What I want is the respect of all," he says, in a tone that exudes both terror and avarice.[17]

Aires mulls over the problem for a while longer. At last, he comes up with two more suggestions. First, "Leave the sign painted the way it is, and under the title have these words written, which will explain the

---

16 Ibid., 138.
17 Ibid., 141.

name: 'Founded in 1860.'" (Custódio's shop was indeed founded in 1860); and second, "Leave the word 'Império' and add underneath, in the middle, these two which don't need to be big letters: 'das leis,' 'of the Law.'" Custódio rejects both, saying, "Since the letters underneath were smaller, they could not be read as quickly and clearly as those above … Thus if a politician or some personal enemy did not quickly grasp the subtitle …" In response to the first suggestion, Custódio remarks that "it would seem that the pastry chef, by emphasizing the date of opening the shop, boasted about being old."[18]

In a satirical fashion, Machado seriously questions the limits of language and its ability to (mis)communicate. Ultimately, the decoding process of communication pertains to those who receive the message and decode it according to their own ideological frameworks. In contemporary terms, Custódio is terrified at the thought of being *cancelled* by his present and future customers. In times of great political divide, a form of cancel culture is always active, ready to call out people and push them towards social ostracism. What Custódio is trying to do is walk on the public tightrope without falling down. To do so successfully, he must use words as carefully as possible. In this regard, he can't put the terms *empire, republic, government, founded in 1860,* or *empire of the law* – with *of the law* in smaller letters – on the shop's sign. If not any of these, what words can he paint on the sign?

Counselor Aires proposes another option, the name of the street, so it would read *Confeitaria do Catete.* He had forgotten, though, that there is another pastry shop located on Catete street. Both shops are, in principle, *do Catete* since both are located there. No one shop can claim exclusivity. Aires gives up at last. He says Custódio should put nothing on the sign,

> unless he [Custódio] wanted to use his own name, "Confeitaria do Custódio." Many people certainly did not know the house by any other name. A name, a very name of the owner, did not have any political or historical significance, not hate or love, nothing that would call the attention of either regime and consequently put into peril his Santa Clara tarts, much less the life of the proprietor and the employees. Why not adopt this solution?[19]

From the terms initially brainstormed – republic, government, empire (founded in 1860, of the law) – to the option of the street name – Catete

---

18 Ibid., 142–43.
19 Ibid., 143.

street – then finally arriving at simply Custódio's name, it's possible to see a movement towards individualization, as if the *solution* to be adopted in response to Custódio's dilemma is the individual. In principle, the individual carries "not hate or love." Ideologies, on the other hand, are replete with both. They function as a means of expression for both. But, Custódio can find a place between the regimes by simply being Custódio. And who is Custódio? To his clientele, Custódio is who he wants to be: liberal one minute, conservative the next; both at same time; or even none of them. When history and historical meaning are continuously spinning and eternally switching, or when nothing is definitive in this world, why must Custódio be a fixed, unchangeable person?

"What Is Definitive in This World?"

When Baroness Natividade, the twins' mother, starts worrying about the rivalry between Pedro and Paulo, she seeks the advice of Counselor Aires. Discussing specifically Paulo with Aires, Natividade asks: "So you think Paulo will always be like this?" To this, Aires responds: "I won't say forever. Nor do I say the contrary. Baroness, you demand definitive answers, but tell me what is definitive in this world, except for your husband's game of whist?"[20]

If nothing is definitive, then "all is fleeting in this world …"

"All Is Fleeting in This World"

"All is fleeting in this world," writes Counselor Aires in his diary on August 24, 1888. And he continues:

> If my eyes were not ailing, I would devote myself to composing another *Ecclesiastes, à la moderne*, although there must not be anything modern since that book. He was already saying that there was nothing new under the sun, and if there was nothing new in those days there has been nothing new since, or ever will be. Everything is thus contradictory and unstable also.[21]

Everything is contradictory; even changes, as they don't really change anything.

---

20 Ibid., 82.
21 Machado de Assis, *Counselor Ayres' Memorial*, 87–88.

"One Also Changes Clothes Without Changing Skin"

The twins' father, Baron de Santos, arrives at Counselor Aires' house on November 15, 1889, bringing news of the fall of the empire: "It's true, counselor, I saw the troops coming down the Rua do Ouvidor, I heard the cries for the republic," he says, agitated, and continues: "The stores are closed and the banks too, and the worst is if they do not open again, and we fall into public disorder. It is a disaster." Counselor Aires wants to calm him down, so he says: "Nothing would change. It was possible that the regime would, but one also changes clothes without changing skin."[22]

Nothing changes: life is repetition.

Life Is Repetition

"Life, on the other hand," writes Counselor Aires on September 30, 1888, in a passage in which he compares life and art,

> Life … is like that, a repetition of acts and gestures, as in receptions, meals, visits, and other amusements; in the matter of work it is the same thing. Events, no matter how much chance may weave and develop them, often occur at the same time and under the same circumstances; so it is with history and the rest.[23]

Is There Any Way Out? Yes, There Is

On March 13, 1889, Counselor Aires wrote in his diary: "There is nothing like the passion of love to make original what is commonplace, and new what is dying of old age." He goes on to mention an old story, that of Adam and Eve from the book of Genesis, and add: the "drama of love, which appears to have been born of the serpent's guile and of man's disobedience, has never yet failed to play to full houses in this world." And here is the key section to note in the passage: "Now and again some poet lends it his tongue, amid the tears of the spectators; only that."[24]

Nothing is new. But the love of art, or the passion for (re-)creation, can "make original what is commonplace." In this sense, the artist is an

---

22 Machado de Assis, *Esau and Jacob*, 144.
23 Ibid., 111.
24 Machado de Assis, *Counselor Ayres' Memorial*, 172–73.

illusionist. Through their artistry, they make the old seem new. They restore the freshness of the world, and, thus, they renew and invigorate *our* sensitive perception of the world. For Machado, in sum, one response to the repetition of history is the recreation of history through an imaginative mind. The act of restoring the newness of the world in art can function as a sort of compensation for the vanity, selfishness, decadence, and corruption which inevitably pervade *our* vulnerable human nature.

Machado and Nietzsche

Comparing Machado and Nietzsche in full would result in another book entirely, and this one is shortly coming to an end. It's possible, though, that some concepts examined in this chapter might make the readers think of Nietzsche. The eternal recurrence of the same, for instance. In this case, it's worth pointing out and briefly commenting on possible links between these two writers.

Repetition as an underlying principle of history preoccupied Machado as well as Nietzsche. Both also identified two basic patterns in this cycle of repetition. The first holds that moral agents (i.e. individuals endowed with moral agency) act permanently in their own self-interest, even when they further the interests of the others. According to this view, there is no such thing as altruism, just various degrees of egoism, or selfishness. The second pattern is the lust for or the will to power, both inwardly, as self-overcoming or self-mastery, and outwardly, as sociopolitical domination. In both patterns, the focus falls on the individual, and not on the community. Machado and Nietzsche adopted the materialistic and metonymical – *pars pro toto* – method of analysis. In this respect, in order to comprehend metaphysical concepts such as *history* or *humanity*, they begin with individuals in particular circumstances, and analyze them as psychologists trying to define a coherent link between behavior and motivation, or appearance and essence (though, *essence*, or essentialism, as opposed to relativism and historicism, is a problematic concept, particularly in Nietzsche but also in Machado's works).

If the present repeats the past, and the future repeats the present, and we, as humans, are inevitably trapped inside this whirl of meaningless repetition, what attitude ought we to adopt, not to escape the whirl but to make it meaningful at least? Again, one answer is art, or defying historical reality through daring imagination. After all, art *is* the realm of meaning *par excellence*. Art, in the broadest sense possible, can re-signify life after time and history have, through repetition, de-signified it. Art, in the broadest sense possible, doesn't mean just writing new poems about old themes; it also means looking at the oneself and at the world with the eyes of a poet: what Nietzsche calls "the art of staging and watching ourselves";[25] or, in other words, the art of aestheticizing life. Because, ultimately, "All the world's a stage," as Jacques says in Shakespeare's *As You Like It*.[26]

As stated above, this is a rough and simplified picture. It's a possible avenue to explore, if you will. We know that Machado had heard about Nietzsche, because Sílvio Romero mentioned the German philosopher once in his 1897 book about (and against) Machado, but it's unlikely that Machado read any of Nietzsche's works.[27] Romero's passing reference indicates that the name of Nietzsche was circulating in Brazil at the turn of the twentieth century. From that point on, other researchers have pointed out similarities between Machado and Nietzsche: José Barreto Filho,[28] Raimundo Magalhães Júnior,[29] Mattoso Câmara Júnior,[30] Raymundo Faoro,[31] and Roberto Schwarz,[32] among others. Most of the commentary refers to Nietzsche in passing, as is true for William Grossman who, in the prologue to his translation of *Brás Cubas*, argues, without providing any specifics, that "there are surely Nietzschean elements in Quincas Borba's philosophy, which Machado ridicules in the latter part of this book."[33]

---

25 Friedrich Nietzsche, *The Gay Science*, trans. Walter Kaufmann (New York: Vintage Books, 1974), 133.
26 William Shakespeare, *As You Like It*, eds. Barbara A. Mowat & Paul Werstine (New York: Simon & Schuster, 2019) 143.
27 Silvio Romero, *Machado de Assis: estudo comparativo de literatura brasileira* (Rio de Janeiro: Tipografia Universal Laemmert, 1897), 257.
28 José Barreto Filho, *Introdução a Machado de Assis*, 2nd edn. (Rio de Janeiro: Agir Editora, 1980), 97–98.
29 Raimundo Magalhães Júnior, *Machado de Assis desconhecido* (Rio de Janeiro: Civilização Brasileira, 1955), 202.
30 Mattoso Câmara Júnior, *Ensaios machadianos: língua e estilo* (Rio de Janeiro: Livraria Acadêmica, 1962), 103–07.
31 Raymundo Faoro, *Machado de Assis: a pirâmide e o trapézio* (São Paulo: Companhia Editora Nacional, 1974), 332; 401–02.
32 Roberto Schwarz, *Ao vencedor as batatas*, 3rd edn. (São Paulo: Duas Cidades, 1988), 139. Also, *Um mestre na periferia do capitalismo* (São Paulo: Duas Cidades, 1990), 166.
33 William Grossman, "Translator's Introduction," *Epitaph of a Small Winner*, Machado de Assis, trans. William Grossman (New York: Noonday, 1952), 13–14.

The affirmation of life as a dimension deprived of metaphysics, or life hypothetically thought without metaphysics, can be seen as another point of intersection. In *Quincas Borba*, for instance, the philosopher Quincas Borba affirms:

> There is no such thing as death. The meeting of two expansions, or the expansion of two forms, can lead to the suppression of one of them, but, strictly speaking, there's no such thing as death. There's life, because the suppression of one is the condition for the survival of the other, and destruction doesn't touch the universal and common principle. From that we have the preserving and beneficial character of war.[34]

Nietzsche, nine years before *Quincas Borba*, had stated the following in *The Gay Science*:

> Life – that is: continually shedding something that wants to die. Life – that is: being cruel and inexorable against everything about us that is growing old and weak – and not only about *us*. Life – that is, then: being without reverence for those who are dying, who are wretched, who are ancient? Constantly being a murderer?[35]

The affirmation of life, a topic that both Machado and Nietzsche develop from their readings of Schopenhauer, can be paradoxically intensified by forces of negative affection. In the Schopenhauerian story "Viver!" ("Life!"), the last man, Ahasuerus, is dying and yet he "still dreams of life." An eagle, upon witnessing the last man dying and dreaming, remarks in the last line of the story: "He [Ahasuerus] only hated life so much because he loved it so dearly."[36]

About a decade earlier, in *Thus Spoke Zarathustra* – also Schopenhauerian in various aspects – Nietzsche put the following words in the mouth of his hero: "At bottom I love only life – and verily, most when I hate it!"[37]

---

34 Machado de Assis, *Quincas Borba*, trans. Gregory Rabassa (New York: Oxford UP, 1998), 13.
35 Friedrich Nietzsche, *The Gay Science*, 100.
36 Machado de Assis, "Life!," *The Collected Stories of Machado de Assis*, trans. Margaret Jull Costa & Robin Patterson (New York: Liveright, 2018), 755.
37 Friedrich Nietzsche, *Thus Spoke Zarathustra*, trans. Adrian del Caro (Cambridge: Cambridge UP, 2006), 84.

"Everything Is the Same"

In *Thus Spoke Zarathustra*, Nietzsche alludes to the book of Ecclesiastes a few times, in different moments of the narrative. In the passage about the Soothsayer – whom many scholars believe to be Schopenhauer in disguise[38] – there is a doctrine circulating among men that proclaims that "everything is empty, everything is the same, everything was!"[39] This wording parodies Ecclesiastes' premises that "all is vanity" ("everything is empty"), "there is no new thing under the sun" ("everything is the same"), and "the thing that has been" ("everything was"). The concept of the eternal recurrence, also present in *Thus Spoke Zarathustra*, reinforces the idea, previously postulated in Ecclesiastes, that "there is no new thing under the sun," and, therefore, *everything is the same*.

"It's the Same Thing"

The story of Rubião in *Quincas Borba* starts in the town of Barbacena, in the province of Minas Gerais, and cyclically finishes in the same place. After being deceived and exploited by his "friends" in the court, after losing his fortune, dignity, and sanity, Rubião makes his way back to his hometown, accompanied by his dog Quincas Borba, ultimately to die there. Both, indeed, come to die, one after the other, just three days apart. First, the man, then the dog. In the last lines of the novel, the narrator tries to bring some sort of consolation and comfort to the reader by saying: "Come now! Weep for the two recent deaths if you have tears. If you only have laughter, laugh! It's the same thing." The stars, like blinking eyes in the sky, are too high up to "discern the laughter or the tears of men."[40]

If history cyclically repeats itself, and if humanity is condemned to repeat history indefinitely, it doesn't matter if we laugh in the face of a tragedy or cry over a fortunate event. In the circle of history, tragedy and fortune are twin siblings, like Esau and Jacob, or Pedro and Paulo, or monarchy and republic, or sanity and insanity. Our feelings towards them won't change anything. Nevertheless, we can't prevent our

---

[38] See Friedrich Nietzsche, *Assim falou Zaratustra*, trans. Paulo César de Souza (São Paulo: Companhia das Letras, 2011), 327.
[39] Friedrich Nietzsche, *Thus Spoke Zarathustra*, 105.
[40] Machado de Assis, *Quincas Borba*, trans. Gregory Rabassa (New York: Oxford UP, 1998), 271.

emotions from rising. So, before the splendor and dullness of the world, let's rejoice, grieve, fight, surrender, confide, mistrust, seek truth, be delusional. Let's weep if we have tears or laugh if we only have laughter. "It's the same thing."

Chapter Eight

The Machado Alphabet

IN THE ENTRIES below, I recap concepts and ideas related to Machado as well as introducing others.

Absenteeism Machado's detractors have accused him of absenteeism. If one considers this concept to be the opposite of social and political activism, the accusation makes sense. Except for a brief period in the beginning of the 1860s – 1861 and 1862, when he wrote the series of *crônicas* entitled *Comentários da semana* – Machado preferred to stay away from public debates related to pressing political issues. Staying away doesn't mean ignoring, though. His fiction incorporates the major historical events of his time, both nationally (the Paraguayan War, Proclamation of the Republic, Abolition of Slavery) and internationally (the Crimean War, Napoleonic Era). But, as a fictionist, particularly in his second phase, his skepticism precluded him from taking a stand, or from taking a *fixed* stand. Nonetheless, it's worth noting that not taking a stand can be an inverse political statement. Think of Melville's Bartleby, for instance – from "Bartleby, the Scrivener: A Story of Wall Street" by Herman Melville, published in 1856. The obstinate refusal of Melville's character to do what he was *supposed* to do has had huge political and cultural implications. Machado, too, said *no* to political activism while still being deeply interested in politics. Nevertheless, Machado said *yes* and embraced – in a subtle and elusively Machadian way – the feminist cause (see letter F).

Bastide The French sociologist Roger Bastide taught at the University of São Paulo from 1937 to 1954. His contributions to Brazilian studies in the field of sociology were rich and invaluable. His books are deemed classics and continue to be reprinted in new editions to this day. While in

Brazil, Bastide read Machado, whom he considered "a master of world literature."[1] Within Machadian studies, Bastide is recognized for at least two remarkable achievements: first, for helping promote Machado in France during the late 1950s and throughout the 1960s and 1970s (Bastide died in 1974); and second, for writing an essay on Machado – "Machado de Assis, paisagista" ("Machado de Assis, the Landscape Painter") – which became a cornerstone of Machadian criticism. Appearing in 1940, "Machado de Assis, paisagista" came to be the first *modern* interpretation of the author. To a significant extent, Bastide's essay redefined the way we read Machado's fiction. Before 1940, Machado had had important interpreters, such as Astrojildo Pereira, Lúcia-Miguel Pereira, and Augusto Meyer. However, none of them was able to reveal an unknown Machado like Bastide did. In 1940, Machado was seen as a writer completely averse to painting the natural landscapes of Brazil and was accused of being anti-nationalist for that. In his essay, Bastide convincingly proves that, even without describing huge tableaux of landscapes in his stories and novels, or even without painting them at all, Machado "worked the miracle of making nature more present in brief than had he painted it across lengthy pages."[2] With an innovative literary technique originally used in painting, known as the "transposition of elements," Machado "renewed the art of landscaping."[3] Apparently absent, Brazilian nature emerges in Machado's stories and novels with great intensity when the reader learns how to look for it (see letter L).[4] Before Bastide, critics aimed to reveal the other Machado, hidden in the interstices of his texts; Bastide, however, successfully revealed "the other of the other." Among the foreign critics of Machado, Bastide stands out as the most important prior to Helen Caldwell. The few but dense pages of "Machado de Assis, paisagista" still await a skilled translation into English.

Crônica Borges praised Poe for inventing a literary genre – the detective story – and, consequently, a literary reader – the reader of detective stories. Neither existed before Poe.[5] Machado didn't invent a new genre or reader, but he did come close. By writing more than 600 *crônicas* over the

---

1 Roger Bastide, "Machado de Assis, paisagista," *Teresa: Revista de literatura brasileira*, 6/7 (2006), 427.
2 Ibid., 425.
3 Ibid., 423.
4 Ibid., 425.
5 Jorge Luis Borges, "El cuento policial," *Obras completas*, 3rd edn., vol. IV (Buenos Aires: Emecé, 2005), 204–13.

course of four decades, he laid the foundations for the genre to evolve and take the shape we now know. Before Machado, there were attempts at *crônica*, mainly by José de Alencar, but not established *cronistas* in Brazil. In this regard, although Machado didn't invent the genre, his consistent contribution undoubtedly defined its modern basis. Similarly, Machado deserves credit for establishing the modern concept of the short story and novel in Brazil. But in these matters, at least, he had access to more models to learn from and build on, particularly in the case of the Brazilian novel.

Digression The dynamics of thought in Machado's style are both sinuous and insinuating thanks to the artful use of digression. As a rhetorical device, digression invites the reader to dance. Readers who accept the invitation dance and laugh. The digressive thought spins while drawing a colorful mosaic of ideas, feelings, and desires, committed not to rigor or truth, but rather to challenging the limits of logic and reason. The digressive method of narrating ultimately problematizes and defies the notion of schematic rationalism and its strict premises.

Emulation "In the month of August 1838," says the narrator, an old clergyman, in *Casa Velha*, "I read the *Memoirs* which another priest, Luis Gonçalves dos Santos, known as Father Perereca, had written about the time of the king [i.e. 1808–21], and it was this book that made up my mind. I found it decidedly second rate, and wanted to show that a member of the Brazilian clergy could produce something better."[6] Machado also wanted to show that a member of the Brazilian *intelligentsia* "could produce something better" than had been managed until that point. Ezra Pound created the slogan "make it new." In relation to his fellow Brazilians, at least, Machado would prefer the motto *make it better*.

Feminism Machado's heroines are models of moral virtue. Moral not in an ethical sense, but rather in a literary or aesthetic sense. They are complex, clever, fearless, perceptive, and strong. They are endowed with will and determination, wit and self-confidence. As such, they challenge the male-dominant social environment, not to pose a threat to it, but rather cunningly to carve out a more dignified space within it. Through his heroines, therefore, Machado makes a powerful political statement against the oppressive patriarchal system while in favor of women's empowerment

---

6 Machado de Assis, *The Old House*, trans. Mark Carlyon (Rio de Janeiro: Cidade Viva, 2010), 45.

and gender equality. Machado's arguable absenteeism (see letter A) – at least here – does not bear out.

Greeks When Machado died in 1908, José Veríssimo wrote in the obituary: "Mulatto, he [Machado] was indeed a Greek from the greatest era [of ancient Greek history]." In a letter, Joaquim Nabuco reproached Veríssimo for the use of the term "mulatto," in referring to Machado, and concluded: "To my eyes, I just saw the Greek in him [Machado]."[7] At the turn of the twentieth century, Greek culture became fashionable in Brazil. Several authors, particularly poets, strove to incorporate references to ancient Greece. The results, overall, were superficial and artificial, "a Greece made out of pasteboard, that is, purely decorative."[8] In order not to make the same mistake as others, Machado, who was indeed a great admirer of ancient Greek culture, took another path: the road of satire, specifically Menippean satire, as had other authors he loved, among them Erasmus, Rabelais, Cervantes, Swift, and Voltaire. José Guilherme Merquior analyzed *Brás Cubas* through the lenses of Menippean satire in a seminal article which is helpful and enlightening.[9] Ultimately, as a stylistic paradigm, Menippean satire constitutes a backbone of Machado's unique style. Nevertheless, the Greece to which Veríssimo and Nabuco alluded in relation to Machado wasn't that of satire. They referred instead to other facets of Machado's personal and literary style, such as elegance, refinement, formalism, range of knowledge, wit, and lightness.

Helena *Helena* is the most Romantic of Machado's novels. The narrative exhibits the vices and virtues of Romanticism – a style in which, oddly enough, vices can become virtues. Perhaps for its Romantic nature, *Helena* was successfully adapted for Brazilian television twice: first, in 1975 (20 episodes), and then in 1987 (stretched across 162 episodes). Other than *Helena*, adaptations of Machado's works for the screen – with few exceptions – have been of questionable quality, not because of the actors and directors involved in the productions, but mostly for the fact that Machado's works, overall, don't seem to be suitable for the screen.

---

7 *Apud* Jean-Michel Massa, *A juventude de Machado de Assis*, trans. Marco Aurélio de Moura Matos (Rio de Janeiro: Civilização Brasileira, 1971), 46.
8 Brito Broca, *A vida literária no Brasil – 1900* (Rio de Janeiro: José Olympio, 1975), 102.
9 José Guilherme Merquior, "Gênero e estilo das 'Memórias Póstumas de Brás Cubas,'" *Colóquio/Letras*, no. 8 (1972), 12–20.

Internationalization Will Machado achieve the international recognition he undoubtedly deserves some day? It's impossible to know. But it doesn't matter. We, as Machado-lovers, will continue working tirelessly, generation after generation, to reach this goal.

Joking, Tragedy, and Formality The moral tale below functions as a digressive cut from *Quincas Borba*'s main narrative. It's a joke about tragedy and formality which, to a degree, encapsulates the entire story of Rubião.

> Once upon a time there was a cottage burning by the side of the road. The owner – a poor ragged wretch of woman – was weeping over her disaster, sitting on the ground a few steps away. Suddenly, a drunken man happened along. He saw the fire, saw the woman, and asked her if that was her house.
> "It's mine, yes, sir, and all I have in this world."
> "Do you mind if I light my cigar from it?"
> The priest who told me this certainly must have edited the original text. You don't have to be drunk to light your cigar on someone else's misfortune.[10]

Kafka Allen Ginsberg reputedly deemed Machado de Assis "another Kafka."[11]

Landscaping In his "Machado de Assis, paisagista," Roger Bastide (see letter B) quotes a famous passage from Chapter XXXII of *Dom Casmurro* in which Bentinho looks at Capitu's eyes, to illustrate the notion of "transposition of elements," whereby nature and character – in this case, Capitu and the sea – become fused:

> They [Capitu's eyes] held some kind of mysterious, active fluid, a force that dragged one in, like the undertow of a wave retreating from the shore on stormy days. So as not to be dragged in, I held on to anything around them, her ears, her arms, her hair spread about her shoulders; but as soon as I returned to the pupils of her eyes again, the wave emerging from them grew towards me, deep and dark, threatening to envelop me, draw me in and swallow me up.[12]

---

10 Machado de Assis, *Quincas Borba*, 168.
11 Despite the great frequency with which Ginsberg's claim is cited, on book covers, flap texts, and reviews, I have not been able to find the primary source.
12 Machado de Assis, *Dom Casmurro*, trans. John Gledson (New York: Oxford UP, 1997), 63.

In the nineteenth-century novel, landscape was commonly used as a backdrop, or functioned like a canvas on a wall, just as it does in this passage from Eça de Queirós's O primo Basílio:

> This room was at the back of the house and gave on unoccupied land, surrounded by a low stockade, full of tall weeds and chance vegetation. Here and there, in the summer-crested verdure, large stones glittered in the heat of the perpendicular sun. One old fig-tree, isolated in the midst of the landscape, spread out its immobile foliage, which, in the white light, took on the dark tints of bronze. Beyond, the backs of other houses could be seen, with verandahs, and washing hanging out to dry. A vague, low, dusty haze thickened the luminous air.[13]

By making the characters somehow embody and resemble nature, Machado's style appears more concise. See, in this respect these lines from Iaiá Garcia, also mentioned by Bastide: "Iaiá walked through the doorway and left; she needed some air, space, light; her soul coveted an immense bath of blue and gold, and the afternoon awaited her clothed in its most beautiful, celestial shades."[14]

Midlife Crisis, or the Forty-Year Crisis This refers to the period from 1878 to 1880 when Machado, supposedly undergoing a crisis, conceived of and wrote Brás Cubas. The lack of biographical context has led critics to speculate as to what enabled Machado to take such a radical turn, going from Iaiá Garcia (1878) to Brás Cubas (1880). Among those who offered clues and shed light on this mysterious period were Jean-Michel Massa, José Guilherme Merquior, Roberto Schwarz, John Gledson, and, more recently, João Cezar de Castro Rocha.

Nationalism "The tropics are less exotic than out of date." Lévi-Strauss wrote this statement in his 1955 Tristes Tropiques, the memoirs of his explorations of remote areas of Brazil during the late 1930s.[15] Machado arrived at basically the same conclusion but almost a century earlier. His notion of nationalism, broadly considered, evolved from and built upon this idea of Brazil being "less exotic than out of date." Another revealing

---

13 Eça de Queirós, Cousin Bazilio, trans. Roy Campbell (New York: Noonday, 1953), 5.
14 Machado de Assis, Iaiá Garcia, trans. Albert I. Bagby, Jr. (Lexington: UP of Kentucky, 1977), 135.
15 Claude Lévi-Strauss, Tristes Tropiques, trans. John Weightman & Doreen Weightman (New York: Penguin, 2012), 87. The original reads: "Les tropiques sont moins exotiques que démodés."

point related to this topic was made by Roger Bastide, who argues that Machado avoided exoticism at all costs because "exoticism corresponds to the act of seeing one's own country through foreigners' eyes."[16]

Opera "Everything is music, my friend. In the beginning was *do*, then from *do* came *re*, etc." says an old Italian tenor to Bentinho in the central digression of *Dom Casmurro* (Chapter IX). "Life is an opera," teaches the Italian tenor. "God is the poet. The music is by Satan." In a famous segment of this digression, Shakespeare is referred to as a "plagiarist."[17] Meanwhile, Machado himself went on *plagiarizing* Shakespeare's *Othello* ...

Polemic "From the start," says the narrator of *Casa Velha*, "I noticed that the minister's son had the quality of knowing how to listen and disagreeing as though he agreed, so that at times his ideas unwittingly appeared to concur with our own."[18] Machado loathed engaging in controversies. To avoid debate, he, too – like the minister's son of *Casa Velha* – "had the quality of knowing how to listen and disagreeing as though he agreed."

Quixotism "I wrote it with the pen of mirth and the ink of melancholy, and it is not difficult to predict what may come of such a union."[19] The inseparable amalgamation of mirth and melancholy, the utterance that inextricably interweaves seriousness and frivolity, the character that exhibits both self-confidence and self-deception – all these strange but provocative combinations were borrowed by Machado from Cervantes's *Don Quixote*, and he creatively utilized them in *Brás Cubas* and other fictional works.

Rio de Janeiro "Machado's literary mapping of Rio reaches back to the St Petersburg of Gogol and Dostoevsky, and anticipates the Dublin of Joyce," states Chris Power, accurately, in *The Guardian*.[20]

Shakespeare "George Bernard Shaw praised Shakespeare's 'gift of telling a story (provided that someone else told it to him first)'. It is not

---

16 Roger Bastide, "Machado de Assis, paisagista," 421.
17 Machado de Assis, *Dom Casmurro*, 18–20.
18 Machado de Assis, *The Old House*, 53.
19 Machado de Assis, *The Posthumous Memoirs of Brás Cubas*, trans. Flora Thomson-DeVeaux (New York: Penguin, 2020), 3.
20 www.theguardian.com/books/booksblog/2013/mar/01/survey-short-story-machado

an entirely unfair remark," argues Shakespearean scholar Stanley Wells.[21] Shaw's remark could equally fairly be applied to Machado.

"To no avail" In *Brás Cubas*'s Chapter LXXII, Brás Cubas metalinguistically declares that he's inclined to "do away with the previous chapter" because there is a "phrase that verges on nonsense" in it, and he has "no intention of providing fodder for future critics." Brás Cubas, then, acting as a sort of a clairvoyant, envisions the future, "seventy years from now," when …

> a scrawny, sallow, gray-headed fellow who loves nothing but books will lean over the previous page to see if he can find the nonsense; he reads it, rereads it, threereads it, disjoints the words, takes out one syllable, then another, yet another and the rest, examines them inside out, from all sides, against the light, dusts them off, wipes them on his knee, washes them, and to no avail; he cannot find the nonsense.
> He is a bibliomaniac …[22]

… And the bibliomaniac is also us, the readers of Machado. We read, reread, and three-read the elusive language of Machado; we strive to grasp it, tame it, control it, but then, with a neat sleight of hand, language regains its power, meaning slips through our fingers, and we have to start all over again.

Useful Ignorance "Literature is the most agreeable way of ignoring life."[23] Machado would probably agree with the *spirit* of this statement, which was written by the Portuguese poet Fernando Pessoa, on an unknown date between the 1910s and 1930s. Life is pain, and the world exists only to be transformed into a beautiful story.

Views on Politics "Notwithstanding the heated political climate of those days, he was not affiliated with either of the two parties but preserved precious friendship in both, and these were on hand to lower him into his grave. Occasionally he did have political opinions of a sort, gathered on the frontiers of liberalism and conservatism at the exact point where the

---

21 Stanley Wells, *William Shakespeare: A Very Short Introduction* (New York: Oxford UP, 2015), 49.
22 Machado de Assis, *The Posthumous Memoirs of Brás Cubas*, 154.
23 Fernando Pessoa, *The Book of Disquiet*, trans. Richard Zenith (New York: Penguin, 2002), 116.

two dominions merge."[24] These words, used to depict Counselor Valle in *Helena*, could be fairly used to describe Machado himself.

Wizard of Cosme Velho (Portuguese: "Bruxo do Cosme Velho") This is the epithet by which Machado is commonly known. Machado and Carolina moved to the neighborhood of Cosme Velho, in Rio, to live in a two-story cottage on Cosme Velho Street in 1884. The couple resided there until their dying days. The origin of the epithet is obscure. According to the most accepted version of they story, Machado used to burn letters and documents in a cauldron in his backyard. In watching this habit of his, his neighbors came up with the nickname *wizard* for Machado, the *wizard of Cosme Velho*. The epithet gained ground in 1959 when Carlos Drummond de Andrade published "A um bruxo, com amor" ("To a Wizard, with Love"), a poem about Machado whose opening line reads: "In a certain house on Cosme Velho Street."

Xerxes In the story "Lágrimas de Xerxes" ("Xerxes' Tears"), Machado employs the *trompe l'oeil* perspective: the narrator imagines a conversation between Shakespeare's characters Juliet, Romeo, and Friar Lawrence, in which Friar Lawrence imagines the sequence of an episode described by Herodotus – that of Xerxes weeping at the sight of his army. The implications of this juxtaposition of intertextualities render "Xerxes' Tears" one of Machado's most complex stories. The tale's opening words read: "Let us suppose (because everything is mere supposition) …"[25] Fiction (Shakespeare) and history (Herodotus) are equally nothing but suppositions; "because everything," in an age of doubt and uncertainty, "is mere supposition."

Yayá Garcia and Counselor Ayres The first Portuguese-language spelling reform occurred in 1911. That year, the letter y was banned from the Portuguese alphabet, and only foreign words from then on could make use of it. For example, one should spell *Byroniano* instead of writing it out as *Baironiano* (Byronian). Machado wrote with y. He originally spelt *yayá* – which is a variant form of *sinhá*, the pronoun used by enslaved individuals to address white people – and *Ayres* as such. This confused the translators. In 1972, Helen Caldwell translated *Memorial de Aires* as

---

24 Machado de Assis, *Helena*, trans. Helen Caldwell (Berkeley: U of California P, 1984), 5–6.
25 Machado de Assis, "Xerxes's Tears," *The Collected Stories of Machado de Assis*, trans. Margaret Jull Costa & Robin Patterson (New York: Liveright, 2018), 819.

Counselor Ayres' Memorial; in 1990, Robert Scott-Buccleuch rendered the same novel as *The Wager: Aires' Journal*. However, Scott-Buccleuch had translated *Iaiá Garcia* as *Yayá Garcia* in 1976, whereas in the following year another translation, signed by Albert I. Bagby, Jr., was released with the title *Iaiá Garcia* (see Appendix One).

Zola, the Main Antagonist "Influence is a beneficent and necessary corollary of creative genius."[26] Different from Romantic authors, Machado never hid his literary sources or influences. The notion of influence is also relevant because it contiguously relates to other pivotal concepts to Machado's poetics – I'm referring to emulation (see letter E), imitation, parody, plagiarism, paraphrasing, intertextuality, misreading, translation, and tradition. In terms of influences, Machado elected a fine group of national and foreign authors, spearheaded by Shakespeare, whom he constantly assimilated and rewrote. Nevertheless, if his creative process, like that of Shakespeare (see letter S), focuses on assimilating and rewriting his sources, he also writes *in opposition* to some, say, anti-sources – the main ones being Émile Zola and the deterministic premises of Naturalism. Machado abhorred Naturalism to the point that the topic was one of the few that could make him lose his "diplomatic" temper. Machado wrote his works, particularly in his second phase, in response to both his sources and his "anti-sources," with the aim of accrediting (or praising) the former as well as discrediting (or opposing) the latter. The following image may not be completely accurate, but we may think of a spectrum with Machado lying at its center between two extremes: Shakespeare, the main influence, at one end; and Émile Zola, the main antagonist, at the other.

---

26 Helen Regueiro Elam, "Influence," *The New Princeton Encyclopedia of Poetry and Poetics*, eds. Alex Preminger & T. V. F. Brogan (Princeton: Princeton UP, 1993), 605.

Coda

Machado's Legacy

MARXISM IS DEAD. It died in November 1989 with the fall of the Berlin Wall. After 1989, Russians used to joke about the death of Marxism by saying that in capitalism men exploit men, while in Marxist socialism it is the other way around[1] – a very Machadian joke, by the way. But – one could argue – Marxism and Marxist socialism, although interconnected, are two distinct concepts: the former is an umbrella term that covers that latter. In this regard, it would be more accurate to affirm that, even though Marxist socialism is dead, Marxism is not; as a tool of critical analysis, Marxism remains useful and valuable to date.

Did Machado read Marx? Most likely, he did not. Nevertheless, there exist areas of intersection, or common interests, between Machado's fiction and Marx's propositions. Simply put, the analysis of how the social-economic system controls human behavior can be seen as a point of convergence. But this isn't the only point on which they concur. The mediator between behavior and the social world is the human mind. And for both Marx and Machado, the social-economic system, beyond controlling human behavior, constitutes a shaping force that molds human psyche and sentiments. In other words, the materialistic basis of capitalism, upon being absorbed by the human mind, created a new way of thinking: the bourgeois mindset. The deep desire that underpins this mindset – the lust for power – wasn't new, but the material conditions for it to emerge certainly were.

---

1   Robert H. Kane, *The Quest for Meaning: Values, Ethics, and the Modern Experience* (Chantilly, VA: Great Courses, 1999), Lecture Seven (Audio).

In his fiction, Machado skillfully intermingled metaphysics (the will to power) and history (post-revolutionary liberalism and capitalism), without losing sight of the local order (the nineteenth-century Brazilian society). One Marxist question Machado's fiction often poses to its readers can be summed up as follows: how does a typical bourgeois respond to the moral inquiries of his own consciousness about his immoral – or at least morally reprehensible – actions? The answer is that the bourgeois consciousness, as an act of self-protection and self-deception, go through a series of argumentative contortions to rationalize his (mis)conduct and, as a result, transform moral vices into virtues. Furthermore, Machado makes this moral *contortionism* a structural component of the narrative through the recurrent employment of digressions and the strategic use of fickle, unreliable narrators, for instance. In this respect, the social-economic structure becomes a structural element that organizes the narrative and makes it a "structural reduction"[2] of its referent – i.e. the social ideas that the narrative intends to portray in fictional form.

Throughout the twentieth century, the concept of *structure* became central in art and literature. Structural, or formal, experiments with the literary discourse gained the status of *aesthetic capital* with the works of novelists such as Joyce, Virginia Woolf, Nabokov, and Cortázar; the theater of Brecht, Beckett, and Ionesco; and the poetry of Mayakovsky, Khlebnikov, Ezra Pound, Cesar Vallejo, and Haroldo de Campos. The roots of this structuralism (or structuralisms) are various and at time elusive, but Marxism undoubtedly plays a significant role in it.

Based on this argument, Machado's fiction and its intuitive links with Marxism can be fairly deemed modernist *avant la lettre*. Whenever one intends to research the twentieth-century modernism movement from a historical perspective, one needs to go back to certain nineteenth-century authors, such as Machado and Dostoevsky. Literarily speaking, both contributed considerably, directly or indirectly, to the foundations of modernism. That was not the case, however, of Dickens and Hugo, and even early Dostoevsky, whose works represent, from a Marxist point of view, the other side of Marxism: that of focusing on and giving voice to the oppressed so that they might, albeit fictionally, rewrite history.

In the Brazilian cultural context, the generation that came immediately after Machado saw him as a formalist in terms of style, and as an aristocrat in respect to moral principles. Even those professing admiration

---

2 Roberto Schwarz, *A Master on the Periphery of Capitalism*, trans. John Gledson (Durham, NC: Duke UP, 2001), 20.

for his works, such as Lima Barreto (1881–1922), Mário de Andrade (1893–1945), and Carlos Drummond de Andrade (1902–1987), felt the necessity of overcoming Machado's works by opening other pathways for Brazilian literature to explore.[3] But the point of departure, for them and others, was Machado. It has always been. To adapt a famous Marx phrase, the specter of Machado has been haunting Brazilian culture ever since his death. Never neutral, Machado's specter has either provoked opposition – when writers reject his style – or assimilation – when authors try to expand his legacy. For over a century, in sum, Machado has been inescapable. His works stand at the very center of Brazilian cultural life. For Lima Barreto, Mário de Andrade, Carlos Drummond de Andrade, and others, Machado must be overcome. For all of us, he cannot be overlooked.

---

3   See Hélio de Seixas Guimarães, *Machado de Assis, o escritor que nos lê* (São Paulo: Editora Unesp, 2017), 82–94.

Appendix One

Machado de Assis in English

Novels

Ressurreição (1872)

Resurrection. Trans. Paulo de Tarso Dantas. s.l.: Amazon Digital Services LLC – KDP Print US, 2019.

Resurrection. Trans. Karen Sherwood Sotelino. Pittsburgh: Latin American Literary Review Press, 2013.

A mão e a luva (1874)

The Hand and the Glove. Trans. Albert I. Bagby, Jr. Lexington: UP of Kentucky, 1970.

Helena (1876)

Helena. Trans. Helen Caldwell. Berkeley: U of California P, 1984.

Iaiá Garcia (1878)

Yayá Garcia. Trans. Robert Scott-Buccleuch. London: Peter Owen, 1976.
Iaiá Garcia. Trans. Albert I. Bagby, Jr. Lexington: UP of Kentucky, 1977.

Memórias póstumas de Brás Cubas (1881)

The Posthumous Memoirs of Braz Cubas. Trans. William Grossman. São Paulo: Editora São Paulo, 1951. Reissued with the title *Epitaph of a Small Winner*. New York: Noonday, 1952; and London: W. H. Allen, 1953.

Posthumous Reminiscences of Braz Cubas. Trans. E. Percy Ellis. Rio de Janeiro: MEC / INL, 1955.
Posthumous Memoirs of Brás Cubas. Trans. Gregory Rabassa. New York: Oxford UP, 1997.
Posthumous Memoirs of Brás Cubas. Trans. Flora Thomson-DeVeaux. New York: Penguin, 2020.
Posthumous Memoirs of Brás Cubas. Trans. Margaret Jull Costa & Robin Patterson. New York: Liveright, 2020.

Quincas Borba (1891)

Philosopher or Dog? Trans. Clotilde Wilson. New York: Noonday, 1954. In the U.K., the edition was entitled *The Heritage of Quincas Borba* (London: W. H. Allen, 1954).
Quincas Borba. Trans. Gregory Rabassa. New York: Oxford UP, 1998.

Dom Casmurro (1899)

Dom Casmurro. Trans. Helen Caldwell. New York: Noonday, 1953. The U.K. edition was released the same year by W. H. Allen.
Dom Casmurro: Lord Taciturn. Trans. Robert Scott-Buccleuch. London: Peter Owen, 1992. (Infamous edition missing nine of the book's 148 original chapters.)
Dom Casmurro. Trans. John Gledson. New York: Oxford UP, 1997.

Esaú e Jacó (1904)

Esau and Jacob. Trans. Helen Caldwell. Berkeley: U California P, 1965.
Esau and Jacob. Trans. Elizabeth Lowe. New York: Oxford UP, 2000.

Memorial de Aires (1908)

Counselor Ayres' Memorial. Trans. Helen Caldwell. Berkeley: U California P, 1972.
The Wager: Aires' Journal. Trans. Robert Scott-Buccleuch. London: Owen, 1990.

Appendix One: Machado de Assis in English 237

Short Stories

This list contains book editions only, no anthologies.[4]

The Psychiatrist and Other Stories. Trans. William L. Grossman & Helen Caldwell. Berkeley: U California P, 1963.
What Went on at the Baroness': A Tale with a Point. Trans. Helen Caldwell. Santa Monica: Magpie Press, 1963.
The Devil's Church and Other Stories. Trans. Jack Schmitt & Lori Ishimatsu. Austin: U Texas P, 1977.
The Alienist. Trans. Alfred J. Mac Adam. San Francisco: Arion Press, 1998.
A Chapter of Hats and Other Stories. Trans. John Gledson. London: Bloomsbury, 2008.
The Old House. Trans. Mark Carlyon. Rio de Janeiro: Cidade Viva, 2010. (Like "O alienista," "Casa velha," or "The Old House," is considered to be neither a tale nor a novel. It falls more appropriately in the category of novella. As "O alienista" appears in this section, I included "Casa velha" here, too.)
The Alienist. Trans. William L. Grossman. Brooklyn: Melville House, 2012. (This is a reissue with minor edits of Grossman's 1963 version of Machado's novella, then entitled "The Psychiatrist.")
The Alienist and Other Stories of Nineteenth-Century Brazil. Trans. John Charles Chasteen. Indianapolis: Hackett, 2013.
Stories. Trans. Rhett McNeil. Champaign: Dalkey Archive Press, 2014.
Midnight Mass and Other Stories. Trans. Juan LePuen. s.l.: Fario, 2014.
Ex Cathedra: Stories by Machado de Assis. Eds. Glenn Alan Cheney, Luciana Tanure, & Rachel Kopit. Various translators. Hanover: New London Librarium, 2014.
Miss Dollar: Stories by Machado de Assis. Trans. Greicy Pinto Bellin & Ana Lessa-Schmidt. Hanover: New London Librarium, 2016.
Trio in A-Minor: Five Stories by Machado de Assis. Trans. Ana Lessa-Schmidt & Glenn Alan Cheney. Hanover: New London Librarium, 2018.
The Collected Stories of Machado de Assis. Trans. Margaret Jull Costa & Robin Patterson. New York: Liveright, 2018.
Machado de Assis: 26 Stories. Trans. Margaret Jull Costa & Robin Patterson. New York: Liveright, 2019. (This is an abbreviated edition of *The Collected Stories of Machado de Assis*.)

---

4 It's worth observing that the first translations of Machado into English appeared in an anthology: *Brazilian Tales*, ed. & trans. Isaac Goldberg (Boston: Four Seasons, 1921). There, Goldberg translated three stories by Machado: "The Attendant's Confession," "The Fortune Teller," and "Life."

The Male Nurse: Original Story by Machado de Assis. Trans. Clara Monnerat. Niterói: Itapuca, 2021.

Crônicas

"Joaquim Maria Machado de Assis: Six *Crônicas* on Slavery and Abolition." Trans. Robert Patrick Newcomb. *Portuguese Studies*, vol. 33, no. 1 (2017): 105–22.

Good Days! The Bons Dias! *Chronicles of Machado de Assis (1888–1889).* Trans. Ana Lessa-Schmidt. Hanover: New London Librarium, n.d. [2018].

Criticism

"Reflections on Brazilian Literature at the Present Moment: The National Instinct." Trans. Robert Patrick Newcomb. *Brasil/Brazil*, vol. 26, no. 47 (2013): 85–101. Reprinted with a headnote in *Journal of World Literature* 3 (2018): 403–16.

"The New Generation." Trans. Robert Patrick Newcomb. *Journal of Lusophone Studies* 1.2 (Autumn 2016): 262–308.

Theater

You, Love, and Love Alone. Trans. Edgar C. Knowlton, Jr. Macau: Imprensa Nacional, 1972. Also printed in *Boletim do Instituto Luis de Camões* 6.3 (1972): 143–75.

Poetry

Brazilian Literature by Isaac Goldberg. New York: Alfred A. Knopf, 1922. Poems: "The Blue Fly" and "Vicious Circle" (pp. 151–53).

Machado de Assis of Brazil: The Life and Times of Machado de Assis by José Bettencourt Machado. New York: Bramerica, 1953. Poems: "Vicious Circle," "The Blue Fly," and "Christmas Sonnet" (pp. 204–08).

The Descent by Ann Stanford. New York: Viking Press, 1970. Poem: "To Carolina" (p. 23). Stanford's translation appears also in *Machado de Assis: The Brazilian Master and His Novels*. By Helen Caldwell. Berkeley: U of California P, 1970 (p. 202).

Poets of Brazil: A Bilingual Selection by Frederick G. Williams. Provo-UT; Salvador; New York: Brigham Young Universities Studies; Editora da

UFBA; Luso-Brazilian Books, 2004. Poems: "Vicious Circle," "The Devil's Wedding," and "To Carolina" (pp. 142–49).

Letters

In *Machado de Assis: The Brazilian Master and His Novels* (Berkeley: U of California P, 1970), Helen Caldwell translated the only two letters that remain from Machado and Carolina's (presumably extensive) correspondence. The letters are from Machado to Carolina and were dated March 1869. In this volume, Caldwell also included two letters to Francisco Ramos Paz dated November 1869, and excerpts of letters to Joaquim Nabuco.

Appendix Two

On Machado de Assis in English (Ten Books and a Bonus)

THIS IS A list of ten books and one essay about Machado de Assis. Like every list, mine is partial, subjective, and imperfect. However, despite its inevitable imperfection, I decided to make it anyway, for I believe that it's better to have a questionable list than not have one at all. Two criteria guided my selection. First, language: the chosen titles were either originally written in English or have been translated into English. Second, plurality of approaches: each author appears just once in the list. Also, by the criterion of plurality, my list does not intend to be a roll call of the top ten books on Machado. Some outstanding studies were left out. The main idea was to offer a representative and versatile range of critical approaches to Machado. It is presented in chronological order of publication.

Ten Books

1. *Machado de Assis of Brazil: The Life and Times of Machado de Assis* by José Bettencourt Machado. New York: Bramerica, 1953.

This is the only biography – in the classic sense of the term – of Machado de Assis in English. It's a little outdated since some of the groundbreaking biographical studies on Machado (Raimundo Magalhães Júnior, Jean-Michel Massa) came after it. Nonetheless, it's still a book worth reading.

2. *The Brazilian Othello of Machado de Assis: A Study of Dom Casmurro* by Helen Caldwell. Berkeley: U of California P, 1960.

This is a classic and a turning point in Machado studies. In one word, indispensable. Moreover, it's the first book – in any language – entirely dedicated to examining one specific work by Machado.

3. *The Deceptive Realism of Machado de Assis: A Dissenting Interpretation of "Dom Casmurro"* by John Gledson. Liverpool: Francis Cairns, 1984.

Building on the work of Roberto Schwarz (*Ao vencedor as batatas* [*To the Victor, the Potatoes*], 1977), Gledson interprets *Dom Casmurro* through historical and sociopolitical lenses. To a degree, Gledson's importance to Machado's reception in the Anglophone world is as great as Helen Caldwell's.

4. *Retired Dreams: "Dom Casmurro," Myth, and Modernity* by Paul B. Dixon. West Lafayette: Purdue UP, 1989.

Dixon examines *Dom Casmurro* through rhetorical and mythical lenses. It's a different approach when compared to those of Caldwell and Gledson. But the results are equally impressive and helpful for the general understanding of the Machado novel.

5. *A Master on the Periphery of Capitalism* by Roberto Schwarz. Trans. John Gledson. Durham, NC: Duke UP, 2001.

A Marxist reading of *Memórias Póstumas de Brás Cubas*. It's a key reference in Machado's studies.

6. *Machado de Assis: Multiracial Identity and the Brazilian Novelist* by G. Reginald Daniel. University Park: Pennsylvania State UP, 2012.

Daniel's study analyzes issues of race in Machado's lifetime and works. One central question which Daniel tries to shed light on is: "To what extent does the apparent lack of racial consciousness in Machado's life and writings actually reflect a *denial* of being a mulatto?" (p. 7)

7. *Machado de Assis and Female Characterization: The Novels* by Earl E. Fitz. Lewisburg, PA: Bucknell, 2015.

Whenever approaching Machado's works from a critical perspective, one has inevitably to deal with his female characters. In this respect, Fitz's offers a solid guide to a broad but deep understanding of Machado's heroines.

8. *Machado de Assis: Towards a Poetics of Emulation* by João Cezar de Castro Rocha. Trans. Flora Thomson-DeVeaux. East Lansing: Michigan State UP, 2015.

Along with Roberto Schwarz and Hélio de Seixas Guimarães, João Cezar de Castro Rocha is among the most reputable living scholars of Machado in Brazil. In this book, he investigates the period from 1878 to 1880, when Machado radically changed the course of his career as a fictionist.

9. *Machado de Assis: A Literary Life* by K. David Jackson. New Haven: Yale UP, 2015.

A critical introduction to Machado that centers on analysis of his main works.

10. *Emerging Dialogues on Machado de Assis*, eds. Lamonte Aidoo & Daniel F. Silva. New York: Palgrave Macmillan, 2016.

A collection of essays that cover a wide range of topics associated with various facets of Machado's oeuvre.

A Bonus

1. "An Outline of Machado de Assis" by Antonio Candido. Trans. Howard Becker. In *On Literature and Society*. Princeton: Princeton UP, 1995.

Antonio Candido's contribution to literary criticism in Brazil can be compared only with that of Machado to Brazilian prose fiction. In this brief and insightful essay, Candido comments on the critical reception of Machado's works while making his own remarks about some of the best-known novels and stories by Machado.

Bibliography

Aidoo, Lamonte & Daniel F. Silva (eds.). *Emerging Dialogues on Machado de Assis*. New York: Palgrave Macmillan, 2016.
Andrade, Mario. "Machado de Assis." In *Aspectos de literatura brasileira*. São Paulo: Martins Editora, 1967, 87–105.
Baptista, Abel Barros. *A formação do nome: Duas interrogações sobre Machado de Assis*. Campinas: Unicamp, 2003.
Barreto Filho, José. *Introdução a Machado de Assis*. 2nd edn. Rio de Janeiro: Agir Editora, 1980.
Bosi, Alfredo. *Machado de Assis*. São Paulo: Publifolha, 2002.
———. *Machado de Assis: O enigma do olhar*. São Paulo: Ática, 2003.
———. *Brás Cubas em três versões: Estudos machadianos*. São Paulo: Companhia das Letras, 2006.
Caldwell, Helen. *The Brazilian Othello of Machado de Assis*. Berkeley: U of California P, 1960.
———. *Machado de Assis: The Brazilian Master and His Novels*. Berkeley: U of California P, 1970.
Calheiros, Pedro. "A recepção de Machado de Assis em Portugal." *Travessia* 27 (1993): 52–95.
Candido, Antonio. "Esquema de Machado de Assis." In *Vários escritos*. São Paulo: Duas Cidades, 1970, 15–32.
Challoub, Sidney. *Machado de Assis: Historiador*. São Paulo: Companhia das Letras, 2003.
Coutinho, Afrânio. *Machado de Assis na literatura brasileira*. 2nd edn. Rio de Janeiro: Livraria São José, 1966.
Daniel, G. Reginald. *Machado de Assis: Multiracial Identity and the Brazilian Novelist*. University Park: Pennsylvania State UP, 2012.
Dixon, Paul B. *Retired Dreams: Dom Casmurro, Myth, and Modernity*. West Lafayette, IN: Purdue UP, 1989.

———. "Machado de Assis, the "Defunto Autor" and the Death of the Author." *Luso-Brazilian Review* 46 (2009): 45–56.
———. *O chocalho de Brás Cubas: Uma leitura de Memórias póstumas*. São Paulo: EDUSP/Nankin, 2009.
———. "Machado's Organic Sense: An Outline of Approaches to *Lição de Botânica*." *Machado de Assis em linha* 26 (2019): 62–76.
———. *Por linhas tortas: Uma leitura de Quincas Borba de Machado de Assis*. São Paulo: Nankin, 2020.
Faoro, Raymundo. *Machado de Assis: A pirâmide e o trapézio*. São Paulo: Companhia Editora Nacional, 1974.
Fitz, Earl E. *Machado de Assis*. Boston: Twayne, 1989.
———. "The Reception of Machado de Assis in the United States during the 1950s and 1960s." *Luso-Brazilian Review* 46 (2009): 16–35.
———. *Machado de Assis and Female Characterization*. Lewisburg: Bucknell UP, 2015.
———. *Machado de Assis and Narrative Theory*. Lewisburg: Bucknell UP, 2019.
Fuentes, Carlos. *Machado de la Mancha*. México DF: Fondo de Cultura Económica, 2001.
Gledson, John. *The Deceptive Realism of Machado de Assis: A Dissenting Interpretation of "Dom Casmurro."* Liverpool: Francis Cairns, 1984.
———. *Machado de Assis: Ficção e história*. Trans. Sonia Coutinho. Rio de Janeiro: Paz e Terra, 1986.
———. *Por um novo Machado de Assis*. Trans. Fernando Py et al. São Paulo: Companhia das Letras, 2006.
Granja, Lúcia. *Machado de Assis: Antes do livro, o jornal*. São Paulo: Unesp, 2018.
Guerini, Andréia, Luana Ferreira de Freitas & Walter Carlos Costa (eds.). *Machado de Assis: Tradutor e traduzido*. Florianópolis: PGET/UFSC; Copiart, 2012.
Guimarães, Hélio de Seixas (ed.). *Teresa: Revista de literatura brasileira* 6/7 (2006) (collection of essays by various authors).
———. *Machado de Assis, o escritor que nos lê*. São Paulo: Unesp, 2017.
Halling, Anna-Lisa. "The Shrew of the Shrewd: Machado de Assis's *Lição de Botânica*." *Machado de Assis em linha* 26 (2019): 77–89.
Jackson, K. David. *Machado de Assis: A Literary Life*. New Haven: Yale UP, 2015.
Lisboa, Maria Manuel. *Machado de Assis and Feminism*. Lewiston: Edwin Mellen Press, 1996.
Machado, José Bettencourt. *Machado of Brazil*. New York: Bramerica, 1953.
Magalhães, Raimundo de, Jr. *Vida e obra de Machado de Assis*. 4 vols. Rio de Janeiro: Civilização Brasileira, 1981.
Maia Neto, José Raimundo. *Machado de Assis: The Brazilian Pyrrhonian*. West Lafayette, IN: Purdue UP, 1994.

Massa, Jean-Michel. *A juventude de Machado de Assis*. Trans. Marco Aurélio de Moura Matos. Rio de Janeiro: Civilização Brasileira, 1971.

———. *Machado de Assis tradutor*. Trans. Oséias Silas Ferraz. Belo Horizonte: Crisálida, 2008.

Matos, Mário. *Machado de Assis: O Homem e a Obra*. São Paulo: Companhia Editora Nacional, 1939.

Merquior, José Guilherme. "Gênero e estilo das *Memórias póstumas de Brás Cubas*." *Colóquio/Letras* 8 (1972): 12–20.

Meyer, Augusto. *Machado de Assis (1935–1958): Ensaios*. 4th edn. Rio de Janeiro: José Olympio, 2008.

Miguel-Pereira, Lucia. *Machado de Assis (Estudo crítico e biográfico)*. São Paulo: Companhia Editora Nacional, 1936.

———. "Machado de Assis e Eça de Queiroz." *Revista de Portugal* 8 (1939): 474–78.

Nunes, Benedito. "Machado de Assis e a filosofia." *Travessia* 19 (1989): 7–23.

Nunes, Maria Luisa. *The Craft of an Absolute Winner*. Westport, CT: Greenwood Press, 1983.

Passos, José Luiz. *Machado de Assis: O romance com pessoas*. São Paulo: Edusp/Nankin, 2007.

Penjon, Jacqueline. "Machado de Assis: Um século de traduções francesas." *E-Letras com Vida* 2 (2019): 188–201.

Pereira, Astrojildo. *Machado de Assis*. São Paulo/Brasília: Boitempo/Fundação Astrojildo Pereira, 2022.

Pinto, Manuel da Costa (ed.). *Cadernos de literatura brasileira* 23/24 (2008): 5–380.

Rocha, João Cezar de Castro (ed.). *The Author as a Plagiarist – The Case of Machado de Assis*. Portuguese Literary & Cultural Studies 13/14 (2005) (collection of essays by various authors).

———. *Machado de Assis: Por uma poética da emulação*. Rio de Janeiro: Civilização Brasileira, 2013.

Schwarz, Roberto. *Ao vencedor as batatas*. 3rd edn. São Paulo: Duas Cidades, 1988.

———. *Um mestre na periferia do capitalismo*. São Paulo: Duas Cidades, 1990.

———. "A poesia envenenada de *Dom Casmurro*." In *Duas meninas*. São Paulo: Companhia das Letras, 1997, 9–41.

Sousa, J. Galante de. *Bibliografia de Machado de Assis*. Rio de Janeiro: MEC/INL, 1965.

Teixeira, Ivan. *Apresentação de Machado de Assis*. São Paulo: Martins Fontes, 1987.

———. *O altar & o trono*. Cotia/Campinas: Ateliê/Unicamp, 2010.

Veríssimo, José. "Machado de Assis, poeta." In *Estudos de literatura brasileira*. 4th ser. Belo Horizonte: Itatiaia/Edusp, 1977, 51–69.

Wisnik, José Miguel. *Machado maxixe: O caso Pestana*. São Paulo: Publifolha, 2008.

Index

Abramo, Cláudio Weber 148
Abreu, Capistrano de 169
"Academias de Sião, As" ["The Academies of Siam"] 166
Adorno, Theodor 12
Aeschylus 165
Aha! moment, the
  in relation to literary digression 190, 191
Alencar, José de 9, 17, 19, 65, 78, 82, 94, 98, 103, 104, 106, 111, 117, 120, 223
Alencar, Mário de 65
"Alienista, O" ["The Alienist"] 22, 31, 116, 157–59, 161–65
Alighieri, Dante 69, 75, 103, 157, 170
Allen, Woody 23
Almeida, Manuel Antônio de 100
Alvarenga, Lucas José de 44
Alvarenga, Manuel Inácio da Silva 49
Alves, Castro 9, 78, 83, 103
Amado, Jorge 18, 20, 21, 31, 32
Americanas [*From America*] 9, 82–84, 94
Andrade, Carlos Drummond de 64, 118, 229, 233
Andrade, Mário 10, 11, 19, 83, 233
"Anel de Polícrates, O" ["Polycrates' Ring"] 165
Angelou, Maya 29
Antes da missa [*Before Mass*] 92
"Apólogo, Um" ["An Apologue"] 55

Araripe Júnior, Tristão de Alencar 82, 106, 107, 169
Arbousse-Bastide, Paul 17
Aristotle 38, 39
Arouet, François-Marie 173, 224
Armstrong, Neil 11
Assis, Francisco José de (Machado's father) 46, 53, 66
Assis, Maria Machado de (Machado's sister) 46, 47
Atwood, Margaret 6
Azevedo, Álvares de 78, 106

Bagby, Jr., Albert I. 230
Balzac, Honoré de 25, 44
Bandeira, Manuel 78
Barbosa, Domingos Caldas 49
Barbosa, Rui 127
Barreto, Afonso Henriques de Lima 49, 118, 129, 233
Barreto Filho, José 217
Barros, Abel Baptista 26
Barroso, Ary 54 n.18
Barth, John 23
Bastide, Roger 17, 18, 20, 221, 222, 227
Baudelaire, Charles 12, 44, 76
Beckett, Samuel 23, 232
Bergson, Henry 96
Berkley, George 38
Berveiller, Michel 18
Blake, William 81

Bloom, Harold 23, 33, 56, 73, 202 n.56
Bocaiúva, Quintino 48, 93, 94, 95, 102, 121
Boisvert, Georges 21
Bolaño, Roberto 73
Borges, Jorge Luis 1–3, 5, 6, 12, 13, 19, 22, 25, 37, 39, 51, 52, 65, 66, 71, 73, 139, 157, 222
Bosi, Alfredo 95
Bote de rapé, O [*The Snuff Box*] 92
"Braços, Uns" ["Those Arms"] 168
Braga, Rubem 118
Branco, Camilo Castelo 59
Brás Cubas see *Memórias póstumas de Brás Cubas*
Braudel, Fernand 17
Brecht, Bertold 232
Brito, Francisco de Paula 48, 49, 66, 72, 77, 92
Brontë sisters (Anne, Emily, and Charlotte) 45
Browning, Elizabeth 45
Burton, Robert 96
Byrd, Charlie 31

Calderón de la Barca, Pedro 19, 37
Caldwell, Helen 21, 29–32, 73, 174, 192–97, 210 n.11, 222, 229
Calheiros, Pedro 26
Câmara Júnior, Mattoso 217
Caminho da porta, O [*The Path to the Door*] 93
Camões, Luis de 157, 170
Campos, Haroldo de 232
Candido, Antonio 17, 21
"Cantiga de esponsais" ["Nuptial Song"] 168
Cardoso, Fernando Henrique 17
Carolina see Novais, Carolina Augusta Xavier de
Carpentier, Alejo 13
Carrol, Lewis 45
Casa velha [*The Old House*] 74, 223, 227
Casanova, Pascale 22
"Caso da vara, O" ["The Case of the Stick"] 83, 167
"Causa secreta, A" ["The Secret Cause"] 168

Caxias, Marquis of see Silva, Luís Alves de Lima e
Cervantes, Miguel de 19, 23, 69, 73, 157, 160, 170, 172, 191, 224, 227
Chateaubriand, René 17
Chekhov, Anton 23, 45, 140, 141, 144, 145, 149
Cicero 132
Coelho Neto, Henrique Maximiano 49, 68
colonizing shadow 25
Columbus, Christopher 11
Comte, Auguste 163
"Confissões de uma viúva moça" ["Confessions of a Young Widow"] 166
Conrad, Joseph 11
Contos fluminenses [*Rio Tales*] 94, 149
Cortázar, Julio 13, 33, 232
Costa, Margaret Jull 22, 34, 165
Coutinho, Afrânio 123
Crespo, Antônio Cândido Gonçalves 49, 59
Crisálidas [*Chrysalises*] 78–80, 84
crônica
  origins and definition 118–25
cultural geopolitics 5–11
Cunha, Euclides da 18, 64

Dante see Alighieri, Dante
"D. Benedita: Um retrato" ["Dona Benedita: A Portrait"] 166
Debussy, Claude 17, 25
Delpech, Adrien 16
Descartes, René 146
Desencantos [*Disenchantment*] 49, 92
Dias, Gonçalves 9, 49, 78, 82, 83, 94
Dickens, Charles 25, 45, 232
Dickinson, Emily 12, 44
Diderot, Denis 189
"Diplomático, O" ["Mr. Diplomat"] 166
Dixon, Paul 96, 97, 101, 202, 203
Dom Casmurro 18, 22, 29, 30, 32–34, 61, 62, 73–75, 81, 175, 180, 191–99, 201–03, 225, 227
Dostoevsky, Fyodor 23, 25, 45, 192, 227, 232
Doumer, Paul 50

"D. Paula" ["Dona Paula"]   166
Dumas, Alexandre   153–55

Ecclesiastes   205, 214, 219
Ellington, Duke   54
Ellis, Alfredo   14
Ellis, E. Percy   22, 31
Emerson, Ralph Waldo   12, 44
"Enfermeiro, O" ["The Caregiver"]   16, 165
"Entre santos" ["Among Saints"]   167
Esaú e Jacó [*Esau and Jacob*]   15, 22, 31, 90, 180, 192, 198, 199, 209, 211
Erasmus (of Rotterdam)   224
"Espelho, O" ["The Mirror"]   141, 144–49, 151, 153, 157, 165
Euripides   165

Falenas [*Moths*]   78–81, 84, 94
Faoro, Raymundo   217
Fernandes, Florestan   17
Ferrante, Elena   6
Fielding, Henry   189
Fitz, Earl   13 n.16, 24, 25, 95–98, 101, 174, 193, 202
Flaubert, Gustave   23, 24, 44
Fonseca, Deodoro da   125, 126
Foucault, Michel   12
France, Anatole   16
Franzen, Jonathan   23
Freire, Junqueira   106
Freud, Sigmund   12, 139, 150, 191
Freyre, Gilberto   10
Frias, Viscount Sanches de   60
Friedenreich, Arthur   54
Fuentes, Carlos   13, 23, 39, 40

Gadamer, Hans-Georg   12
Gama, Basílio da   82
Garcia, José Maurício Nunes   44 n.9
García Márquez, Gabriel   7, 13, 32, 33
Garnier, Hippoyte   14, 15
Garrett, Almeida   169
Genesis   215
Genette, Gérard   22
Getz, Stan   31
Gilberto, João   31, 64
Ginsberg, Allen   23, 225

Giraldi, Giovanni Battista   73
Gledson, John   33, 147–49, 226
Goethe, Johann Wolfgang von   19, 24, 69, 157, 170, 172
Gogol, Nikolai   23, 45, 227
Goldberg, Isaac   30, 165
Gonzaga, Tomás António   44, 44 n.9
González Echevarría, Roberto   24
Grieco, Agripino   110
Grossman, William   22, 30, 31
Gueroult, Martial   17
Guimarães, Bernardo   82

Halling, Anna-Lisa   96, 101
Hardwick, Elizabeth   23
Hardy, Thomas   23, 45
Hart, Stephen   199, 200
Hawthorne, Nathaniel   12, 44, 100
Hegel, Georg Wilhelm Friedrich   109, 139, 146, 150, 206
Heidegger, Martin   12
Heine, Heinrich   44, 75
Helena   32, 63, 65, 74, 94, 173, 176, 177, 224, 229
Hénaux, Victor   72, 92
Hernández, José   19
Herodotus   229
Highland, Alexandrina   14, 15
Histórias da meia-noite [*Midnight Tales*]   94, 149
Histórias sem data [*Undated Stories*]   149
Hoje avental, amanhã luva [*Today an Apron, Tomorrow a Glove*]   72, 73, 76
"Homem célebre, Um" ["A Famous Man"]   168
Homer   4, 130
Hourcade, Pierre   18
Hugo, Victor   44, 69, 75, 232

Iaiá Garcia   32, 63, 64, 74, 94, 111, 112, 173, 176, 180, 181, 226
"Ideal do crítico, O" ("The Critic's Ideal")   105, 114
"Ideias sobre o teatro" ["Ideas on Theater"]   87, 88, 90
"Ideias vagas"   104
"Imortal, O" ["The Immortal"]   167

"Instinto de nacionalidade" ["Instinct of Nationality"]   20, 82, 93, 94, 104, 107–10, 175, 177
intermediation
   the Catholic culture of authoritative   42
Ionesco, Eugène   232
Ivo, Lêdo   37

Jabès, Edmond   28
Jackson, David   13, 102
James, Henry   23, 44, 117
João VI (of Portugal) *also* D. João (Prince Regent)   48, 142, 147, 162, 170
Jobim, Antônio (Tom) Carlos   64
Johnson, Samuel   19
Joyce, James   4, 227, 232
Junqueiro, Guerra   59

Kafka, Franz   12, 23, 25, 157, 192, 225
Khlebnikov, Velimir   232

Lacan, Jacques   12
Lamartine, Alphonse de   131
latinité project   16, 17
Lavalade, René Chadebec de   18, 22
Lebesgue, Philéas   17
Léry, Jean de   17
Lévi-Strauss, Claude   17, 18, 226
Lição de botânica [*A Botany Lesson*]   68 n.37, 93, 95–102, 156
Lima, Oliveira   16
"Lira chinesa" ["Chinese Lire"]   80
Lisboa, Antônio Francisco   44
Lispector, Clarice   32, 64, 118
literary canon   3–5
   a pragmatic approach to   4, 5
literary criticism
   concept of *modern* literary criticism   104–06
Longfellow, Henry   127, 128
Lope de Vega, Félix   19
Luther, Martin   43

Machado, Maria Leopoldina (Machado's mother)   46, 47
"Machete, O"   168
Magalhães, Gonçalves de   82, 104

Magalhães Júnior, Raimundo   217
Maistre, Xavier de   115, 170, 171, 189
Mann, Thomas   158, 159
Mão e a luva, A [*The Hand and the Glove*]   32, 63, 74, 94, 173, 176, 178
"Mariana"   167
Marvell, Andrew   96
Marx, Karl   45, 109, 139, 150, 206, 231, 233
Massa, Jean-Michel   20, 21, 60, 61, 76, 226
Matos, Gregório de   44 n.9
Mauro, Humberto   55
Mayakovsky, Vladimir   232
Mello, Augusto Ernesto de Castilho e   107, 108
Melo, Custódio de   126–28
Melo, Sebastião José de Carvalho e   43
Melville, Herman   12, 23, 44, 221
Memorial de Aires [*Counselor Aires's Memorial*]   22, 192, 198–200
Memórias póstumas de Brás Cubas [*Posthumous Memoirs of Brás Cubas*]   14–16, 18, 22–24, 26, 30–34, 39, 51, 63–65, 67, 72, 75, 79, 86, 90, 99, 104, 106, 110, 111, 113, 114, 117, 132, 163, 169–74, 180, 182, 186, 188, 191, 198, 199, 201–03, 207, 217, 224, 226–28
Memórias póstumas de Brás Cubas as a response to Eça de Queirós's *O primo Basílio*   110-16, 163, 171
Mendes, Odorico   75
Merquior, José Guilherme   224, 226
mestiçagem vs. miscegenation   10 n.13
Métailié, Anne-Marie   21, 22
Meyer, Augusto   222
Miguel-Pereira, Lúcia   21, 27, 74, 176, 187, 188, 222
Miomandre, Francis de   18
"Missa do galo" ["Midnight Mass"]   28, 150, 151, 153, 156, 157, 165
Mistérios sociais, Os [*The Social Mysteries*] by Augusto César de Lacerda
   Machado's report on   89–91
Monbeig, Pierre   17
Montaigne, Michel de   132

Monte-Alverne, Francisco de   104
Montello, Josué   34
"Musa consolatrix" ["Consolatrix Muse"]   79

Nabokov, Vladimir   232
Nabuco, Joaquim   53 n.18, 54, 59, 224
Najac, Émile de   72, 74
Não consultes médico [*Don't Consult a Doctor*]   93
Napoleão, Artur   60
Napoleon III   127
Nascimento, Edson Arantes do   64
Neruda, Pablo   25
Neto, Coelho   17
Nietzsche, Friedrich   12, 44, 69, 70, 150, 177, 178, 216-19
"No alto" ["At the Top"]   84-86
"Noite de almirante" ["Admiral's Night"]   167
Novais, Carolina Augusta Xavier de (Machado's wife)   19, 21, 50, 51, 56, 58-65, 68, 70, 111, 131, 171, 229
Novais, Faustino Xavier de   21, 59-61
Novais, Miguel   14

"Óbito, Um" ["A Death"]   131
Ocidentais [*Occidentals*]   84, 86
"Ode de Anacreonte, Uma" ["An Ode by Anacreon"]   80, 92
Ortigão, Ramalho   111
Orwell, George   192
Otaviano, Francisco   75
Owen, Peter   34

Páginas recolhidas [*Collected Pages*]   149
"Pai contra mãe" ["Father Against Mother"]   83, 167
"Pálida Elvira" ["Pale Elvira"]   80
Papéis avulsos [*Miscellaneous Papers*]   149
Pascal, Blaise   115, 163, 173
Patai, Daphne   28 n.43
Patrocínio, José do   49
Patterson, Robin   22, 34, 165
Pedro I (of Brazil)   122, 127
Pedro II (of Brazil)   45, 104, 125, 162
Peixoto, Afrânio   18
Peixoto, Floriano   126-28

Pelé *see* Nascimento, Edson Arantes do
Pereira, Astrojildo   222
Pereira, Bento Barroso   62
Pereira, Maria José Mendonça Barroso (Machado's godmother)   46, 47, 62
Pereira, Olympio da Silva   53
Pérez Galdós, Benito   40
Pertence, José Paulo Sepúlveda   197
Pessoa, Fernando   65, 76, 228
Picasso, Pablo   17
Pignatari, Décio   1, 2, 20, 21
"Pílades e Orestes" ["Pylades and Orestes"]   165
Piquet, Julio   15
Pirandello, Luigi   18
Plato   139, 164
Poe, Edgar Allan   12, 13, 23, 25, 44, 75, 81, 95, 139, 162, 170, 222
Pombal, Marquis of *see* Melo, Sebastião José de Carvalho e
Porto-Alegre, Manuel Araújo de   104
Pound, Ezra   223, 232
Power, Chris   227
Prévost, Abbé   194
Pritchett, V. S.   23
Protocolo, O [*Protocol*]   93
Proust, Marcel   18, 23
Pujol, Alfredo   114

Queda que as mulheres têm para os tolos [*The Weakness Women Have for Fools*]   49, 72, 73, 92
Queirós, Eça de   26-28, 40, 65, 110-15, 117, 132, 163, 226
Quevedo, Francisco de   19
Quincas Borba   22, 30, 32, 33, 116, 178-80, 191, 198, 201-03, 218, 219, 225
Quiroga, Horacio   25

Rabassa, Gregory   22, 32, 33
Rabelais, François   224
Ramos, Graciliano   18
Rego, José Lins do   18, 55
Relíquias de casa velha [*Relics from an Old House*]   95, 149
Ressurreição [*Resurrection*]   61, 63, 75, 81, 94, 173-76, 202 n.58

Index

Ribeiro, Luis Filipe 148, 150
Ricard, Xavier de 17
Ricardo, Cassiano 55
Richards, A. I. 39
Rilke, Rainer Maria 12
Rimbaud, Arthur 44
Rio, João do 49
Rocha, Fernando 167
Rocha, João Cezar de Castro 226
Rodrigues, José Carlos 107
Romero, Sílvio 55, 106, 107, 217
Rosa, João Guimarães 20, 26, 28, 32, 37, 64, 192
Roth, Philip 23
Rousseau, Jean-Jacques 172, 173, 205
Rushdie, Salman 7, 23

"Sabina" 83
Samosata, Lucian of 115
Samoyault, Tiphaine 22
Sand, George 44
Santos, Hemetério dos 67, 68
Santos-Dumont, Alberto 64
Saramago, José 26–28
Sarmiento, Domingo Faustino 19
Scarpa, Gustavo 192, 193, 197
Schopenhauer, Arthur 69, 169, 171, 172, 191, 218, 219
Schwarcz, Lilia 52
Schwarz, Roberto 217, 226
Schweblin, Samanta 6
Scott-Buccleuch, Robert 34, 230
"Senhora, Uma" ["A Lady"] 166
"Segredo de Augusta, O" ["Augusta's Secret"] 166
"Sereníssima república, A (Conferência do cônego Vargas)" ["The Most Serene Republic (Canon Vargas's Lecture)" 166, 167
Shakespeare, William 12, 19, 23, 24, 39, 62, 68, 73, 75, 81, 84–86, 96, 109, 146, 157, 166, 170, 172, 174, 194, 205, 206, 206 n.2, 217, 227, 229
Shaw, George Bernard 227
Silva, Luís Alves de Lima e 122
Silva, Maria Inês da (Machado's stepmother) 46, 47, 66–68

Silveira, Joaquim Alberto de Sousa da (Machado's godfather) 62
Soares, Antônio Joaquim de Macedo 104, 169 n.3
Socrates 4
solae doctrine
  the five Protestant 42
"Sonnet" (first poem published by Machado) 48
Sontag, Susan 2, 3, 13, 23, 33
Sophocles 165
Sousa, Antônio Gonçalves Teixeira e 49
Sousa, João Cardoso de Menezes e 75, 82
Sterne, Lawrence 23, 25, 81, 115, 170–72, 189, 191
Storm, Theodor 45
Stowe, Harriet Beecher 11, 44
succès d'estime
  Machado de Assis as a 23, 27
Swift, Jonathan 23, 81, 170, 189, 224

Taunay, Alfredo 17
Thackeray, William 179
Thomson-DeVeaux, Flora 22, 180 n.23
Thoreau, Henry David 12, 44
Tolstoy, Leo 25, 45
"Trio em lá menor" ["Trio in A Minor"] 168
Tu, só tu, puro amor... [*Thou, Only Thou, Pure Love...*] 93, 102
Turgenev, Ivan 45
Twain, Mark 12

"Última folha" ["Last Leaf"] 79
"Última jornada" ["The Last Journey"] 83
Updike, John 23

Vallejo, Cesar 232
van Gogh, Vincent 12
Vargas, Getúlio 9, 10, 54, 55
Vargas Llosa, Mario 13
Várias histórias [*Assorted Stories*] 14, 16, 149
Vattier, Gustave 72, 74
Veloso, Caetano 54 n.18
Verissimo, Érico 24

Veríssimo, José 53, 53 n.18, 83, 106, 107, 224
Verissimo, Luis Fernando 118
"Verme, O" ["The Worm"] 80–82
"Versos a Corina" ["Verses to Corina"] 80
Vieira, Antônio 43 n.9
"Vieux pays, Un" ["An Old Country"] 80
Villa-Lobos, Heitor 25
Virgil 103
"Virginius" 167
"Visita de Alcibíades, Uma" ["A Visit from Alcibiades"] 165, 167
"Viver!" ["Life!"] 165, 171
Voltaire *see* Arouet, François-Marie
von Besa, Curt Busch 14

von Hahn-Hahn, Ida 44
von Martius, Karl Friedrich Phillip 9–11

Wells, Stanley 228
Whitman, Walt 25, 44
Williams, Frederick G. 59
Wilson, Clotilde 30, 31
Wittgenstein, Ludwig 4
Wood, Michael 23, 156
Woolf, Virginia 232

Xenophon 210, 210 n.11, 212
Xerxes 229

Zola, Émile 44, 112, 114–16, 132, 163, 230

TAMESIS BOOKS

Founding Editors
†J. E. Varey
†Alan Deyermond

General Editor
Stephen M. Hart

Advisory Board
Andrew M. Beresford
Zoltán Biedermann
Celia Cussen
Efraín Kristal
Jo Labanyi
María E. López
Thea Pitman
Julius Ruiz
Alison Sinclair
Jonathen Thacker
Isabel Torres
Noël Valis

www.ingramcontent.com/pod-product-compliance
Lightning Source LLC
Jackson TN
JSHW061114250625
86703JS00004B/48